Street by Street

C000160619

BOLTON

HORWICH, WALKDEN, WESTHOUGHTON

Adlington, Aspull, Atherton, Blackrod, Edgworth, Farnworth,
Kearsley, Little Lever, Swinton, Tottington, Tyldesley

2nd edition October 2007
© Automobile Association Developments Limited 2007

Original edition printed May 2002

This product includes map data licensed from Ordnance Survey® with the permission of the Controller of Her Majesty's Stationery Office. © Crown copyright 2007. All rights reserved. Licence number 100021153.

The copyright in all PAF is owned by Royal Mail Group plc.

Published by AA Publishing (a trading name of Automobile Association Developments Limited, whose registered office is Fanum House, Basing View, Basingstoke, Hampshire RG21 4EA. Registered number 1878835).

Produced by the Mapping Services Department of The Automobile Association. (A03490)

A CIP Catalogue record for this book is available from the British Library.

Printed by Oriental Press in Dubai

The contents of this atlas are believed to be correct at the time of the latest revision. However, the publishers cannot be held responsible or liable for any loss or damage occasioned to any person acting or refraining from action as a result of any use or reliance on any material in this atlas, nor for any errors, omissions or changes in such material. This does not affect your statutory rights. The publishers would welcome information to correct any errors or omissions and to keep this atlas up to date. Please write to Publishing, The Automobile Association, Fanum House (FH12), Basing View, Basingstoke, Hampshire, RG21 4EA. E-mail: streetbystreet@theaa.com

Ref: ML203z

Key to map pages	ii-iii
Key to map symbols	iv-1
Enlarged map pages	2-3
Main map pages	4-57
Index – towns & villages	58
Index – streets	59-80
Index – featured places	81-83
Acknowledgements	83

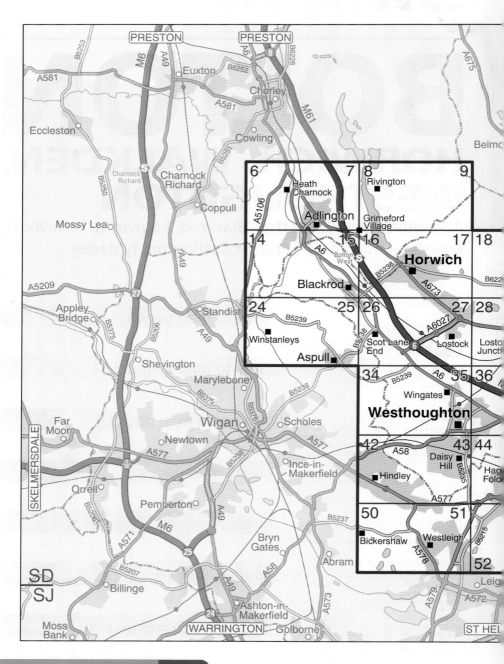

Enlarged scale pages 1:10,000 6.3 inches to 1 mile

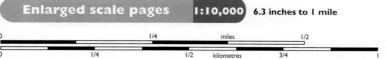

0   1/4   miles   1/2

0   1/4   1/2   kilometres   3/4   1

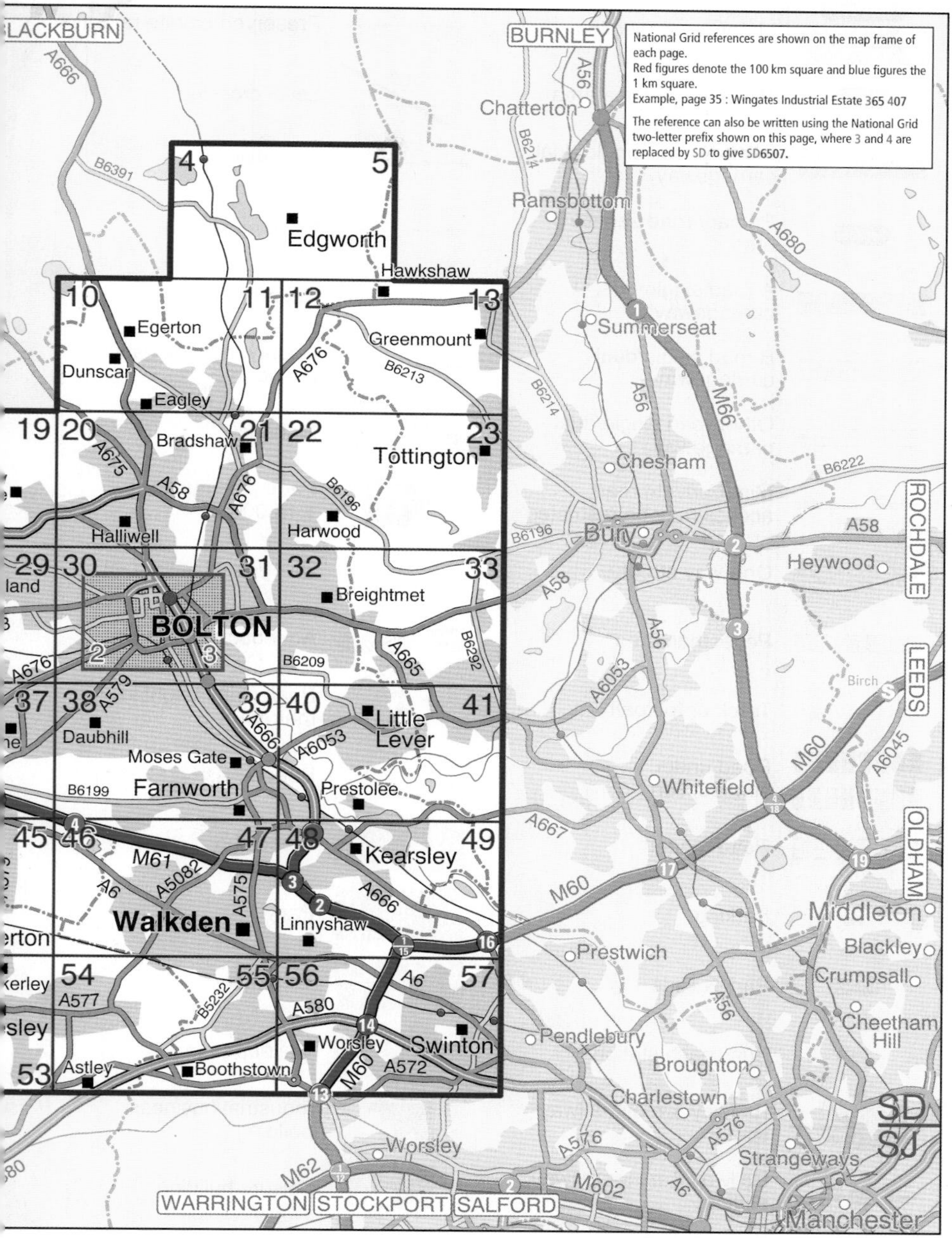

National Grid references are shown on the map frame of each page.
Red figures denote the 100 km square and blue figures the 1 km square.
Example, page 35 : Wingates Industrial Estate 365 407

The reference can also be written using the National Grid two-letter prefix shown on this page, where 3 and 4 are replaced by SD to give SD6507.

LACKBURN — A666 — B6391

BURNLEY — A56 — B6214

Chatterton

Ramsbottom

Summerseat

A680

4 **5**

Edgworth

Hawkshaw

Greenmount

10 **11 12** **13**

Egerton — Dunscar — Eagley — A676 — B6213

Chesham

B6222

ROCHDALE

A58

Heywood

Birch

LEEDS

A6045

19 20 21 22 23

Bradshaw — Tottington — A675 — A58 — A676 — B6196

Halliwell — Harwood

Bury — A58 — B6196 — A56

29 30 31 32 33

BOLTON — Breightmet — B6209 — A665 — B6292 — A6053 — A676

37 38 39 40 41

Daubhill — Little Lever — A579 — A666 — A6053

Moses Gate — Prestolee

Farnworth — B6199

Whitefield — A667 — M60

OLDHAM

Middleton

Blackley

Crumpsall

45 46 47 48 49

M61 — A5082 — A6 — A575 — A666 — Kearsley

Walkden — Linnyshaw

M60 — Prestwich — A56

Cheetham Hill

54 55 56 57

A577 — B5232 — A580 — A6 — Worsley — Swinton — A572

Pendlebury — Broughton — Charlestown

SD SJ

53

Astley — Boothstown — M60

Worsley — A576 — A6 — Strangeways

M62 — M60 — A572 — M602

WARRINGTON STOCKPORT SALFORD

Manchester

4.2 inches to 1 mile — **Scale of main map pages 1:15,000**

0 — 1/4 — miles — 1/2 — 3/4 — 1

0 — 1/4 — 1/2 — kilometres 3/4 — 1 — 1 1/4 — 1 1/2

iv

Junction 9	Motorway & junction
Services	Motorway service area
	Primary road single/dual carriageway
Services	Primary road service area
	A road single/dual carriageway
	B road single/dual carriageway
	Other road single/dual carriageway
	Minor/private road, access may be restricted
← ←	One-way street
	Pedestrian area
	Track or footpath
	Road under construction
⌐ ‒ ‒ ‒ ‒ ¬	Road tunnel
P	Parking
P+🚌	Park & Ride
🚌	Bus/coach station
	Railway & main railway station
	Railway & minor railway station
⊖	Underground station
⊖	Light railway & station

+++++++++	Preserved private railway
LC	Level crossing
•—•—•—•	Tramway
‒ ‒ ‒ ‒ ‒	Ferry route
....	Airport runway
‒ · ‒ · ‒ · ‒	County, administrative boundary
▼▼▼▼▼▼▼	Mounds
17	Page continuation 1:15,000
	River/canal, lake, pier
	Aqueduct, lock, weir
465 ▲ Winter Hill	Peak (with height in metres)
	Beach
	Woodland
	Park
† † † † † † † † † †	Cemetery
	Built-up area
	Industrial/business building
	Leisure building
	Retail building
	Other building

City wall	City wall	Castle	Castle
A&E	Hospital with 24-hour A&E department		Historic house or building
PO	Post Office	Wakehurst Place (NT)	National Trust property
	Public library	M	Museum or art gallery
i	Tourist Information Centre		Roman antiquity
i	Seasonal Tourist Information Centre		Ancient site, battlefield or monument
	Petrol station, 24 hour Major suppliers only		Industrial interest
†	Church/chapel		Garden
	Public toilets		Garden Centre Garden Centre Association Member
	Toilet with disabled facilities		Garden Centre Wyevale Garden Centre
PH	Public house AA recommended		Arboretum
	Restaurant AA inspected		Farm or animal centre
Madeira Hotel	Hotel AA inspected		Zoological or wildlife collection
	Theatre or performing arts centre		Bird collection
	Cinema		Nature reserve
	Golf course		Aquarium
▲	Camping AA inspected	V	Visitor or heritage centre
	Caravan site AA inspected		Country park
	Camping & caravan site AA inspected		Cave
	Theme park		Windmill
	Abbey, cathedral or priory		Distillery, brewery or vineyard

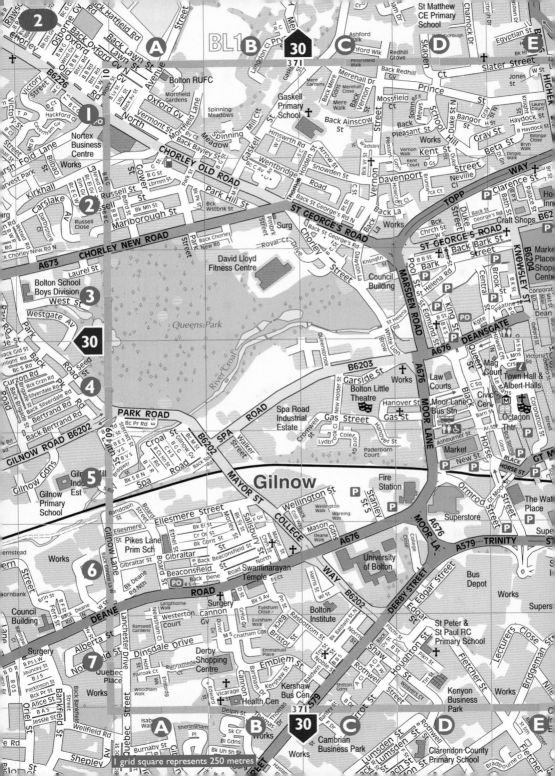

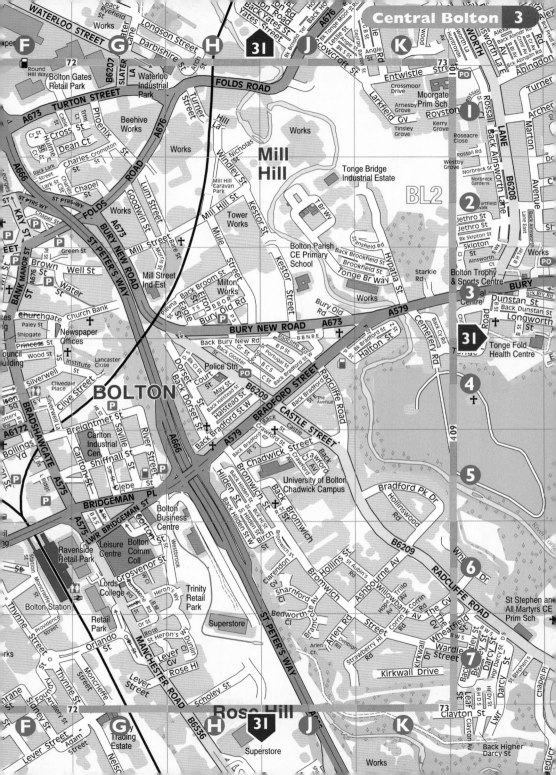

Crowthorn Road

Crowthorn Road

Works

Broadhead Rd

E **F** **G** **H**

75 76

18

Blackburn

Bury

1

Broadhead Road

Plantation

2

17

Road

Hawkshaw

Edgworth

Greenacres Cl

Red Earth
Farm

3
e

Hol
Fole

Edgeworth
Vale

Edgworth
CC

Bury Road

4

Edgworth
odist
School

Witton Weavers

Way

416

Hawkshaw Lane

ton
toms

Bury Road

Higher House
Farm

5

The Gardens

Knotts Brow

75 76

E **F** ⧨**12** **G** **H**

lead

Bottom o' th'
Knotts Brow

Hawkshaw Lane

Blackburn

Bolton

Hawksh

6

Sevenoaks

Burgh

Holy Cross
RC High
School

Park
Golf Club

BOLTON

Woodside

Chester
Avenue **C**

The Cedars

Lower Burgh Way

Dale
Vw

A

Winchester

Duxbury
59

Hall

Worcester Pl

D

ROAD

The
Willows

3 58

Woodlands Meadow

Firtree

Burgh
Hall

The Dr

Rufford

Cl

Cades

Yewtree
Cl

River Yarrow

Duxbury
Park

Golf Course

A5106

Martins Av

I

15_{puth}

Duxbury Jubilee
Park Golf Club

**Heath
Charnock**

Burgh Lane

2

Gilbertson
Road

WIGAN LANE

Grundy's Lane

Shade
Lane

Rawlinson

WESTHOUGHTON ROAD

Leeds and Liverpool Canal

A6

The Asshawes

3

Grundy's   Lane

Lane

Rawlinson L

4 14

Mercer

Dnsw

Ct

K/ngslea

4

A5106

Coppull Hall Lane

5

4 13

Jolly Tar Lane

WIGAN LANE

Stonor

Adl
Pri

3 58

59

A

A5106

B

14

C

Sandringham
Close

Lewis Close

Sandy Rd

Carrington

Park

Acresfield

Road

Chapel St

D

Castle House
La

Balmoral

Windsor
Av

Warwick
St

Cemetery

1 grid square represents 500 metres

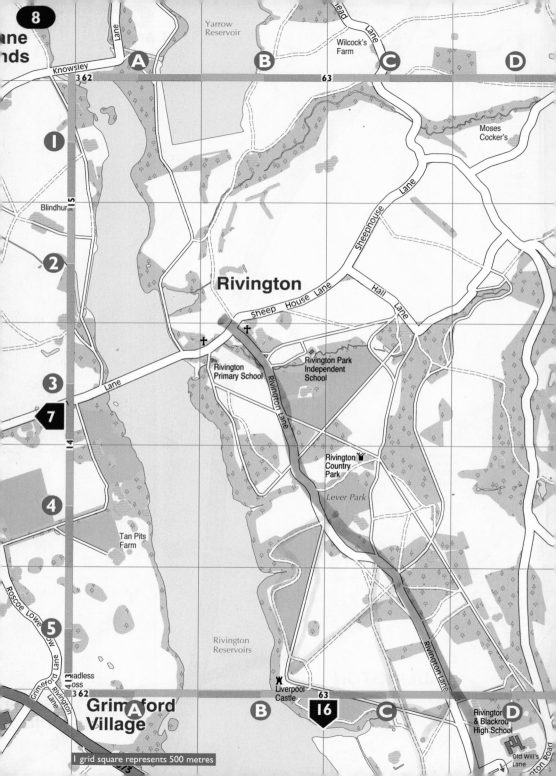

E F G H

65 66

Stoops

I

Blackburn
Lancashire County

Belmont Road

15

456
▲
Wint 2

*Rivington
Moor*

Lancashire County
Bolton

3

14

*Rivington
Pike*

4

5

413

George's Lane

65 66

E F 17 G H

Wilderswood

E   F   G   H

77   78

**Holcombe
Brook**

Hawkshaw

Spenleach Lane

Redisher Lane

Redisher
Close

BOLTON   ROAD   A676

Holly Mount

BL8

Greenmount

Greenmount
Primary School

Kimble
Cl

Holly Mount
RC Primary
School

Croichley
Fold

Chapel
Gardens

HOLCOMBE ROAD

B6215

Byron Road

Keats Road

Avondale Dr

Kendal Rd

Kendal Road West

Holcombe
Brook Sports Club

Woodhey R

Mayfield Rd

Castle Gv

Brooklands Rd

Westgate Av

Stretton Road

Southfield Road

B6214

PO

Vernon
Medica

Vernon Rd

Andrew Cl

Newton Dr

Beech Gv

Nabbs
Way

Hunt Fold Drive

Larkfield Cl

Greenpark Cl

Greenleys Crs

Brookside Crs

Greenside

Greenside Cl

Brookside Dr

Station Rd

Royston

Holcombe Road

Greenmount
CC

Shepherd   Street

B6213

Cann Street

Cann St

Woodstock Dr

Thornley

Claybank Dr

Leigh Cl

Cliff AV

Claybank Dr

TURTON ROAD

Victoria St

Brookhouse

Osws Cl

Quakers
Fld

Mill   Street

Works

Hawthorn
Crescent

Old Doctors
Street

Chapel St

Royds Street

Kirklees Street

Beryl Av

St Kirklees

Rhine Cl

Avallon

Laburnum Av

Burgundy Dr

Rhine Cl

Primrose
Bank

Harwood Road

Harwood
Crescent

Wesley Street

Spring Street

PO

Spring Cl

Spring V
St

Spring V Dr

Laurel Street

Ryecroft AV

Victoria Works

Tottington
Health Centre

Old S Rd

E   F   **23**   G   H

TOTTINGTON

Tottington High
School

MARKET STREET

Sunny Bower St

First St

Wilbnk St

I

1

2

3

14

4

5

413

E F G H

69 70

Scout Road

Horrocks Hill Farm

Coal Pit Road

I

Cunliffe's Farm

Smithills Dean Road

Longshaw Ford Road

2

Barrow

St Peters Smithills Dean CE Primary School

Smithills Hall Museum

Bridge

Barrow Bridge

Limefield Close

Limefield Road

Smithills Dean Road

3

Bolton Sixth Form College North Campus

20

Firth Street

Fourth St

Second Street

Third St

First St

BVM Lea Ter

Lowthine Av

Bazley Street

Redcar Road

Jesmond Road

Myrton Rd

Abercorn Road

Smithills School

Golf Course

Riversleigh Close

Road

Road

Smithills

Croft

Woodburn Dr

Whitster's Hollow

Road

Brookdean Cl

Uban Crs

Raved

Whalley Avenue

Lightbounds Road

Moss Bank Park

Lumwood

Forest Road

4

Harpers Lane

Hollin Hey Road

Dunsop Drive

Worston Av

Johnson Fold Community Primary School

Capitol Cl

Garwick Rd

Kenwood Road

Moss Lane

Mulholme

Riefield

Harpers La

Belayse Cl

Harpers

nson Fold

Lightbounds Av

Gargrave Av

Chipping Road

BANK

Canons Close

Beechfield Road

Barcroft

Bowland Drive

Montserrat Road

Gisburn Av

Shackleton

Tattersall Av

Oakenclough Dr

Lombridge Crs

Grisedale Cl

MOSS

WAY

Harper's Lane

Hollywood Road

Back Church Rd N

Brentford Avenue

Highfield Rd

Thornley Av

Kngs Av

Snn Rd

Sunnybank Rd

HORLEY OLD ROAD

Craven Place

Delph Hill Terrace

ynson Rd

Knott Lane

Mallet Crs

Maria Crs

Breasdale Rd

smithi lls Drive

PO

Heaton CC

Heaton CC

Doffcocker

Back Church Lane

Moorland Gv

Brookland Grove

Church Road Primary School

Orwell

church Road

PO

Hazelwood Road

Restnybank Cl

Shelbourne Avenue

Clough Street

New Barn Street

Mansfield Gv

Merlin Grove

Mellor Gv

Cuthile Grove

St Kngs

Brentford Avenue

Fenkford

5

Delph Hl

Delph HI

New Cft Rd

Wolsby Rd

Church Road

Moorside Road

Woodstock Drive

Abbotsford

Shelbourne Avenue

Rawlyn Road

70

Back Arnold Terrace

Doffcocker Lodge Nature Reserve

DOFF

29

KER BROW

CHORLEY OLD ROAD

B6226

Health Centre

Bro Fo

E F G H

69

MOSS BANK WAY A58

Heaton Avenue

Ripon

Thornton Avenue

Millstone Avenue

Normandale

Whitecroft

Sheil

Heaton-Med

Conway

Stranley Road

Stratford

Nuffield Av

PO

St

Lewis St

Seathle

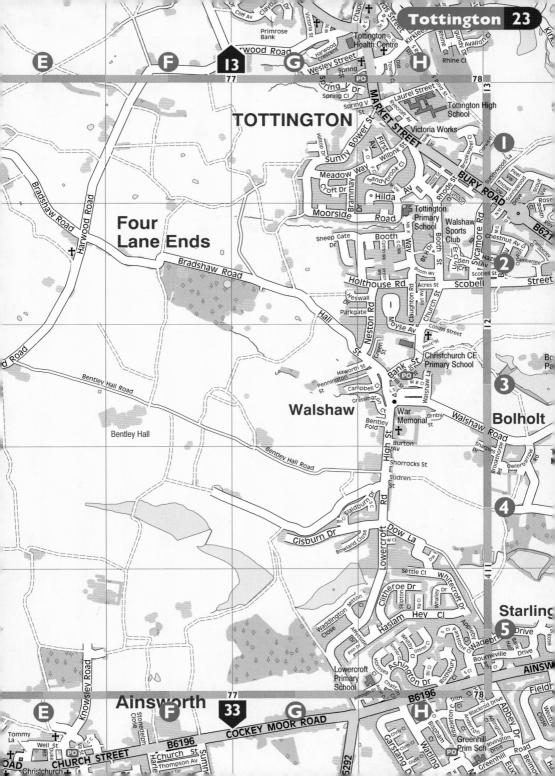

24

CHORLEY

A5106

3 58

A　　**B**　　14　　**C**　**Bolton: Wigan**　　**D**

59

Arley Lane

Wigan Golf Club

Golf Course

Arley Lane

Pennington La

Pennington Lane

Brookside Road

WC

Gareham Cl

Devon Dr

Alden Cl

Works

Essex Rd

S C

PO

Works

Worthington Lakes Business Park

Arley Lane

1

RED ROCK LANE   B5239   SCHOOL LANE

2

Rowton Ri

Red Rock

06

09

Lurdin La

Ridge Av

3

Richmond Cl

H Av

Works

08

Winstanleys

Pendlebury Lane

Pendlebury Lane

4

Douglas Vw

Wigan Lane

Pendlebury Lane

Sennicar Lane

A49

ere Oaks chool

5

Douglas Vw

Sennicar Lane

Sennicar Lane

Works

Wigan RUFC

Douglas Valley Business Park

WN1

Leeds & Liverpool Canal

School Lane

Golf Course

Haigh Hall Golf Complex

Haigh Coun Park

mfield Rd

Scott Av

Penbury Rd

Bethersden Rd

Newenden Rd

Old La

Ashford Rd

Larkfield Av

Walter

Whitley

06

07

LANE

3 58

A　　**B**　　**C**　　**D**

59

Brook Mill Lane

Wingates Road

Broomhey Avenue

Judd Terrace

Cranbrook Way

Hazelwood Rd

Elwood Cl

Hall   Lane

Woodfield

1 grid square represents 500 metres

26

Road
Castlecroft Av.
Vauze House
C
Chidgrove
orn Wy
Greenbarn
Vaze Va
Thursfor
Grove
Shawa
Close

A
362
Cemetery
Blackrod
Station
Works

Moss

B
Lane

16
63

C

D

Hillside
Avenue

MANCHESTER ROAD

Corston Grove

STATION ROAD

Greenbarn Way

B5408

Highfield Rd
Meadow Wy

1

90

Blackrod
Primary School

Red Moss

Midd

2

MANCHESTER ROAD

Hope Street

BLACKROD BY-PASS ROAD

Park Hall
Farm

Scot Lane End
CE Prim Sch

King
Cheethams

M61

3

25

Eskdale Av
Newlands
Drive

Dorning Street

B5408

MANCHESTER

Ramada
Hotel

80

Scot Lane
End

Scot Lane
Industrial
Estate

4

SCOT
LANE

Bolton
Wigan

ROAD

Hilton House

A6

A6027

5

Corfe C
Renfrew Rd
Lincoln Dr
Fold

362
407

Brinsop Hall Lane

Brinsop
Hall

Cooper
Turning

A6

B5239

ASPUL

A

BOLTON

B

34
63

C

DICCONSON

LANE

D
Dodd
Indust
Estat

Bode Lane

I grid square represents 500 metres

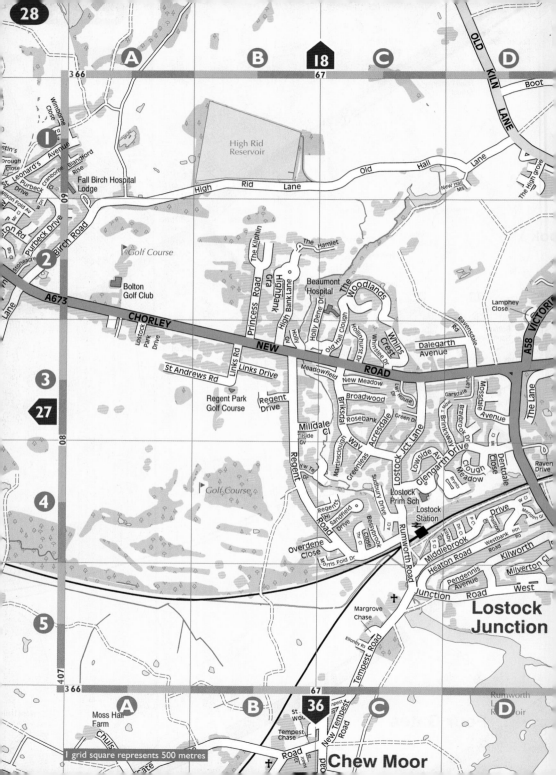

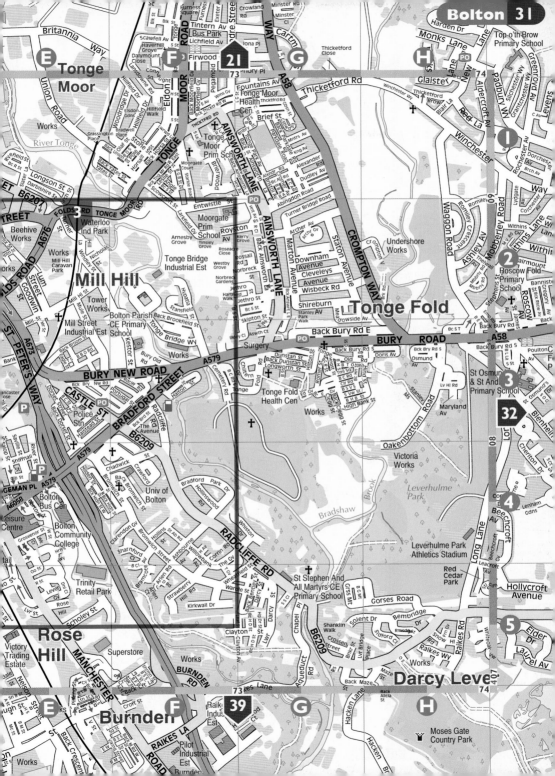

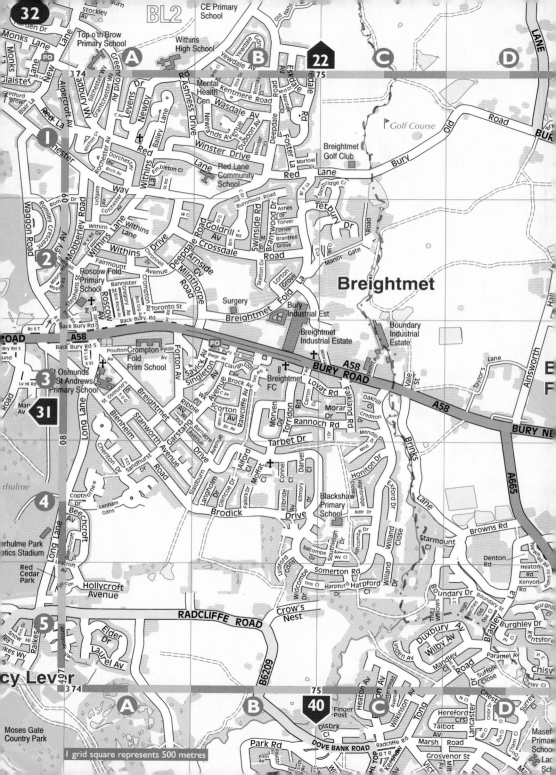

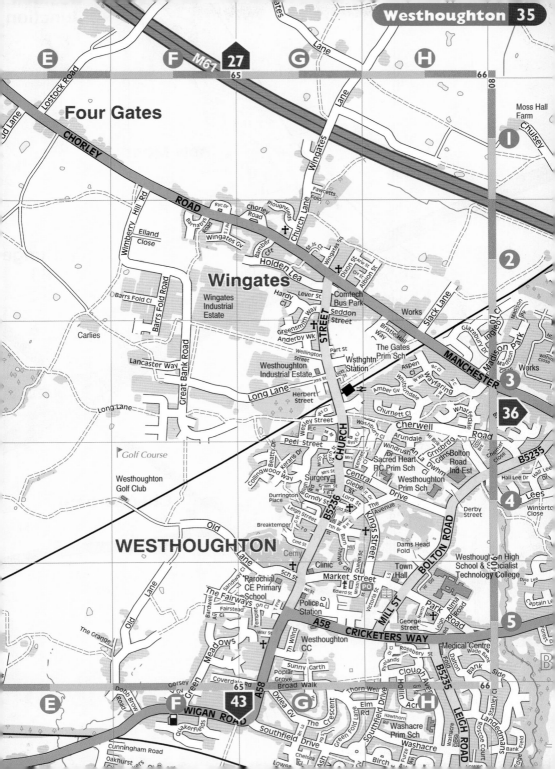

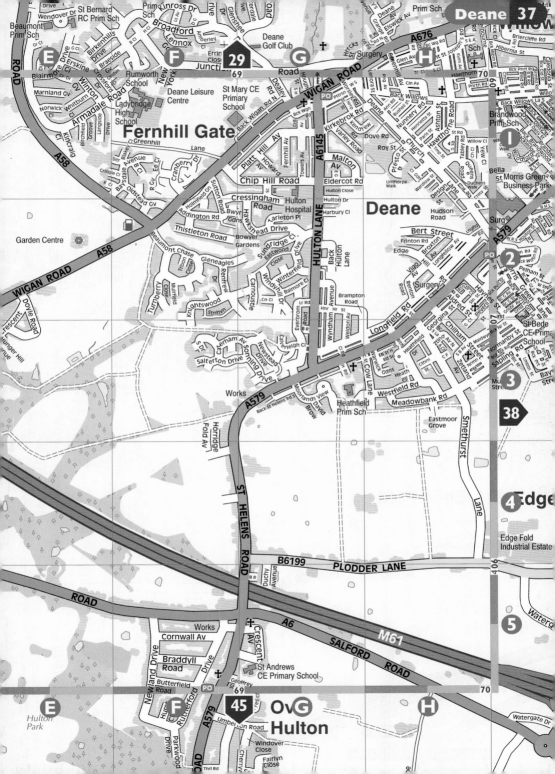

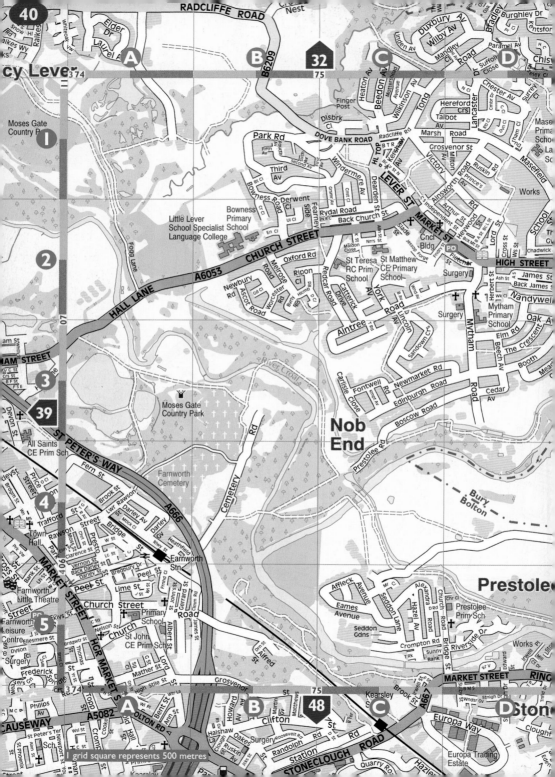

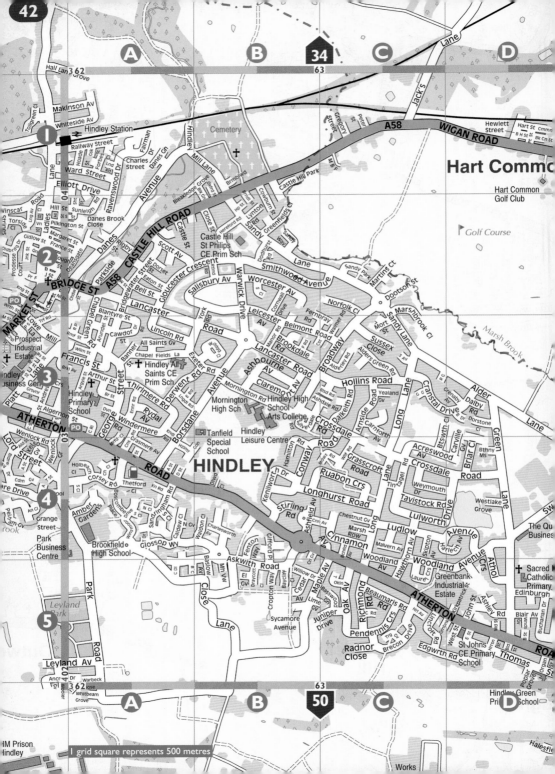

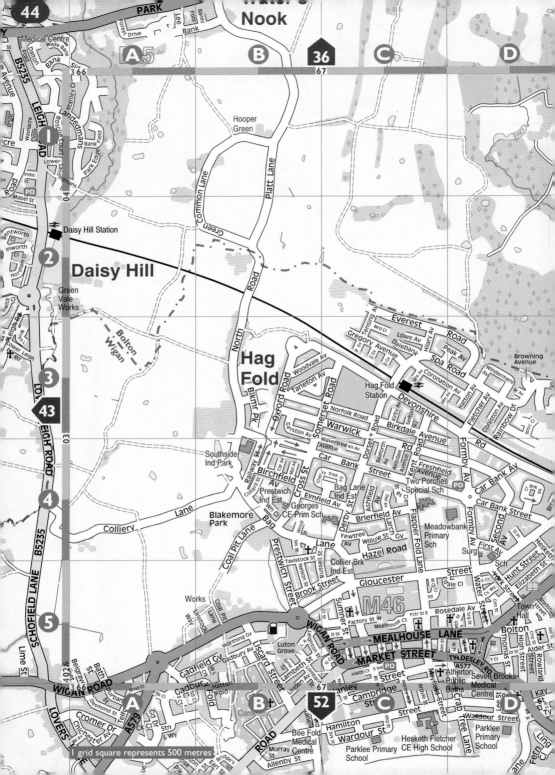

A6

M61

SALFORD ROAD

E

F

G

H

Works

Cornwall Av

Crescent Av

Braddyll Drive

St Andrews CE Primary School

37

Newland Drive

Hurst Cl

Butterfield Road

Rutherford Drive

Parkwood Drive

A579

NEWBROOK ROAD

69

PO

Frey Street

Mountmores Cl

Umberton Road

Over Hulton

Windover Close

Fairlyn Close

Cherrwood Av

Fairlyn Drive

Watergate Dr

I

70

04

Israel's Farm

Rosemary Lane

Back Lane

Thrl Rd

Reynolds Drive

Firs

Road

Rv Cl

Cl3

DS

Sandacre Cl

2

High Bank

Park Bank

Mrnngtn Rd

Brkdl

Shurdington Road

Breeze Hill Road

Makants Close

Carthmere Rd

Wellington Rd

The Close

Woodlands Dr

Breeze Hill

Hill Crest

Rutland Av

Lansdowne Road

3

Leadbeater's Farm

03

46

Woodside View

Hill Top

Low Green

Broadway

Highfield Pl

Millbrook Av

Greenfield Rd

Warren Close

Chiltern Av

Belvedere

Green Hall Prim Sch

Green Hall Cl

Meadow Bank Av

Avenue

Springate

Hillside

Eisdon Drive

Brksd Cl

Ascot Dr

Cumberland Road

Marlborough Rd

Central Av

4

Oliver Fold

Engine Lane

Carr

Brook Drive

Upton Road

Belmont

Atherton Station

A579

Marlew

BOLTON ROAD

Weston St

Crosby Street

Marton Drive

Douglas Street

Shakerley Lane

Hertford Drive

Lancaster Avenue

Prim Sch

Birch Rd

Beech St

Sycamore Rd

Douglas Park

5

402

Chowbent Prim Sch

Chanters Avenue

Peel Cl

Mary's

ATHERTON

Cornwall Av

Durham Cl

Essex Pl

Dorset Av

Somerset Av

Laxey

Ramsey Rd

Douglas Road

E

F

53

69

70

G **Shakerley** H

Arley Way

Crawford

Rutland Road

York Av

Devon

Wstmr Rd

Leicester Brk Cl

Shakerley CE Primary School

Old Mill Brook

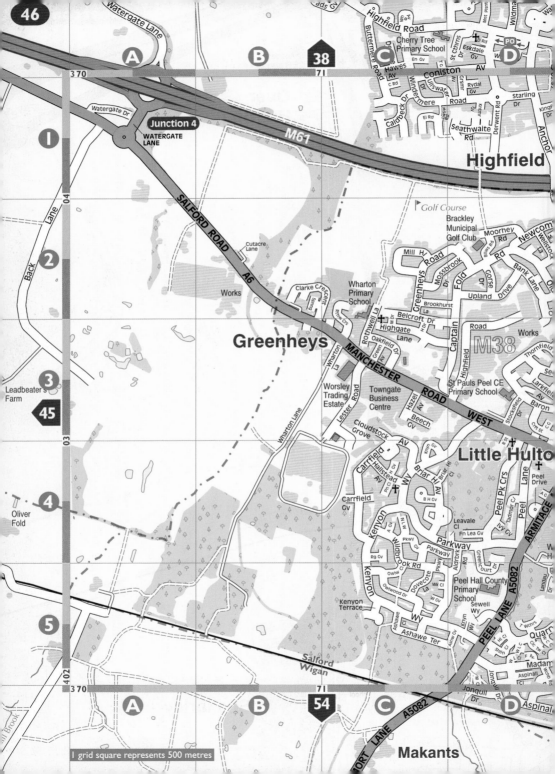

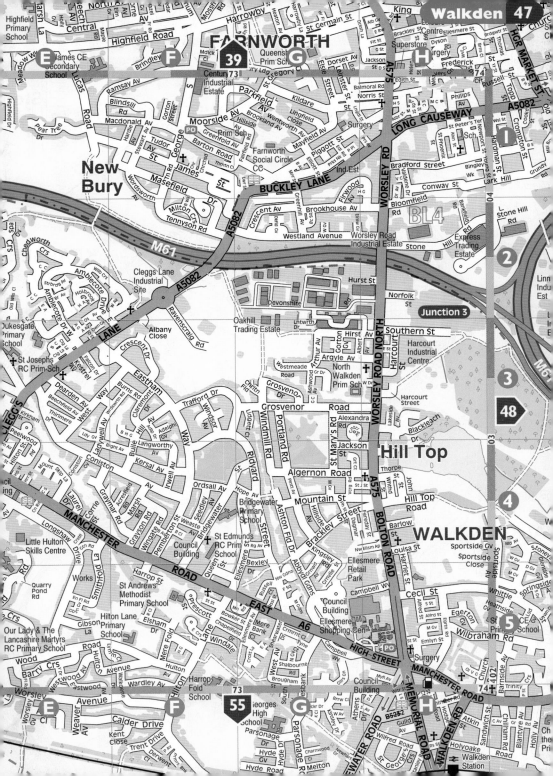

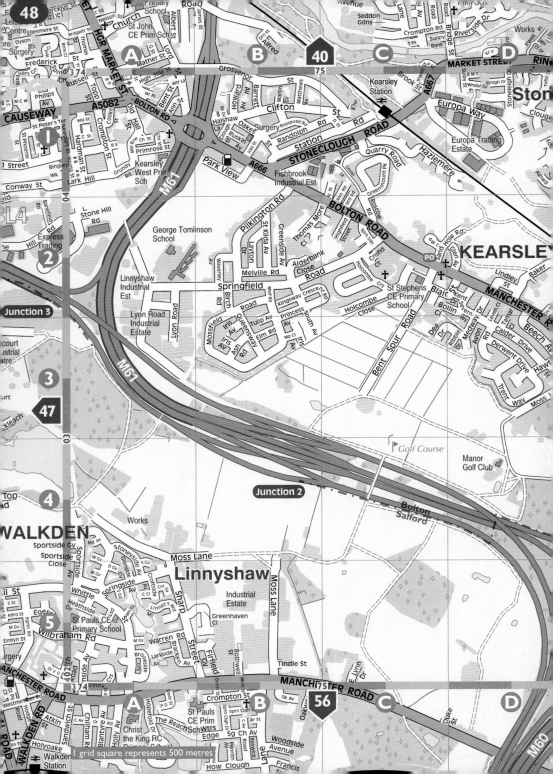

48

CAUSEWAY

A5082

BL4

Junction 3

3

47

4

WALKDEN

Linnyshaw

5

40
75

MARKET STREET

Kearsley
Station

Europa Way

Europa Trading
Estate

KEARSLEY

MANCHESTER R

Stonecough ROAD

A666

A667

BOLTON ROAD

Park View

George Tomlinson
School

Linnyshaw
Industrial
Est

Lyon Road Industrial
Estate

Springfield

Fishbrook
Industrial Est

St Stephens
CE Primary
School

Golf Course

Manor
Golf Club

Junction 2

Bolton
Salford

Moss Lane

Industrial
Estate

Greenhaven

St Pauls CE
Primary School

Wilbraham Rd

MANCHESTER ROAD

56

MANCHESTER ROAD

St Pauls
CE Prim Sch

Woodside
Avenue

Walkden
Station

| grid square represents 500 metres

A   B   C   D

M60

M61

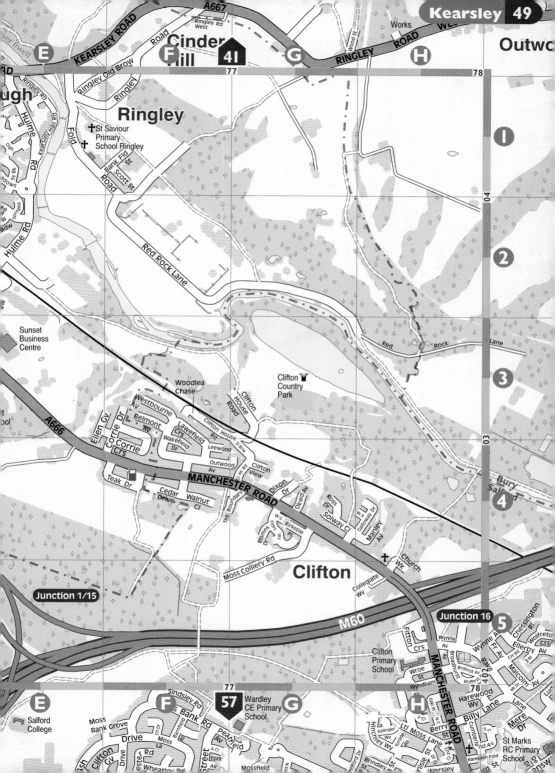

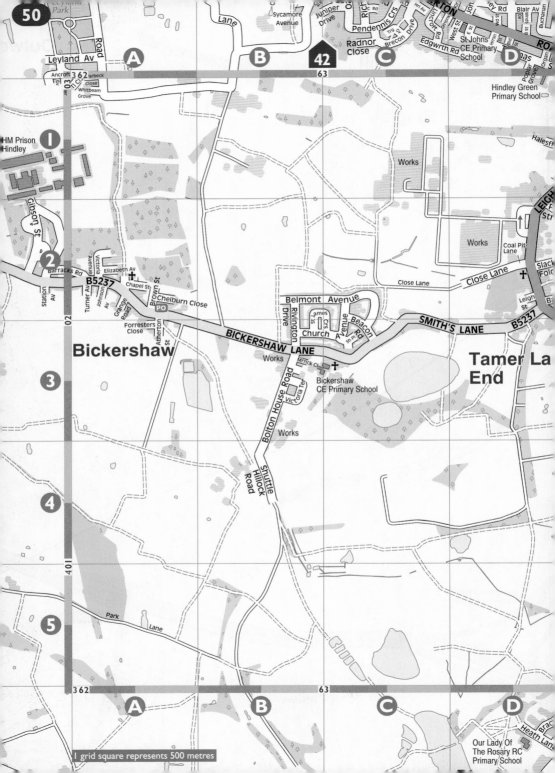

Howe Bridge

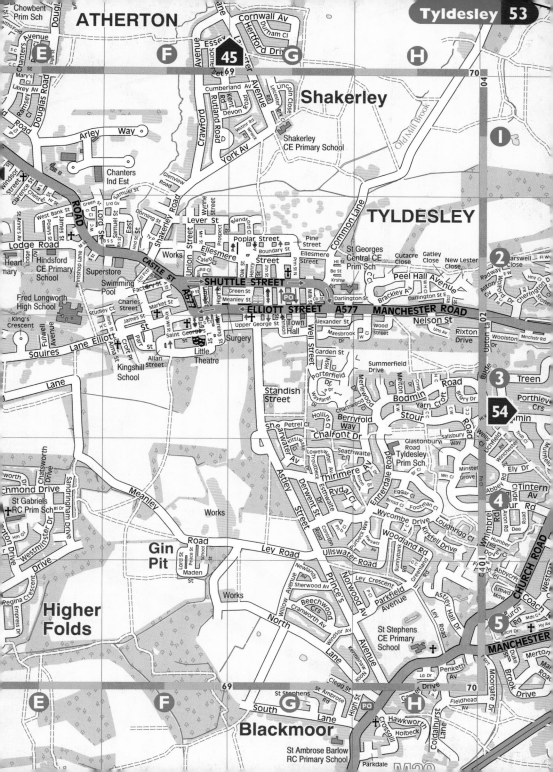

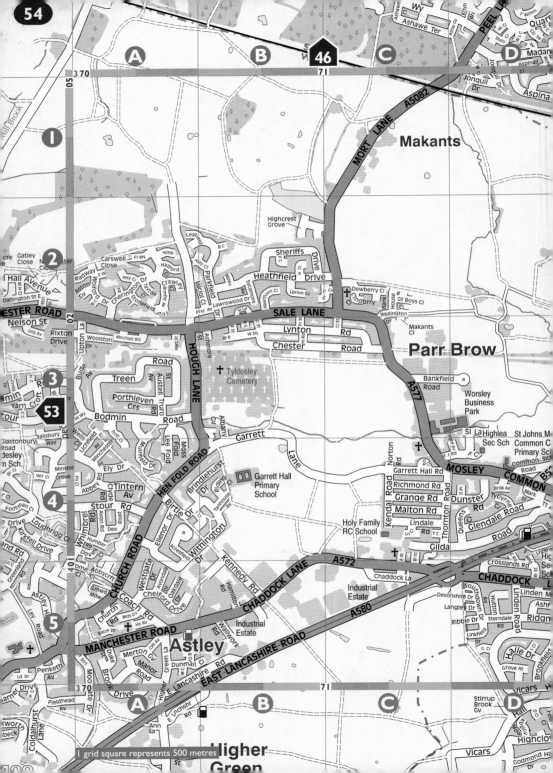

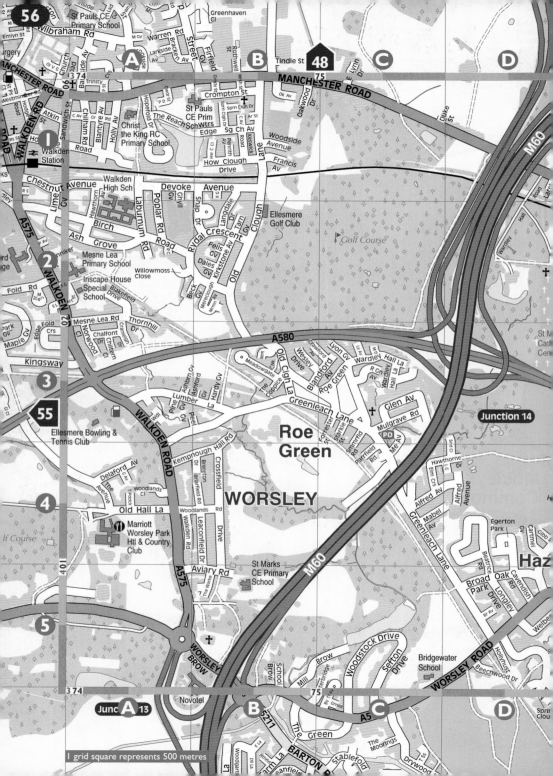

Adlington	7 F5	Deane	37 H2	Hill Top	47 H4	Pennington Green	34 A
Affetside	12 D4	Doffcocker	19 G5	Hilton House	26 C4	Pickley Green	51
Ainsworth	33 F1	Dunscar	10 B3	Hindley	42 A4	Prestolee	40
Anderton	7 F4	Eagley	10 C5	Hindley Green	43 E4	Red Rock	24
Aspull	25 H5	Edge Fold	38 A4	Hindsford	52 D1	Ringley	49
Astley	54 A5	Edgworth	5 E3	Holcombe Brook	13 H1	Rivington	8
Astley Bridge	20 C3	Egerton	10 C2	Hollins	38 B5	Roe Green	56
Atherton	45 E5	Ellenbrook	55 E3	Horrocks Fold	10 A5	Rose Hill	31
Bank Top	21 E2	Farnworth	39 F5	Horwich	17 F2	Scot Lane End	26
Barrow Bridge	19 G3	Fernhill Gate	37 F1	Howe Bridge	52 B2	Shakerley	53
Bickershaw	50 A3	Firwood Fold	21 G4	Hunger Hill	36 D2	Sharples	20
Black Lane	33 H4	Four Gates	35 E1	Johnson Fold	18 D4	Side of the Moor	22 A
Blackrod	15 G4	Four Lane Ends	23 F2	Kearsley	48 D2	Stoneclough	48
Bolton	3 G4	Gilnow	2 B5	Lever-Edge	38 B3	Swinton	57
Boothstown	55 E5	Gin Pit	53 F4	Lilford	52 A5	Tamer Lane End	50
Bottom o' th' Moor	17 G4	Great Lever	39 E2	Linnyshaw	48 A5	Tonge Fold	31
Bradley Fold	32 D3	Greenheys	46 B3	Little Hulton	46 D4	Tonge Moor	21
Bradshaw	21 G1	Greenmount	13 G2	Little Lever	40 D1	Toppings	11
Breightmet	32 C2	Grimeford Village	16 A1	Little Scotland	15 E5	Tottington	23
Bromley Cross	21 E1	Hag Fold	44 B3	Lostock	27 G4	Turton Bottoms	5
Brownlow Fold	30 A1	Haigh	25 F3	Lostock Junction	28 D5	Tyldesley	53
Burnden	39 E1	Halfway Houses	33 E4	Makants	54 C1	Walkden	47
Chapeltown	11 H1	Hall i' th' Wood	21 E3	Markland Hill	29 E2	Wallsuches	17
Chequerbent	36 C4	Halliwell	20 C4	Middlebrook	26 D2	Walshaw	23
Chew Moor	36 C1	Harper Green	39 F4	Mill Hill	3 H2	Wardley	57
Cinder Hill	41 F5	Hart Common	42 D1	Montcliffe	17 H2	Water's Nook	36
Clifton	49 G5	Harwood	22 C4	Moorside	57 F4	Westhoughton	35
Cooper Turning	26 D5	Harwood Lee	22 A2	Moses Gate	39 G3	Westleigh	51
Cox Green	10 D3	Hawkshaw	13 E1	Mosley Common	55 E4	Wilderswood	17
Daisy Hill	44 A2	Hazelhurst	56 D5	New Bury	47 E1	Willows	30
Dales Brow	57 F5	Heath Charnock	6 C2	Newtown	57 G2	Wingates	35
Dangerous Corner	51 E1	Heaton	29 G2	Nob End	40 C3	Winstanleys	24
Darcy Lever	31 H5	Higher Folds	53 E5	Over Hulton	45 G1	Worsley	56
Daubhill	38 A1	Highfield	46 D1	Parr Brow	54 C3		

USING THE STREET INDEX

Street names are listed alphabetically. Each street name is followed by its postal town or area locality, the Postcode District, the page number, and the reference to the square in which the name is found.

Standard index entries are shown as follows:

Abbey CI *BOLS/LL* BL3 ....**37** H3

Street names and selected addresses not shown on the map due to scale restrictions are shown in the index with an asterisk:

Acresfield CI *HOR/BR* BL6 * **15** G4

GENERAL ABBREVIATIONS

ACC	ACCESS	CTS	COURTS	HGR	HIGHER	MTN	MOUNTA
ALY	ALLEY	CTYD	COURTYARD	HL	HILL	MTS	MOUNTAI
AP	APPROACH	CUTT	CUTTINGS	HLS	HILLS	MUS	MUSE
AR	ARCADE	CV	COVE	HO	HOUSE	MWY	MOTORW
ASS	ASSOCIATION	CYN	CANYON	HOL	HOLLOW	N	NOR
AV	AVENUE	DEPT	DEPARTMENT	HOSP	HOSPITAL	NE	NORTH EA
BCH	BEACH	DL	DALE	HRB	HARBOUR	NW	NORTH WE
BLDS	BUILDINGS	DM	DAM	HTH	HEATH	O/P	OVERPA
BND	BEND	DR	DRIVE	HTS	HEIGHTS	OFF	OFFI
BNK	BANK	DRO	DROVE	HVN	HAVEN	ORCH	ORCHA
BR	BRIDGE	DRY	DRIVEWAY	HWY	HIGHWAY	OV	OV
BRK	BROOK	DWGS	DWELLINGS	IMP	IMPERIAL	PAL	PALA
BTM	BOTTOM	E	EAST	IN	INLET	PAS	PASSA
BUS	BUSINESS	EMB	EMBANKMENT	IND EST	INDUSTRIAL ESTATE	PAV	PAVILI
BVD	BOULEVARD	EMBY	EMBASSY	INF	INFIRMARY	PDE	PARA
BY	BYPASS	ESP	ESPLANADE	INFO	INFORMATION	PH	PUBLIC HOU
CATH	CATHEDRAL	EST	ESTATE	INT	INTERCHANGE	PK	PA
CEM	CEMETERY	EX	EXCHANGE	IS	ISLAND	PKWY	PARKW
CEN	CENTRE	EXPY	EXPRESSWAY	JCT	JUNCTION	PL	PLA
CFT	CROFT	EXT	EXTENSION	JTY	JETTY	PLN	PLA
CH	CHURCH	F/O	FLYOVER	KG	KING	PLNS	PLAIN
CHA	CHASE	FC	FOOTBALL CLUB	KNL	KNOLL	PLZ	PLA
CHYD	CHURCHYARD	FK	FORK	L	LAKE	POL	POLICE STATIC
CIR	CIRCLE	FLD	FIELD	LA	LANE	PR	PRIN
CIRC	CIRCUS	FLDS	FIELDS	LDG	LODGE	PREC	PRECIN
CL	CLOSE	FLS	FALLS	LGT	LIGHT	PREP	PREPARATO
CLFS	CLIFFS	FM	FARM	LK	LOCK	PRIM	PRIMA
CMP	CAMP	FT	FORT	LKS	LAKES	PROM	PROMENA
CNR	CORNER	FTS	FLATS	LNDG	LANDING	PRS	PRINCE
CO	COUNTY	FWY	FREEWAY	LTL	LITTLE	PRT	PO
COLL	COLLEGE	FY	FERRY	LWR	LOWER	PT	POI
COM	COMMON	GA	GATE	MAG	MAGISTRATE	PTH	PA
COMM	COMMISSION	GAL	GALLERY	MAN	MANSIONS	PZ	PIAZ
CON	CONVENT	GDN	GARDEN	MD	MEAD	QD	QUADRA
COT	COTTAGE	GDNS	GARDENS	MDW	MEADOWS	QU	QUEE
COTS	COTTAGES	GLD	GLADE	MEM	MEMORIAL	QY	QUA
CP	CAPE	GLN	GLEN	MI	MILL	R	RIVE
CPS	COPSE	GN	GREEN	MKT	MARKET	RBT	ROUNDABO
CR	CREEK	GND	GROUND	MKTS	MARKETS	RD	ROA
CREM	CREMATORIUM	GRA	GRANGE	ML	MALL	RDG	RID
CRS	CRESCENT	GRG	GARAGE	MNR	MANOR	REP	REPUBLI
CSWY	CAUSEWAY	GT	GREAT	MS	MEWS	RES	RESERVO
CT	COURT	GTWY	GATEWAY	MSN	MISSION	RFC	RUGBY FOOTBALL CLU
CTRL	CENTRAL	GV	GROVE	MT	MOUNT	RI	RI

.... RAMP	SPR .... SPRING
.... ROW	SQ .... SQUARE
.... SOUTH	STN .... STATION
.... SCHOOL	ST .... STREET
.... SOUTH EAST	STR .... STREAM
.... SERVICE AREA	STRD .... STRAND
.... SHORE	SW .... SOUTH WEST
.... SHOPPING	TDG .... TRADING
.... SKYWAY	TER .... TERRACE
.... SUMMIT	THWY .... THROUGHWAY
.... SOCIETY	TNL .... TUNNEL
.... SPUR	TOLL .... TOLLWAY

TPK .... TURNPIKE	VLG .... VILLAGE
TR .... TRACK	VLS .... VILLAS
TRL .... TRAIL	VW .... VIEW
TWR .... TOWER	W .... WEST
U/P .... UNDERPASS	WD .... WOOD
UNI .... UNIVERSITY	WHF .... WHARF
UPR .... UPPER	WK .... WALK
V .... VALE	WKS .... WALKS
VA .... VALLEY	WLS .... WELLS
VIAD .... VIADUCT	WY .... WAY
VIL .... VILLA	YD .... YARD
VIS .... VISTA	YHA .... YOUTH HOSTEL

OSTCODE TOWNS AND AREA ABBREVIATIONS

.... Atherton	CHLYE .... Chorley east/
.... Bolton	Adlington/Whittle-le-Woods
LE .... Bolton east	EDGW/EG ...... Edgeworth/Egerton
.S/LL .. Bolton south/Little Lever	FWTH .... Farnworth
LY/EC .... Chorley/	HOR/BR ...... Horwich/Blackrod
Eccleston	LEIGH .... Leigh

LHULT .... Little Hulton	WALK .... Walkden
RAD .... Radcliffe	WCN .... Wigan
RAMS .... Ramsbottom	WGNE/HIN ... Wigan east/Hindley
SWIN .... Swinton	WHTN .... Westhoughton
TOT/BURYW ... Tottington/Bury west	
TYLD .... Tyldesley	

Index - streets

Abb - Ash

A

bey Cl BOLS/LL BL3 ... 37 H3
RAD M26 ... 33 G5
bey Cl RAD M26 ... 41 G1
beycroft Cl TYLD M29 ... 54 A5
beydale Gdns WALK M28 ... 47 G4
bey Dr SWIN M27 ... 57 G3
bey Gv CHLYE PR6 ... 7 E5
bey La LEIGH WN7 ... 51 F2
beylea Dr WHTN BL5 ... 36 A3
bey Rd TYLD M29 ... 54 A4
bey Sq LEIGH WN7 ... 51 F2
bey St LEIGH WN7 ... 51 H5
bingdon Wy LEIGH WN7 ... 51 F2
ot Cft WHTN BL5 ... 43 H2
bot's Fold Rd WALK M28 ... 55 F4
botsford Rd BOL BL1 ... 29 G1
bott St BOLS/LL BL3 ... 30 C5
OR/BR BL6 ... 16 D3
ercorn Rd BOL BL1 ... 19 H4
ernethy St HOR/BR BL6 ... 17 F5
ngdon Rd BOLE BL2 ... 31 G2
ian Rd BOL BL1 ... 20 A5
aham St HOR/BR BL6 ... 16 D3
cia Av SWIN M27 ... 57 G5
worth Rd SWIN M27 ... 57 G2
e Fld BOLE BL2 ... 21 H3
esdale HOR/BR BL6 ... 28 C4
esfield CHLY/EC PR7 ... 14 D1
YLD M29 ... 54 A4
esfield Cl HOR/BR BL6 * ... 15 G4
esfield Rd LHULT M38 ... 47 F4
es St TOT/BURYW BL8 ... 23 H2
e St RAD M26 ... 41 G2
eswood Av WGNE/HIN WN2 ... 42 C4
am St BOLS/LL BL3 ... 30 D5
lington Rd BOLS/LL BL3 ... 37 F2
elaide St BOLS/LL BL3 ... 38 B1
HLYE PR6 ... 7 E4
WIN M27 ... 57 F4
elphi Dr LHULT M38 ... 47 F3
elphi Gv LHULT M38 ... 47 F3
elphi St RAD M26 ... 33 H5
sham Dr BOL BL1 ... 30 D1
ington St BOLS/LL BL3 ... 38 B2
ian Rd BOL BL1 ... 20 A5
etside Dr TOT/BURYW BL8 ... 23 G5
eck Av RAD M26 ... 40 C5
scow Av HOR/BR BL6 ... 27 H2
sdale Av ATH M46 ... 44 C4
DGW/EG BL7 ... 4 D2
sdale Rd BOLS/LL BL3 ... 38 C3
se Rd HOR/BR BL6 ... 15 F4
sley Gv WALK M28 ... 55 H1
slie Rd BOL BL1 ... 29 G1
sworth Av HOR/BR BL6 ... 27 G1
sworth Ct BOLE BL2 ... 31 G3
sworth Hall Rd BOLE BL2 ... 32 D5
sworth La BOLE BL2 ... 31 G2
sworth Rd BOLS/LL BL3 ... 40 C2
AD M26 ... 33 H5
sworth St BOL BL1 ... 20 A5
tree Rd BOLS/LL BL3 ... 40 C3
e Dr BOLE BL2 ... 21 F2
eworth St WHTN BL5 ... 35 G3
1 St BOL BL1 ... 20 B4
any Cl LHULT M38 ... 47 F3

Albany Gv TYLD M29 ... 54 B3
Albermarle Rd SWIN M27 ... 57 G4
Alberta St BOLS/LL BL3 ... 30 A5
Albert Av WALK M28 ... 47 H3
Albert Colliery Est
   WGNE/HIN WN2 * ... 50 B3
Albert Gv FWTH BL4 ... 39 H5
Alberton Cl WGNE/HIN WN2 ... 25 G4
Albert Rd FWTH BL4 ... 39 H5
Albert Rd West BOL BL1 ... 29 G2
Albert St BOLS/LL BL3 * ... 40 D2
   EDGW/EG BL7 ... 10 B1
   FWTH BL4 ... 40 A5
   HOR/BR BL6 ... 16 D3
Albion St BOLS/LL BL3 ... 30 D5
   FWTH BL4 ... 48 C2
   SWIN M27 ... 35 G2
Aldbury Ter BOL BL1 * ... 30 B1
Alderbank HOR/BR BL6 ... 16 B4
Alderbank Cl FWTH BL4 ... 48 B2
Alderbrook Rd LHULT M38 ... 46 D5
Aldercroft Av BOLE BL2 ... 31 H1
Alder Dr SWIN M27 ... 57 E2
Alderfold St ATH M46 ... 44 D5
Alder La WGNE/HIN WN2 ... 42 D3
Alderley Av BOL BL1 ... 20 C2
Alderley Rd WGNE/HIN WN2 ... 42 C3
Alderminster Av LHULT M38 ... 47 E3
Alders Green Rd
   WGNE/HIN WN2 ... 42 C3
Alder St ATH M46 ... 44 D5
   BOLS/LL BL3 ... 38 D2
Aldersyde St BOLS/LL BL3 ... 38 B2
Alderton Dr WHTN BL5 ... 43 G2
Aldford Dr ATH M46 ... 45 E3
Aldford Gv BOLE BL2 ... 32 D5
Aldred St BOLS/LL BL3 ... 37 H2
   LEIGH WN7 ... 51 G3
Aldsworth Dr BOLS/LL BL3 ... 38 C1
Alexander Briant Ct
   FWTH BL4 * ... 47 G1
Alexander Rd BOLE BL2 ... 31 G1
Alexander St TYLD M29 ... 53 G3
Alexandra Rd FWTH BL4 ... 48 C2
   HOR/BR BL6 ... 27 G2
   RAD M26 ... 40 C5
   WALK M28 ... 47 G3
Alexandra St BOLS/LL BL3 * ... 38 B1
   FWTH BL4 ... 47 H1
Alexandria Dr WHTN BL5 ... 36 B5
Alford Cl BOLE BL2 ... 32 B4
Alfred Av WALK M28 ... 56 D4
Alfred St BOLS/LL BL3 ... 31 F5
   EDGW/EG BL7 ... 10 B1
   FWTH BL4 ... 39 H3
   FWTH BL4 ... 40 B5
   TYLD M29 ... 53 F2
   WALK M28 ... 47 H5
Algernon Rd WALK M28 ... 47 G4
Algernon St SWIN M27 ... 57 F3
Alice St BOLS/LL BL3 ... 30 A5
Allan St TYLD M29 ... 53 F3
Allenby Gv WHTN BL5 ... 43 G1
Allenby Rd SWIN M27 ... 57 E5
Allenby St ATH M46 ... 52 B1
Allendale Gdns BOL BL1 ... 20 C5
Allen St BOLS/LL BL3 ... 40 C1
   RAD M26 ... 41 H2
Allerton Cl WHTN BL5 ... 36 A4

Allesley Cl WHTN BL5 ... 36 A4
All Saints Gv WGNE/HIN WN2 ... 42 A3
All Saints' St BOL BL1 ... 2 E2
Allsopp St BOLS/LL BL3 ... 2 E6
Alma Rd WHTN BL5 ... 35 H5
Alma St ATH M46 ... 44 C5
   BOLS/LL BL3 ... 38 A1
   BOLS/LL BL3 ... 40 D2
   FWTH BL4 * ... 48 D3
   LEIGH WN7 ... 51 G3
   RAD M26 ... 33 H5
   TYLD M29 ... 53 F3
Almond Gv BOL BL1 * ... 20 D4
Almond St BOL BL1 ... 20 D3
   FWTH BL4 ... 39 G5
Alnwick Cl WGNE/HIN WN2 ... 25 H5
Alpine Dr LEIGH WN7 ... 51 E3
Alston Lea ATH M46 ... 45 E4
Alston St BOLS/LL BL3 * ... 38 C2
Amber Gdns WGNE/HIN WN2 ... 42 A4
Ambergate ATH M46 ... 52 D1
Amber Gv WHTN BL5 ... 35 H3
Amberley Cl BOLS/LL BL3 ... 29 F5
Amblecote Dr East
   LHULT M38 ... 47 E2
Amblecote Dr West
   LHULT M38 ... 47 E2
Ambleside Cl BOLE BL2 ... 22 B3
Ambrose Av LEIGH WN7 ... 51 G2
Anchor La FWTH BL4 ... 46 D1
Ancroft Dr WGNE/HIN WN2 ... 42 A5
Anderby Wk WHTN BL5 ... 35 G3
Anderton Cl TOT/BURYW BL8 ... 33 H1
Anderton St BOLS/LL BL3 * ... 16 C2
Anderton La HOR/BR BL6 ... 16 A4
Anderton St CHLY/EC PR7 ... 7 E5
Andrew Cl TOT/BURYW BL8 ... 13 H3
Andrew La BOL BL1 ... 20 D1
Anfield Rd BOLS/LL BL3 ... 38 C3
Angelo St BOL BL1 ... 20 B4
Angle St BOLE BL2 ... 31 F1
Anglezarke Rd CHLYE PR6 ... 7 E5
Anglia Gv BOLS/LL BL3 ... 38 A1
Angus Av LEIGH WN7 ... 51 E5
Annis Rd BOLS/LL BL3 ... 37 H1
Ann St FWTH BL4 ... 48 A1
   LEIGH WN7 ... 51 G3
Ansdell Rd HOR/BR BL6 ... 17 E3
Anson Av SWIN M27 ... 57 G5
Anson Rd SWIN M27 ... 57 G5
Anson St BOL BL1 ... 20 D4
Anyon Vls HOR/BR BL6 * ... 16 D3
Appleby Cl TOT/BURYW BL8 ... 23 H5
Appleby Gdns BOLE BL2 * ... 31 E1
Appledore Dr BOLE BL2 ... 22 B5
Appleton La WHTN BL5 ... 35 H4
Aqueduct Rd BOLS/LL BL3 ... 39 G1
Arbor Gv LHULT M38 ... 46 C4
Archer Av BOLE BL2 ... 31 G2
Archer Gv BOLE BL2 ... 31 G2
Archer St WALK M28 ... 54 C5
Arch St BOL BL1 ... 3 H1
Ardens Cl SWIN M27 ... 57 F1
Ardley Rd HOR/BR BL6 ... 17 E3
Arena Ap HOR/BR BL6 ... 27 E3
Argo St BOLS/LL BL3 ... 38 B1
Argyle Av WALK M28 ... 47 G3
Argyle St ATH M46 ... 52 C1
   SWIN M27 ... 57 G4
   WGNE/HIN WN2 ... 42 B4

Arkholme WALK M28 ... 55 E3
Arkwright Cl BOL BL1 ... 30 A1
Arkwright St HOR/BR BL6 ... 17 E5
Arlen Ct BOLE BL2 ... 3 J7
Arlen Rd BOLE BL2 ... 3 J7
Arley La WGN WN1 ... 24 B1
Arley Wy ATH M46 ... 53 E1
Arlington Av SWIN M27 ... 57 F5
Arlington St BOLS/LL BL3 ... 38 D2
Armadale Rd BOLS/LL BL3 ... 37 E1
Armitage Av LHULT M38 ... 46 D4
Armitage Gv LHULT M38 ... 46 D4
Armstrong St HOR/BR BL6 ... 17 E5
Arncot Rd BOL BL1 ... 20 D2
Arnesby Gv BOLE BL2 ... 3 K1
Arnfield Dr WALK M28 ... 55 F5
Arnold Rd EDGW/EG BL7 ... 10 D4
Arnold St BOL BL1 ... 20 B5
Arnside Gv BOLE BL2 ... 32 A2
Arnside Rd WGNE/HIN WN2 ... 42 C3
Arran Cl BOLS/LL BL3 ... 29 E5
Arran Gv RAD M26 ... 33 G5
Arrowhill Rd RAD M26 ... 33 H2
Arrow St BOL BL1 ... 2 C1
Arthur Av WALK M28 ... 47 G3
Arthur La BOLE BL2 ... 22 D5
Arthur St BOLS/LL BL3 ... 40 C2
   FWTH BL4 ... 39 H5
   SWIN M27 ... 57 F4
   WALK M28 ... 55 H2
   WALK M28 ... 56 B1
   WGNE/HIN WN2 ... 42 A3
Artillery St BOLS/LL BL3 ... 3 F7
Arundale WHTN BL5 ... 35 H3
Arundel Dr LEIGH WN7 ... 51 H5
Arundel St BOL BL1 ... 20 C2
   SWIN M27 ... 57 E2
   WGNE/HIN WN2 ... 42 A3
Ascot Dr ATH M46 ... 45 E4
Ascot Rd BOLS/LL BL3 ... 40 B2
Ashawe Cl LHULT M38 ... 46 C5
Ashawe Gv LHULT M38 ... 46 D5
Ashawe Ter LHULT M38 ... 46 C5
Ashbank Av BOLS/LL BL3 ... 29 E4
Ashbee St BOL BL1 ... 20 C4
Ashbourne Av BOLE BL2 ... 3 K6
   WGNE/HIN WN2 ... 42 B3
Ashbourne Cl LEIGH WN7 ... 51 F2
Ashbourne Gv WALK M28 ... 56 A3
Ashburn Cl HOR/BR BL6 ... 27 F2
Ashburner St BOL BL1 ... 2 D5
Ashbury Cl BOLS/LL BL3 ... 2 C7
Ashby Cl FWTH BL4 ... 39 F2
Ashby Gv LEIGH WN7 ... 51 E3
Ashcombe Dr BOLE BL2 ... 32 C4
   RAD M26 ... 33 F5
Ashcott Cl HOR/BR BL6 ... 28 D5
Ashcroft St WGNE/HIN WN2 ... 42 A4
Ashdale Av BOLS/LL BL3 ... 29 E5
Ashdale Rd WGNE/HIN WN2 ... 42 B3
Ashdene Crs BOLE BL2 ... 21 H3
Ashdown Dr BOLE BL2 ... 21 G4
   WALK M28 ... 54 D4
Ash Dr SWIN M27 ... 57 E1
Asher St BOLS/LL BL3 ... 38 A2
Ashes Dr BOLE BL2 ... 32 B2
Ashfield Av ATH M46 ... 44 C4
   WGNE/HIN WN2 ... 42 B4
Ashfield Dr WGNE/HIN WN2 ... 25 G5
Ashfield Gv BOL BL1 ... 21 E1

Ashfield Rd *CHLYE* PR6 ....7 F4
Ashford Av *SWIN* M27 ....57 E5
  WALK M28 ....54 D5
Ashford Cl *BOLE* BL2.....................22 A3
Ashford Gv *WALK* M28..................56 B3
Ashford Wk *BOL* BL1......................30 C1
Ash Gv *BOL* BL1 ....29 H2
  BOLE BL2.....................................22 B4
  RAMS BL0....................................13 H1
  WALK M28 ....56 A2
  WHTN BL5 ....43 G1
Ashington Cl *BOL* BL1...................19 H4
Ashington Dr *TOT/BURYW* BL8 .....33 G1
Ashlands Av *WALK* M28.................55 E4
  WALK M28 ....57 E5
Ash Lawns *BOL* BL1 ....29 H3
Ash Leigh Dr *BOL* BL1...................29 E2
Ashley Av *BOLE* BL2......................31 H2
  SWIN M27 ....57 F5
Ashley Crs *SWIN* M27....................57 F4
Ashley Dr *LEIGH* WN7...................51 E3
  SWIN M27 ....57 F5
Ashley Rd *WGNE/HIN* WN2 ....42 D5
Ashling Ct *TYLD* M29.....................54 A2
Ashmore St *TYLD* M29...................54 B3
Ashness Cl *HOR/BR* BL6.................16 B4
Ashness Dr *BOLE* BL2....................32 A1
Ashover Cl *BOL* BL1.......................20 D1
Ashridge Cl *HOR/BR* BL6..............28 C4
Ash Rd *FWTH* BL4..........................48 B3
Ash St *BOLE* BL2 ....3 G5
  TYLD M29....................................53 G2
Ashton Field Dr *WALK* M28...........47 G4
Ashton St *BOLS/LL* BL3.................37 H1
  BOLS/LL BL3.................................40 D2
Ashurst Cl *BOLE* BL2.....................22 B4
Ashwell St *BOLE* BL2 *...................21 F4
Ashwood *RAD* M26........................48 D1
Ashwood Av *WALK* M28.................47 G3
Ashworth Av *BOLS/LL* BL3.............41 E2
Ashworth La *BOL* BL1....................20 D2
Ashworth St *FWTH* BL4.................39 G5
  WGNE/HIN WN2..........................34 A2
Asia St *BOLS/LL* BL3 ....39 E2
Askrigg Cl *ATH* M46......................52 A3
Askwith Rd *WGNE/HIN* WN2 ....42 B5
Aspen Cl *WHTN* BL5......................35 H3
Aspinall Cl *HOR/BR* BL6................27 E1
  WALK M28 ....46 D5
Aspinall Crs *WALK* M28.................54 D1
Aspinall St *HOR/BR* BL6................27 F1
Aspinall Wy *HOR/BR* BL6..............27 F1
The Asshawes *CHLYE* PR6...............6 D3
Aster Av *FWTH* BL4 ....39 E4
Astley Hall Dr *TYLD* M29...............53 H5
Astley La *BOL* BL1 ....20 B4
Astley Rd *BOLE* BL2.......................22 A2
Astley St *BOL* BL1..........................20 C5
  TYLD M29....................................53 G4
Aston Gv *TYLD* M29.......................54 A2
Athens Dr *WALK* M28.....................55 G1
Atherfield *BOLE* BL2.......................22 A3
Atherleigh Gv *LEIGH* WN7............51 H4
Atherleigh Wy *LEIGH* WN7............51 H1
Atherton Av *WGNE/HIN* WN2........42 C5
Atherton St *CHLY/EC* PR7.............15 E1
  WGNE/HIN WN2..........................50 A3
Athlone Av *BOL* BL1......................20 B2
Athol Crs *WGNE/HIN* WN2............42 D4
Atholl Cl *BOLS/LL* BL3...................29 F4
Atkinson Av *BOLS/LL* BL3.............39 F2
Atkin St *WALK* M28........................55 H1
Auberson Rd *BOLS/LL* BL3............38 B2
Auburn St *BOLS/LL* BL3.................38 B2
Augustus St *BOLS/LL* BL3.............39 E1
Austin's La *HOR/BR* BL6................27 H1
Avallon Cl *TOT/BURYW* BL8 ....13 H5
Avebury Cl *HOR/BR* BL6................27 H1
Avenue St *BOL* BL1..........................2 A1
The Avenue *BOLE* BL2......................3 J4
  CHLYE PR6....................................7 E4
  LEIGH WN7.................................51 H5
  WALK M28 ....56 A4
  WHTN BL5 ....35 H4
Averhill *WALK* M28 ....55 F3
Aviary Rd *WALK* M28......................56 A5
Avocet Cl *LEIGH* WN7....................52 A5
Avoncliff Cl *BOL* BL1.....................20 B4
Avon Cl *WALK* M28........................55 E1
Avondale Dr *RAMS* BL0..................13 H2
  TYLD M29....................................54 A3
Avondale Rd *FWTH* BL4.................38 D5
Avondale St *BOL* BL1....................30 A1
Avonhead Cl *HOR/BR* BL6.............16 C5
Avon Rd *FWTH* BL4 ....48 D3
  TYLD M29....................................54 A4
Avon St *BOL* BL1...........................29 H1
Axelholme Ct *HOR/BR* BL6...........16 B4
Aylesbury Crs *WGNE/HIN* WN2 ....51 E1

Aylesford Wk *BOL* BL1 *................30 C1
Ayr St *BOLE* BL2.............................21 F3
Ayrton Gv *LHULT* M38...................47 E3

B

Babylon La *CHLYE* PR6 ....7 G3
Back Abingdon Rd *BOLE* BL2.........31 G1
Back Adrian Rd *BOL* BL1................20 A5
Back Adrian Rd East *BOL* BL1 * 20 A5
Back Ainscow St *BOL* BL1................2 C1
Back Ainsworth La *BOLE* BL2.........31 G2
Back Ainsworth La East
  BOLE BL2.....................................31 G2
Back Ainsworth St *BOL* BL1 *........20 B5
Back Alder St *BOLS/LL* BL3............38 D2
Back Alexander Rd *BOLE* BL2.........31 G1
Back Alexandra St
  BOLS/LL BL3.................................38 A1
Back Alfred St *BOLS/LL* BL3 *........39 F1
  BOLS/LL BL3.................................40 D2
Back Alicia St *BOLS/LL* BL3............39 H1
Back All Saints' St *BOL* BL1 ....3 F2
Back Alston St *BOLS/LL* BL3...........38 C2
Back Anglia Gv *BOLS/LL* BL3.........38 A1
Back Annis Rd *BOLS/LL* BL3...........37 H1
Back Anson St *BOL* BL1 *...............20 D4
Back Apple Ter *BOL* BL1 *..............20 B5
Back Argo St *BOLS/LL* BL3.............38 B1
Back Arlington St *BOLS/LL* BL3......38 D2
Back Arnold St *BOL* BL1 ....20 A5
Back Arnold Ter *BOL* BL1...............29 F1
Back Ashbee St *BOL* BL1................20 C4
Back Ashford Wk *BOL* BL1 *...........30 C1
Back Ash St *BOLE* BL2.....................3 G5
Back Ashton St *BOLS/LL* BL3 *.......37 H1
Back Ashworth La *BOL* BL1............20 D2
Back Astley St *BOL* BL1..................20 C5
Back Augustus St
  BOLS/LL BL3 *..............................39 E1
Back Augustus St West
  BOLS/LL BL3.................................38 D1
Back Avenue St *BOL* BL1 *...............2 C1
Back Avondale St *BOL* BL1 *...........30 A1
Back Baldwin St *BOLS/LL* BL3 *......2 C7
Back Baldwin St North
  BOLS/LL BL3...................................2 C7
Back Banbury St *BOLE* BL2............31 G1
Back Bankfield St *BOLS/LL* BL3 .....30 A5
Back Bantry St *BOLS/LL* BL3..........30 C5
Back Barbara St *BOLS/LL* BL3.........38 B1
Back Bark St *BOL* BL1......................2 D3
Back Bashall St *BOL* BL1................30 A2
Back Battenberg Rd *BOL* BL1.........30 A2
Back Baxendale St *BOL* BL1...........30 A2
Back Bayley St *BOL* BL1 *................2 A1
Back Baythorpe St *BOL* BL1 *.........20 D5
Back Baytorpe St North
  BOL BL1 *....................................20 D4
Back Beaconsfield St
  BOLS/LL BL3...................................2 A6
Back Beaconsfield Ter
  BOLE BL2 *..................................31 F1
Back Bedford St *BOL* BL1................2 C3
Back Beech St *BOL* BL1...................20 D5
Back Beechwood St
  BOLS/LL BL3.................................38 D2
Back Belmont Rd *BOL* BL1.............20 C2
Back Belmont Rd East *BOL* BL1......20 C2
Back Bennett's La *BOL* BL1............20 A5
Back Bennett's La East *BOL* BL1.....20 A5
Back Bentinck St *BOL* BL1.............29 H1
Back Bentley St *BOLE* BL2.............31 G5
Back Bertrand Rd *BOL* BL1............30 A4
Back Beverley Rd *BOL* BL1............30 A2
Back Blackbank St *BOL* BL1...........30 D5
Back Blackburn Rd East
  EDGW/EG BL7.............................10 B1
Back Blackburn Rd West
  BOL BL1......................................20 C4
  EDGW/EG BL7 *...........................10 C4
Back Blackburn St *BOL* BL1...........20 D4
Back Blackwood St
  BOLS/LL BL3.................................39 E1
Back Bolton St *BOL* BL1.................20 D5
Back Boundary St *BOL* BL1............20 B5
Back Bowen St *BOL* BL1 *..............29 H1
Back Bowness Rd *BOLS/LL* BL3......38 B1
Back Bradford Rd *BOLS/LL* BL3......39 E2
Back Bradford Rd West
  BOLS/LL BL3.................................39 E2
Back Bradford St *BOLE* BL2.............3 K4
Back Bradford St East *BOLE* BL2......3 J4
Back Bradford St South
  BOLE BL2......................................3 H5

Back Bradford St West
  BOLE BL2......................................3 J4
Back Bradshaw *BOLE* BL2..............21 G3
Back Bradshaw Brow West
  BOLE BL2 *..................................21 G3
Back Bradshawgate *BOL* BL1 ....3 F4
Back Bradshaw Rd East
  BOLE BL2.....................................21 H2
Back Brandon St *BOLS/LL* BL3.......38 B1
Back Brandon St North
  BOLS/LL BL3.................................38 B1
Back Brandwood St
  BOLS/LL BL3.................................38 A1
Back Bridgeman St
  BOLS/LL BL3.................................38 C1
Back Bridge St *BOL* BL1.................30 A3
Back Brindley St *BOL* BL1...............20 D3
Back Brink's Pl *BOL* BL1 *................2 C3
Back Bristol Av *BOLE* BL2..............31 G1
Back Bristol St *BOLS/LL* BL3...........2 B7
Back Broach St *BOLS/LL* BL3..........38 C1
Back Broad o' th' La *BOL* BL1 *.....20 C3
Back Bromwich St *BOLE* BL2...........3 J5
Back Brookfield St *BOLE* BL2...........3 J3
Back Broom St *BOLE* BL2................3 H3
Back Burnaby St *BOLS/LL* BL3........30 B5
Back Burnham Av *BOL* BL1............29 G1
Back Bury New Rd *BOLE* BL2 *........3 H4
Back Bury New Rd East
  BOLE BL2......................................3 J4
Back Bury Old Rd *BOLE* BL2...........3 H3
Back Bury Rd *BOLE* BL2.................31 H3
Back Bury Rd East *BOLE* BL2.........31 G3
Back Bury Rd South *BOLE* BL2.......31 H3
Back Bushell St *BOLS/LL* BL3 *.......37 H1
Back Calder St *BOLS/LL* BL3...........38 C2
Back Caledonia St
  BOLS/LL BL3.................................30 A5
Back Calvert St *BOLS/LL* BL3..........38 D2
Back Canada St *BOL* BL1...............20 B5
  HOR/BR BL6.................................16 D4
Back Carl St *BOL* BL1.....................20 B5
Back Carter St *BOLS/LL* BL3...........39 E1
Back Castle St *BOLE* BL2..................3 J4
Back Cecilia St *BOLS/LL* BL3...........39 E1
Back Cecil St *BOLE* BL2....................3 J4
Back Cemetery Rd East
  BOLE BL2......................................3 K3
Back Cestrian St *BOLS/LL* BL3 *......38 D2
Back Chalfont St *BOL* BL1..............20 D5
Back Chapel St *HOR/BR* BL6 *.......17 E4
  TOT/BURYW BL8.........................13 H5
Back Chapman St *BOL* BL1............29 H1
Back Charles Holden St *BOL* BL1....2 A5
Back Chaucer St *BOL* BL1..............30 B1
Back Cheapside *BOL* BL1................2 E4
Back Chorley New Rd *BOL* BL1........2 A2
Back Chorley New Rd North
  BOL BL1......................................29 H3
Back Chorley Old Rd *BOL* BL1.......29 H1
Back Chorley Old Rd North
  BOL BL1......................................29 H1
Back Chorley Old Rd South
  BOL BL1......................................29 G1
Back Chorley St *BOL* BL1 *..............2 C3
Back Chorley St East *BOL* BL1 *......2 C2
Back Church Av *BOLS/LL* BL3.........38 A1
Back Church Rd *BOL* BL1...............19 G5
  BOL BL1......................................20 A5
Back Church Rd North *BOL* BL1.....19 H5
  BOL BL1 *....................................20 A5
Back Church St *BOL* BL1..................2 D2
  BOLS/LL BL3.................................40 C2
Back Clarendon Rd *BOLE* BL2........31 G3
Back Clarke St *BOL* BL1 *...............30 A2
Back Clay St East
  EDGW/EG BL7 *...........................11 E5
Back Clay St West
  EDGW/EG BL7 *...........................11 E5
Back Clegg's Buildings *BOL* BL1 *..2 C2
Back Clegg St *BOLE* BL2.................31 G3
Back Cloister St *BOL* BL1 *.............20 A5
Back Clyde St *BOL* BL1...................20 C5
Back Cobden St *BOL* BL1...............20 B4
Back Colenso Rd *BOLE* BL2 *.........31 H3
Back College Wy *BOLS/LL* BL3........2 B5
Back Columbia Rd *BOL* BL1 *.........30 A2
Back Common St *WHTN* BL5..........42 D1
Back Coniston St *BOL* BL1 *...........20 D4
Back Coop St *BOL* BL1...................20 C3
Back Corson St *BOLS/LL* BL3..........39 H3
Back Cotton St *BOL* BL1.................20 B5
Back Cox Green Rd North
  EDGW/EG BL7.............................10 D4
Back Crawford Av *BOLE* BL2...........3 J5
Back Crawford St *BOLE* BL2 *..........3 J5
Back Crescent Av *BOL* BL1...............2 B2
Back Crescent Rd *BOLS/LL* BL3......39 E1

Back Crescent Rd West
  BOLS/LL BL3.................................39
Back Croft La *BOLS/LL* BL3............39
Back Cromer Av *BOLE* BL2.............31
Back Croston St *BOLS/LL* BL3.........38
Back Crown St *HOR/BR* BL6...........16
Back Crumpsall St North
  BOL BL1......................................20
Back Cundey St *BOL* BL1 *.............30
Back Curzon Rd *BOL* BL1...............30
Back Cyril St *BOLS/LL* BL3 *...........31
Back Daisy St *BOLS/LL* BL3............38
Back Darley St *FWTH* BL4...............40
Back Darwen Rd North
  EDGW/EG BL7.............................10
  EDGW/EG BL7.............................11
Back Darwen Rd South
  EDGW/EG BL7.............................11
Back Darwin St *BOL* BL1................20
Back Deal St *BOLS/LL* BL3 *...........38
Back Deane Church La
  BOLS/LL BL3.................................37
Back Deane Church La West
  BOLS/LL BL3.................................37
Back Deane Rd *BOLS/LL* BL3..........30
Back Deane Rd North
  BOLS/LL BL3...................................2
Back Derby St *BOLS/LL* BL3.............2
  BOLS/LL BL3.................................38
Back Design St *BOLS/LL* BL3 *.......37
Back Devonshire Rd *BOL* BL1.........29
Back Dijon St *BOLS/LL* BL3............38
Back Dijon St North
  BOLS/LL BL3.................................38
Back Dobie St *BOLS/LL* BL3 *.........39
Back Doffcocker Brow
  BOL BL1......................................29
Back Dorset St *BOLE* BL2.................3
Back Dougill St *BOL* BL1................29
Back Dougill St South *BOL* BL1......29
Back Drummond St *BOL* BL1 *.......20
Back Ducie Av *BOL* BL1..................30
Back Duncan St *HOR/BR* BL6 *.......17
Back Dunstan St *BOLE* BL2............31
Back Duxbury St *BOL* BL1 *...........20
Back Earnshaw St
  BOLS/LL BL3.................................38
Back Eastbank St *BOL* BL1.............20
Back Eckersley Rd *BOL* BL1............20
Back Edditch Gv *BOLE* BL2.............31
Back Eden St *BOL* BL1....................20
Back Edgmont Av
  BOLS/LL BL3.................................38
Back Ellesmere Rd *BOLS/LL* BL3.....38
Back Ellesmere St *BOLS/LL* BL3.......2
Back Elmwood Gv *BOL* BL1 *.........30
Back Elmwood Gv West
  BOL BL1......................................30
Back Emmett St *HOR/BR* BL6........16
Back Empire Rd *BOLE* BL2..............31
Back Empress St *BOL* BL1..............29
Back Ena St *BOLS/LL* BL3 *............39
Back Ernest St *BOL* BL1....................2
Back Eskrick St *BOL* BL1 *..............20
Back Eskrick St East *BOL* BL1.........20
Back Eskrick St South *BOL* BL1.......20
Back Eskrick St West *BOL* BL1........20
Back Essingdon St *BOLS/LL* BL3.....38
Back Essingdon St South
  BOLS/LL BL3.................................38
Back Eustace St *BOLS/LL* BL3.........39
Back Euxton St *BOLS/LL* BL3..........38
Back Everton St North
  BOL BL1 *....................................20
Back Ewart St *BOL* BL1 *................20
Back Fairhaven Rd *BOL* BL1...........20
Back Fair St *BOLS/LL* BL3...............38
Back Fern St East *BOLS/LL* BL3.......30
Back Fletcher St *RAD* M26 *...........48
Back Flora St *BOLS/LL* BL3 *...........38
Back Florence Av *BOL* BL1..............20
Back Fortune St *BOLS/LL* BL3.........31
Back Frances St *BOL* BL1................20
Back Frank St *BOL* BL1 *.................20
Back Fylde St *BOLS/LL* BL3............39
Back Gainsborough Av
  BOLS/LL BL3.................................38
Back Garside Gv *BOL* BL1 *............20
Back Gaskell St *BOL* BL1..................2
Back Gaskell St East *BOL* BL1 *........2
Back Gaythorne St *BOL* BL1 *.........20
Back George Barton St
  BOLE BL2.....................................31
Back George St *BOLS/LL* BL3..........2
  HOR/BR BL6.................................17
Back Gibraltar St *BOLS/LL* BL3........2
Back Gibraltar St South
  BOLS/LL BL3...................................2
Back Gilnow Gv *BOL* BL1.................2

k Gilnow La West
OLS/LL BL3 ....30 A4
k Gilnow Rd BOL BL1 ....30 A4
k Glen Av BOLS/LL BL3 * 29 H5
k Glen Bott St BOL BL1 * 20 B5
k Gloster St BOLE BL2 ....3 H4
k Goldsmith St BOLS/LL BL3 ....38 B1
k Gordon Av BOLE BL2 ....30 A5
k Gorses Mt BOLE BL2 ....31 G5
k Grafton St BOL BL1 ....2 A1
k Grantham Cl BOL BL1 * 30 C1
k Grasmere St BOL BL1 ....20 D5
k Greenhalgh St
OLS/LL BL3 ....40 C2
k Greenland Rd
OLS/LL BL3 ....38 D2
k Green La BOLS/LL BL3 ....39 F3
k Green La South
OLS/LL BL3 ....38 D2
k Gregory Av BOLE BL2 ....32 A2
k Grendon St BOLS/LL BL3 ....38 A2
k Gresham St BOL BL1 * 20 D4
k Grove St BOL BL1 ....20 B5
k Hadwin St BOL BL1 * 30 D1
k Halliwell Rd BOL BL1 ....20 C5
k Halliwell Rd South
OL BL1 ....20 B5
k Halstead St BOLE BL2 ....3 H4
k Hargreaves St BOL BL1 ....20 C5
k Harper's La South
OL BL1 * 19 H5
k Hartington Rd BOL BL1 * 30 A2
k Hart St WHTN BL5 ....42 D1
k Hatfield Rd BOL BL1 ....30 A1
k Hawthorne Rd
OLS/LL BL3 ....37 H1
k Hawthorne Rd East
OLS/LL BL3 ....29 H5
k Hawthorn Rd West
OLS/LL BL3 ....29 H5
k Haydn St BOL BL1 ....20 B5
k Haydock St BOL BL1 ....2 E1
k Hengist St BOLE BL2 ....31 G3
k Hennon St BOL BL1 ....30 D1
k Henrietta St
OLS/LL BL3 ....37 H1
k Henry Lee St BOLS/LL BL3 ....38 A2
k High Bank St BOLE BL2 ....31 G3
k Higher Darcy St BOLE BL2 .....31 G5
k Higher Shady La West
DGW/EG BL7 ....11 F5
k Higher Swan La
OLS/LL BL3 ....38 B2
k Higher Swan La West
OLS/LL BL3 ....38 B2
k High St BOLS/LL BL3 ....38 C1
DGW/EG BL7 ....4 C5
k High St South
OLS/LL BL3 ....38 C1
k High St West
OLS/LL BL3 ....38 C1
k Hilden St BOLE BL2 ....3 H5
k Hilden St West BOLE BL2 ....3 H5
k Hind St BOLE BL2 ....31 G3
k Holland St BOL BL1 ....20 D3
k Holland St East BOL BL1 * 20 D3
k Holly Pl BOL BL1 ....20 D3
k Holly St BOL BL1 ....20 D3
k Hopefield St BOLS/LL BL3 ....38 B1
k Horeb St East
OLS/LL BL3 ....30 B5
k Horsa St BOLE BL2 ....31 F1
k Horsa St North
OLE BL2 * 31 F1
k Hotel St BOL BL1 * 2 E3
k Hough La East
DGW/EG BL7 ....11 E5
k Howarden St BOL BL1 * 20 C2
k Howcroft St
OLS/LL BL3 ....38 B1
k Hughes St BOL BL1 ....20 B5
k Hulton La BOLS/LL BL3 ....37 G3
k Hulton La South
OLS/LL BL3 ....37 G3
k Hulton La West
OLS/LL BL3 ....37 G1
k Hurst St BOLS/LL BL3 ....38 A2
k Huxley St BOL BL1 ....20 A5
k Irlam St BOL BL1 ....20 C4
k Irlam St North BOL BL1 * 20 C4
k Ivy Bank Rd BOL BL1 ....20 C2
k Ivy Rd BOL BL1 ....30 A1
k Ivy Rd West BOL BL1 * 20 A5
k James St BOLS/LL BL3 ....40 D2
k Jauncey St BOLS/LL BL3 ....2 A5
k John Brown St BOL BL1 * 2 B2
k John Cross St
OLS/LL BL3 * 38 C1
k Johnson St BOL BL1 * 3 F5

Back Keighley St BOL BL1 ....20 A5
Back Kendal Rd BOL BL1 ....30 A2
Back Kingholm Gdns
BOL BL1 * 30 B1
Back Kingsley St BOL BL1 ....20 B5
Back King St North
EDGW/EG BL7 ....10 D4
Back King St South BOLE BL2 ...21 H2
Back Knowsley Rd BOL BL1 * 19 H5
Back Knowsley St BOL BL1 ....2 E3
Back Kylemore Av
BOLS/LL BL3 * 29 H5
WHTN BL5 ....45 H2
Back Lark St BOL BL1 ....3 F2
Back Latham St BOL BL1 ....20 D5
Back Lawn St BOL BL1 ....30 A1
Back Leachfield St BOL BL1 ....20 B4
Back Leach St BOLS/LL BL3 ....30 C5
Back Lee Av BOLS/LL BL3 ....38 C2
Back Lena St BOL BL1 ....20 D5
Back Lenora St BOLS/LL BL3 .....29 H5
Back Lever Edge La
BOLS/LL BL3 ....38 A3
BOLS/LL BL3 ....38 D2
Back Lever Edge La South
BOLS/LL BL3 ....38 C2
Back Lever St BOLS/LL BL3 ....30 D5
BOLS/LL BL3 ....38 D1
Back Lever St North
BOLS/LL BL3 ....40 C1
Back Lever St South
BOLS/LL BL3 ....38 C1
Back Lightburne Av BOL BL1 .....29 H3
Back Lilly St BOL BL1 ....2 A1
Back Lincoln Rd BOL BL1 * 30 A2
Back Lindley St BOLS/LL BL3 * ..40 D2
Back Longden St BOL BL1 ....30 A2
Back Longfield Rd
BOLS/LL BL3 ....37 H2
Back Long La BOLE BL2 ....32 A3
Back Longsight North
BOLE BL2 ....22 A2
Back Longsight South
BOLE BL2 ....21 H2
Back Longworth Rd
EDGW/EG BL7 ....10 B1
Back Lord St BOLS/LL BL3 ....40 D2
Back Loxham St BOLS/LL BL3 ...39 H3
Back Lumsden St BOLS/LL BL3 ..30 C5
Back Lytton St BOL BL1 ....30 B1
Back Lytton St BOL BL1 ....30 B1
Back Mackenzie St BOL BL1 ......20 B5
Back Malvern Av BOL BL1 ....29 G1
Back Manchester Rd BOLE BL2 ...3 G6
BOLS/LL BL3 ....39 G3
Back Manchester Rd East
BOLE BL2 * 3 G7
Back Manchester Rd South
BOLS/LL BL3 ....39 E1
Back Manchester Rd West
BOLS/LL BL3 ....39 F1
Back Maple St BOLS/LL BL3 * 2 B7
Back Marion St South
BOLS/LL BL3 ....39 G3
Back Market St BOLS/LL BL3 .....40 D2
RAD M26 ....48 D1
Back Markland Hill La BOL BL1 ..29 F1
Back Markland Hill La East
BOL BL1 * 29 F1
Back Markland Hill La West
BOL BL1 * 29 F1
Back Marlborough St BOL BL1 ....2 A2
Back Marsh Fold La BOL BL1 * ...30 A2
Back Mary St BOLS/LL BL3 * 2 B7
Back Mawdsley St BOL BL1 ....2 E4
Back Maxwell St BOL BL1 ....20 C3
Back Maybank St BOLS/LL BL3 ..30 B5
Back Mayfield Av BOLS/LL BL3 ..39 F2
Back Mayor St BOL BL1 * 2 A5
Back Maze St BOLS/LL BL3 ....31 G5
Back McDonna St BOL BL1 ....20 A4
Back McKean St BOLS/LL BL3 ....39 E1
Back McKean St North
BOLS/LL BL3 ....39 E1
Back Melbourne Rd
BOLS/LL BL3 ....30 A5
Back Mellor Gv BOL BL1 * 29 H1
Back Mellor Gv West BOL BL1 * .29 H1
Back Melrose Av BOL BL1 * 29 G1
Back Melville St BOLS/LL BL3 ....39 E2
Back Mercia St BOLS/LL BL3 ......30 A5
Back Meredith St BOLS/LL BL3 ..38 D2
Back Merle Gdns BOL BL1 * 2 C1
Back Methwold St BOLS/LL BL3 *38 A1
Back Milford Rd BOLS/LL BL3 ....38 C2
Back Miller St BOL BL1 * 20 C3

Back Mill St North
EDGW/EG BL7 * 10 D4
Back Mill St South
EDGW/EG BL7 * 10 D4
Back Minorca St BOLS/LL BL3 * .38 C1
Back Moorfield Gv BOLE BL2 .....31 F1
Back Mornington Rd East
BOL BL1 ....30 A2
Back Morris Green La
BOLS/LL BL3 ....38 A3
Back Morris Green La East
BOLS/LL BL3 ....38 A3
Back Moss Ter BOL BL1 * 2 E2
Back Mowbray St BOL BL1 * 29 H1
Back Murton Ter BOL BL1 ....20 D3
Back Musgrave Rd BOL BL1 ....30 A2
Back Musgrave Rd North
BOL BL1 ....30 A2
Back Nebo St BOLS/LL BL3 ....38 B1
Back Nelson St BOLS/LL BL3 * ...17 F4
Back Nevada St BOL BL1 ....30 C1
Back Newhall La BOL BL1 ....29 G1
Back Newport Rd
BOLS/LL BL3 ....39 E1
Back Newport St BOL BL1 * 2 E5
Back Newton St BOL BL1 ....20 C5
Back Nixon Rd BOLS/LL BL3 ......38 A2
Back Normanby St
BOLS/LL BL3 ....38 A3
Back Norris St BOLS/LL BL3 * 40 C2
Back Northern Gv BOL BL1 ....30 A1
Back Nunnery Rd
BOLS/LL BL3 * 37 H1
Back Nut St BOL BL1 ....20 B5
Back Olaf St BOLE BL2 ....31 F1
Back Olga St BOL BL1 ....20 B5
Back Olga St North BOL BL1 * 20 B5
Back Oriel St BOLS/LL BL3 ....30 A5
Back Osborne Gv BOL BL1 ....30 D1
Back Owen's Rw HOR/BR BL6 ....17 E4
Back Oxford Gv North BOL BL1 ..30 A1
Back Packer St BOL BL1 ....20 A5
Back Palace St BOL BL1 ....2 E2
Back Palm St BOL BL1 ....20 D4
Back Parkdale Rd BOLE BL2 ......31 G1
Back Parkfield Rd BOLS/LL BL3 .39 E2
Back Parkinson St
BOLS/LL BL3 * 30 A5
Back Park Rd BOL BL1 ....2 A4
BOL BL1 ....30 A3
Back Park St BOL BL1 ....2 A2
Back Park Vw BOL BL1 ....20 D1
Back Park View Rd
BOLS/LL BL3 * 38 A1
Back Partington St
BOLS/LL BL3 ....38 A3
Back Patterson St
BOLS/LL BL3 * 37 G1
Back Peabody St BOLS/LL BL3 * .38 C1
Back Peace St BOLS/LL BL3........30 B5
Back Pedder St BOL BL1 ....30 A1
Back Penarth Rd BOLS/LL BL3 * .37 H1
Back Pennington Rd
BOLS/LL BL3 ....38 D2
Back Peveril St BOLS/LL BL3 .....37 H2
Back Pikes La West
BOLS/LL BL3 ....30 A5
Back Pine St BOL BL1 ....20 D5
Back Pleasant St BOL BL1 ....2 D1
Back Poplar Av BOL BL1 ....20 D3
Back Portugal St BOLE BL2 ....3 J4
Back Primrose St BOL BL1 * 20 D3
Back Primula St BOL BL1 ....20 D3
Back Progress St BOL BL1 * 30 D1
Back Queensgate BOL BL1 ....30 A2
Back Queen St BOL BL1 * 2 D5
Back Radcliffe Rd East
BOLE BL2 ....2 J3
Back Railway Vw CHLY/EC PR7 ..15 E1
Back Raimond St BOL BL1 ....20 A4
Back Rainshaw St BOL BL1 ....20 D3
Back Randal St BOLS/LL BL3 * ...38 B1
Back Range St BOLS/LL BL3 * 38 B1
Back Raphael St BOL BL1 ....30 B1
Back Rawlinson St
HOR/BR BL6 * 16 D3
Back Rawson Rd BOL BL1 ....30 A1
Back Rawson Rd North BOL BL1 .30 A1
Back Redhill Gv BOL BL1 ....2 C1
Back Ribblesdale Rd
BOLS/LL BL3 ....38 B1
Back Richelieu St BOLS/LL BL3 .39 E1
Back Rigby La North
BOLE BL2 * 21 G1
Back Rigby La South BOLE BL2 ..21 G1
Back Rishton La BOLS/LL BL3 ....38 D2
Back Rishton La East
BOLS/LL BL3 ....38 D2

Back Rock Av BOL BL1 ....20 A4
Back Roland St BOLS/LL BL3 .....30 A5
Back Romer St BOLE BL2 ....31 G3
Back Rosamond St
BOLS/LL BL3 ....38 A1
Back Roscow Av BOLE BL2 ....32 A2
Back Roseberry St BOLS/LL BL3 .38 A1
Back Rossini St BOL BL1 ....20 B4
Back Rowena St BOLS/LL BL3 * .39 G3
Back Rowland St BOLS/LL BL3 * .37 H2
Back Roxalina St BOLS/LL BL3 ...38 C1
Back Rudolph St BOLS/LL BL3 ...38 D2
Back Rumworth St
BOLS/LL BL3 ....38 B1
Back Rushton Rd BOL BL1 * 29 H1
Back Russell Cl BOL BL1 * 30 A2
Back Russell St BOL BL1 ....30 A2
Back Rutland Gv BOL BL1 ....30 A1
Back Ryefield St BOL BL1 ....31 E1
Back St Ann St BOL BL1 ....30 C1
Back St Augustine St BOL BL1 ...20 B5
Back St George's Rd BOL BL1 * ...2 D2
Back St George's Rd North
BOL BL1 ....2 B2
Back St Helens Rd
BOLS/LL BL3 * 38 B1
Back St Helens Rd South
BOLS/LL BL3 ....37 H3
BOLS/LL BL3 ....37 H3
Back St Philip's Av BOLS/LL BL3 .38 B1
Back St Thomas St East
BOL BL1 * 20 B5
Back Salisbury St BOLS/LL BL3 ...2 B5
Back Salisbury Ter BOLE BL2 .....31 H3
Back Sandon St West
BOLS/LL BL3 * 38 B1
Back Sandy Bank Rd
EDGW/EG BL7 ....4 D4
Back Sapling Rd BOLS/LL BL3 * .37 H3
Back Sapling Rd South
BOLS/LL BL3 ....37 H3
Back Scowcroft St BOLE BL2 .....31 F1
Back Settle St BOLS/LL BL3 ....38 B2
Back Settle St North
BOLS/LL BL3 ....38 C2
Back Seymour Rd BOL BL1 ....20 D4
Back Shakerley Rd TYLD M29 * ..53 F2
Back Sharman St BOLS/LL BL3 ...31 F5
Back Sherwood St BOL BL1 ....20 D4
Back Shipton St BOL BL1 ....29 H1
Back Short St ATH M46 ....53 E2
Back Silverdale Rd BOL BL1 ....30 A3
Back Skipton St BOLE BL2 ....31 G2
Back Smethurst La
BOLS/LL BL3 ....37 H3
Back Smethurst La West
BOLS/LL BL3 ....37 H3
Back Sofa St BOL BL1 ....29 H1
Back Soho St BOL BL1 ....2 E5
Back Somerset Rd BOL BL1 ....29 H3
Back Somerville St BOL BL1 * 20 A4
Back South St BOLS/LL BL3 ....38 C2
Back South View St BOLE BL2 ...31 G3
Back Spa Rd BOL BL1 ....2 A5
Back Spa Rd North BOL BL1 * 2 A5
Back Spa Rd West BOL BL1 * 2 A5
Back Springfield St
BOLS/LL BL3 ....39 F1
Back Spring Gdns BOL BL1 * 2 E5
Back Stainsbury St
BOLS/LL BL3 ....38 A1
Back Stewart St BOL BL1 ....30 C1
Back Stone St BOLE BL2 * 31 F1
Backstone St BOLE BL2 ....31 F1
Back Sunlight Rd BOL BL1 ....30 A3
Back Sunning Hill St
BOLS/LL BL3 ....38 B1
Back Sunnyside Rd BOL BL1 ......20 A5
Back Swan La BOLS/LL BL3 * 38 B1
Back Tavistock Rd BOL BL1 ....2 A5
Back Thicketford Rd BOLE BL2 * .31 G1
Back Thicketford Rd West
BOLE BL2 ....31 F1
Back Thomasson Cl BOL BL1 .....30 C1
Back Thorns Rd BOL BL1 ....20 C4
Back Thorn St BOL BL1 ....20 D5
Back Thorpe St BOL BL1 ....20 B5
Back Thurnham St
BOLS/LL BL3 ....38 A2
Back Tonge Moor Rd BOLE BL2 .21 F5
Back Tonge Moor Rd East
BOLE BL2....................................21 G4
BOLE BL2....................................31 F1
Back Tonge Old Rd BOLE BL2 ....31 G3
Back Tong Rd BOLS/LL BL3 ....40 C1
Back Tottington Rd East
BOLE BL2 ....22 A2
Back Tudor St BOLS/LL BL3 ....38 A1
Back Turton Rd East BOLE BL2 ..21 G2

Back Turton Rd West *BOLE* BL2 ....21 G3
Back Uganda St *BOLS/LL* BL3....38 A2
Back Ulleswater St *BOL* BL1.......20 D5
Back Union Rd *BOLE* BL2............31 E1
Back Unsworth St South
  BOLS/LL BL3 ....30 B5
Back Uttley St *BOL* BL1............20 B5
Back Venice St *BOLS/LL* BL3.......38 A1
Back Vernon St *BOL* BL1............2 C2
Back Vernon Rd *BOL* BL1 * 2 C2
Back Vickerman St *BOL* BL1.......20 B5
Back Victoria St *BOL* BL1...........30 A1
Back Victoria Gv North *BOL* BL1 .30 A1
Back Victory St East *BOL* BL1.....30 A2
Back View St *BOLS/LL* BL3..........30 B5
Back Vincent St *BOL* BL1............2 A5
Back Vine St *BOL* BL3 * 20 C4
Back Viola St *BOL* BL1..............20 C4
Back Waldeck St *BOL* BL1..........30 A2
Back Walnut St *BOL* BL1............20 D4
Back Wapping St *BOL* BL1 * 20 D5
Back Wardle St *BOLE* BL2............3 K7
Back Water St *EDGW/EG* BL7......10 B2
Back Waverley Rd *BOL* BL1.........20 C4
Back Webster St *BOLS/LL* BL3 * ...39 F1
Back Westbank St *BOL* BL1.........2 B2
Back Westbourne Av
  BOLS/LL BL3 ....39 E2
Back Weston St North
  BOLS/LL BL3 ....39 E1
Back Weston St South
  BOLS/LL BL3 ....38 D1
Back Westwood Rd *BOL* BL1 * 30 A2
Back Whittle Gv *BOL* BL1 * 29 H1
  BOLS/LL BL3 ....37 G1
Back Wigan Rd *BOLS/LL* BL3.......29 H5
  BOLS/LL BL3 ....37 G1
Back Wigan Rd North
  BOLS/LL BL3 ....37 G1
Back Wigan Rd South
  BOLS/LL BL3 * 29 H5
Back Willows *BOLS/LL* BL3.........37 H1
Back Willows La *BOLS/LL* BL3......38 B1
Back Willows La North
  BOLS/LL BL3 ....37 G1
Back Willows La South
  BOLS/LL BL3 ....38 A1
Back Wilmot St *BOL* BL1 * 20 A4
Back Wilton St *BOL* BL1.............20 D4
Back Windermere St *BOL* BL1......20 D4
Back Windsor Gv *BOL* BL1..........30 C1
Back Wolfenden St *BOL* BL1 * 20 C5
Back Woodbine Rd
  BOLS/LL BL3 ....38 A2
Back Woodfield St
  BOLS/LL BL3 ....39 E2
Back Woodgate St *BOLS/LL* BL3..39 E2
Back Wood St *HOR/BR* BL6.........17 E4
Back Worcester St *BOL* BL1.........30 C1
Back Wordsworth St *BOL* BL1......20 B5
Back Worsel St *BOLS/LL* BL3.......38 A1
Back Worsel St North
  BOLS/LL BL3 * 39 E3
Back Wright St *HOR/BR* BL6........16 D3
Back Wynne St *BOL* BL1.............20 C5
Back Yates St *BOLE* BL2.............31 E1
Badder St *BOL* BL1..................2 E2
Bag La *ATH* M46.....................44 B4
Bagot St *SWIN* M27..................57 E2
Bagshaw La *WGNE/HIN* WN2.......34 A3
Bailey Fold *WHTN* BL5...............36 B5
Bailey La *BOLE* BL2..................32 A1
Baines St *BOL* BL1...................29 H2
Bain St *SWIN* M27....................57 H4
Baker St *FWTH* BL4..................48 D2
Balcary Gv *BOL* BL1.................29 H2
Baldrine Dr *WGNE/HIN* WN2.......42 D3
Baldwin St *BOLS/LL* BL3............2 C7
  WGNE/HIN WN2 ....42 D5
Balfern Cl *WHTN* BL5...............35 G4
Balfern Fold *WHTN* BL5.............35 G4
Balfour St *BOLS/LL* BL3.............2 A6
Balliol St *SWIN* M27..................57 G3
Balmoral *CHLY/EC* PR7.............14 C1
Balmoral Av *BOLS/LL* BL3...........40 C2
Balmoral Cl *HOR/BR* BL6............17 F5
Balmoral Dr *LEIGH* WN7............52 D5
Balmoral Rd *FWTH* BL4.............37 G2
Balmore Cl *BOLS/LL* BL3............37 G2
Balshaw Cl *BOLS/LL* BL3...........30 A5
Bamber Cft *WHTN* BL5..............35 G4
Bamber Wk *BOLS/LL* BL3 * 30 B5
Bamburgh Cl *RAD* M26..............33 E5
Bampton Cl *WHTN* BL5..............35 G4
Banbury Ms *SWIN* M27.............57 F2
Banbury St *BOLE* BL2...............31 G1
Bancroft Rd *SWIN* M27..............57 G2
Bangor St *BOL* BL1...................2 D1
Banker St *BOLS/LL* BL3.............31 G5
Bank Fld *WHTN* BL5..................44 A1

Bankfield Cl *BOLE* BL2...............33 E1
Bankfield Dr *WALK* M28.............55 E5
Bankfield Rd *FWTH* BL4.............47 H2
  TYLD M29 ....54 C3
Bankfield St *BOLS/LL* BL3...........38 A1
Bankhall St *WGNE/HIN* WN2.......50 D2
Bank Field St *RAD* M26..............49 F1
Bank Hey *WHTN* BL5 * 35 H5
Bank House Cl *TYLD* M29...........54 C2
Bank La *LHULT* M38..................46 D2
Bank Meadow *HOR/BR* BL6.......17 E3
Bank Side *WHTN* BL5................35 H5
Bank Stanway Av *BOLS/LL* BL3....2 B6
Bank St *BOL* BL1......................3 F3
  CHLY/EC PR7 ....6 D5
  EDGW/EG BL7 ....4 C5
  FWTH BL4 ....39 H5
  TOT/BURYW BL8 ....23 H3
Bank Top Gv *BOL* BL1..............21 E2
Bank Wd *BOL* BL1...................29 F3
Banner St *WGNE/HIN* WN2.........42 A3
Bannister St *BOLE* BL2..............32 A2
Bantry St *BOLS/LL* BL3..............30 C5
Barbara Av *BOLS/LL* BL3............37 G3
Barbara St *BOLS/LL* BL3............38 B1
Barberry Bank *EDGW/EG* BL7......10 B2
Barbury Cl *LEIGH* WN7..............51 H4
Barchester Av *BOLE* BL2...........32 A1
Barcroft Rd *BOL* BL1................19 H5
Bardon Cl *BOL* BL1 * 30 B1
Bardsley Cl *BOLE* BL2...............21 H2
Bardwell Av *WHTN* BL5.............35 F5
Bare St *BOL* BL1......................3 H2
Barford Gv *HOR/BR* BL6............27 H1
Bark St *BOL* BL1......................2 D3
  FWTH BL4 ....48 D3
Bark St East *BOL* BL1...............2 E3
Bar La *BOL* BL1.......................20 C2
Barley Brook Meadow *BOL* BL1...20 D1
Barlow St *WALK* M28 * 48 A5
Barlow Park Av *BOL* BL1...........20 B2
Barlow St *HOR/BR* BL6..............17 E5
  WALK M28 ....47 H4
Barnabys Rd *WHTN* BL5............35 F2
Barn Acre *HOR/BR* BL6.............26 A1
Barnacre Av *BOLE* BL2..............32 B3
Barn Ct *BOLE* BL2 * 21 G5
Barncroft Dr *HOR/BR* BL6..........17 H4
Barncroft Rd *FWTH* BL4............39 H5
Barnes Cl *FWTH* BL4................39 H5
Barnes Dr *FWTH* BL4................38 D4
Barnes St *FWTH* BL4................39 F4
Barnes Ter *FWTH* BL4...............48 C1
Barnet Rd *BOL* BL1..................19 H5
Barnfield Cl *EDGW/EG* BL7.........10 C2
  RAD M26 ....41 G2
  TYLD M29 ....53 F2
Barnfield Dr *WALK* M28.............55 F5
  WHTN BL5 ....36 A4
Barnfield Rd *SWIN* M27..............57 F1
Barn Hl *WHTN* BL5...................35 G4
Barn Hill Ter *WHTN* BL5.............35 G4
Barn Meadow *EDGW/EG* BL7......4 D4
Barnsdale Cl *BOLE* BL2..............33 E1
Barnside Av *WALK* M28..............56 A1
Barnston Cl *BOL* BL1.................20 D3
Barn St *BOL* BL1......................2 D4
Barn Vw *CHLY/EC* PR7..............14 C5
Barnwood Cl *BOL* BL1 * 30 C1
Barnwood Dr *BOL* BL1..............30 C1
Barnwood Ter *BOL* BL1.............30 C1
Baron Fold Crs *LHULT* M38.........46 D3
Baron Fold Gv *LHULT* M38.........46 D3
Baron Fold Rd *LHULT* M38 * 46 D3
Baron Wk *BOLS/LL* BL3..............41 E2
Barrett Av *FWTH* BL4................48 B1
Barrie St *LEIGH* WN7................51 F3
Barrie Wy *BOL* BL1..................21 F3
Barrisdale Cl *BOLS/LL* BL3..........29 F5
Barron Meadow *LEIGH* WN7.......51 F4
Barrow Bridge Rd *BOL* BL1........19 G4
Barrows St *BOL* BL1..................2 E5
Barrowshaw Cl *WALK* M28.........55 G1
Barrs Fold Cl *WHTN* BL5............35 F2
Barrs Fold Rd *WHTN* BL5...........35 F3
Barry Crs *WALK* M28.................47 E5
Barsham Dr *BOLS/LL* BL3...........2 B7
Barton Fold *FWTH* BL4...............47 F1
Barton St *FWTH* BL4.................48 A1
Barwell Sq *FWTH* BL4...............39 F3
Bashall St *BOL* BL1..................30 A2
Basil St *BOLS/LL* BL3.................2 C7
Baslow Av *WGNE/HIN* WN2.........42 B5
Basswood Gn *WGNE/HIN* WN2 ....42 A5
Bateman St *HOR/BR* BL6............17 F5
Batheaston Gv *LEIGH* WN7.........51 F4
Bath St *ATH* M46....................44 A5
  BOL BL1 ....2 E2
Batridge Rd *EDGW/EG* BL7.........4 A2

Batsmans Dr *SWIN* M27............49 G4
Battenberg Rd *BOL* BL1............30 A2
Baxendale St *BOL* BL1..............20 C5
Baxter's Rw *WGNE/HIN* WN2......50 D1
Baycliff Cl *WGNE/HIN* WN2.........42 B5
Bayley Ct *BOL* BL1...................2 A1
Baysdale Av *BOLS/LL* BL3...........37 F1
Bayswater St *BOLS/LL* BL3.........38 A3
Baythorpe St *BOL* BL1...............20 D4
Bazley St *BOL* BL1...................19 F4
Beacon Cl *ATH* M46.................52 A1
Beacon Rd *WGNE/HIN* WN2.......50 C3
Beaconsfield St *BOLS/LL* BL3......2 A6
Beatrice Rd *BOL* BL1.................30 A2
  WALK M28 ....56 D4
Beatrice St *FWTH* BL4...............39 F5
  HOR/BR BL6 ....16 D3
  SWIN M27 ....57 G2
Beatty Dr *WHTN* BL5................35 G4
Beaufort St *SWIN* M27..............57 F4
Beaumaris Cl *WGNE/HIN* WN2 ....42 C5
Beaumont Av *HOR/BR* BL6.........17 E3
Beaumont Cha *BOLS/LL* BL3.......37 F2
Beaumont Dr *BOLS/LL* BL3.........29 E5
Beaumont Rd *HOR/BR* BL6.........16 D3
  HOR/BR BL6 ....29 E4
Beck Gv *WALK* M28..................56 B2
Beckside *TYLD* M29..................53 E3
Bede St *BOL* BL1.....................20 A5
Bedford Av *SWIN* M27 * 57 G4
  WALK M28 ....55 G2
Bedford Dr *ATH* M46................52 A2
Bedford St *BOL* BL1..................2 A2
  EDGW/EG BL7 ....10 B2
Bedworth Cl *BOLE* BL2...............3 J7
Beech Av *ATH* M46..................45 E5
  BOLS/LL BL3 ....40 D3
  CHLYE PR6 ....7 F4
  FWTH BL4 ....39 E5
  FWTH BL4 ....48 D3
  HOR/BR BL6 ....27 C1
  RAD M26 ....41 H5
  WALK M28 ....55 E5
Beech Cl *BOLS/LL* BL3..............21 G1
Beechcroft Av *BOLE* BL2...........31 H4
Beechcroft Gv *BOLE* BL2............32 A4
The Beeches *ATH* M46 * 44 D5
  BOL BL1 ....20 B1
Beechfield Av *LHULT* M38...........47 E3
  WGNE/HIN WN2 ....42 C4
Beechfield Rd *BOL* BL1..............19 H5
Beech Gv *LHULT* M38................46 C3
Beech St *ATH* M46..................45 E5
  BOL BL1 ....20 D5
  EDGW/EG BL7 ....4 D4
  SWIN M27 ....57 H4
Beechwood Crs *TYLD* M29.........53 G5
Beechwood Dr *WALK* M28.........56 D5
Beechwood St *BOLS/LL* BL3........38 D2
Beedon Av *BOLS/LL* BL3............40 C1
Bee Fold La *ATH* M46...............52 C1
Beehive Gn *WHTN* BL5..............36 B4
Beeston Cl *BOL* BL1.................21 E1
Beeston Gv *LEIGH* WN7.............52 D4
Begonia Av *FWTH* BL4...............39 E4
Belayse Cl *BOL* BL1..................19 H5
Belcroft Cl *LHULT* M38..............46 C2
Belcroft Gv *LHULT* M38 * 46 C3
Belford Dr *BOLS/LL* BL3.............38 C3
Belgrave Crs *HOR/BR* BL6..........17 F4
Belgrave Gdns *BOL* BL1............20 A5
Belgrave St *ATH* M46...............44 A5
  BOL BL1 ....20 A5
Belgrave St South *BOL* BL1........30 C1
Bellairs St *BOLS/LL* BL3.............38 A5
Bella St *BOLS/LL* BL3................38 A1
Bellfield Vw *BOL* BL1................21 E4
Bellingham Cl *TOT/BURYW* BL8...23 H5
Bellpit Cl *WALK* M28.................55 C4
Bell St *LEIGH* WN7...................51 F2
  WGNE/HIN WN2 ....42 A2
Bellwood *WHTN* BL5.................43 E1
Belmont Av *ATH* M46...............45 F4
  SWIN M27 ....49 F3
  WGNE/HIN WN2 ....50 B2
Belmont Dr *WGNE/HIN* WN2.......25 G3
Belmont Rd *BOL* BL1.................20 B1
  CHLYE PR6 ....7 F5
  HOR/BR BL6 ....9 E3
  WGNE/HIN WN2 ....42 B3
Belmont Vw *BOLE* BL2..............22 B3
Belvedere Av *ATH* M46.............45 F4
Belvedere Cl *LEIGH* WN7...........52 D4
Belvedere Rd *CHLYE* PR6...........7 F4
Belvoir St *BOLE* BL2.................31 G3
Bembridge Dr *BOLS/LL* BL3........31 E5
Bennet St *RAD* M26.................41 F1
Bennett's La *BOL* BL1................20 A5
Benson St *EDGW/EG* BL7...........4 D4

Bentham Cl *TOT/BURYW* BL8......23
Bent Hill St *BOLS/LL* BL3 * 37
Bentinck St *BOL* BL1................29
  FWTH BL4 39
Bentley Ct *FWTH* BL4...............39
Bentley Fold *TOT/BURYW* BL8....23
Bentley Fold Cottages
  TOT/BURYW BL8 * 23
Bentley Hall Rd
  TOT/BURYW BL8 39
Bent Spur Rd *FWTH* BL4...........48
Bent St *FWTH* BL4..................48
Bentworth Cl *WHTN* BL5...........43
Beresford Av *BOLS/LL* BL3.........30
Berkeley Crs *RAD* M26..............30
Berkeley Rd *BOL* BL1................20
Berlin St *BOLS/LL* BL3...............20
Bernard Gv *BOL* BL1.................20
Berne Av *HOR/BR* BL6..............17
Bernice St *BOL* BL1..................20
Berryfold Wy *TYLD* M29............53
Berry St *CHLYE* PR6.................7
  SWIN M27 57
Bertha St *BOL* BL1..................20
Bertrand Rd *BOL* BL1................30
Bert St *BOLS/LL* BL3.................37
Berwick Cl *WALK* M28...............54
Beryl Av *TOT/BURYW* BL8.........13
Beryl St *BOL* BL1.....................20
Bessybrook Cl *HOR/BR* BL6........28
Beta St *BOL* BL1......................2
Bethany Ms *WGNE/HIN* WN2......42
Beverley Rd *BOL* BL1................30
  BOLS/LL BL3 40
Bewick St *BOLE* BL2.................21
Bewley Gv *LEIGH* WN7.............52
Bexhill Cl *BOLS/LL* BL3..............41
Bexhill Dr *LEIGH* WN7...............51
Bexley Dr *LHULT* M38...............47
Bexley St *WGNE/HIN* WN2.........42
Bickershaw Dr *WALK* M28.........55
Bickershaw La *WGNE/HIN* WN2...50
Bickley Gv *TYLD* M29................54
Bideford Dr *BOLE* BL2...............32
Bidford Cl *TYLD* M29................53
Bidston Cl *TOT/BURYW* BL8.......23
Big Fold *HOR/BR* BL6 * 15
Bilbao St *BOL* BL1...................30
Billinge Cl *BOL* BL1...................2
Billy La *SWIN* M27...................57
Binbrook Wk *BOLS/LL* BL3.........38
Bingham St *SWIN* M27..............57
Bingley Wk *FWTH* BL4..............47
Birch Av *WHTN* BL5.................43
Birches Rd *EDGW/EG* BL7..........4
Birchfield *BOLE* BL2..................22
Birchfield Av *ATH* M46..............44
Birchfield Dr *WALK* M28............55
Birchfield Gv *BOLS/LL* BL3.........37
Birchfold Cl *LHULT* M38.............38
Birchgate Wk *BOLS/LL* BL3........30
Birch Rd *ATH* M46...................45
  FWTH BL4 48
  LEIGH WN7 51
  WALK M28 55
Birch St *BOLE* BL2...................3
  TYLD M29 * 53
Birch Tree Wy *HOR/BR* BL6.......27
Birkdale Av *ATH* M46................44
Birkdale Gdns *BOLS/LL* BL3........30
Birkenhills Dr *BOLS/LL* BL3.........29
Birkett Cl *BOL* BL1...................20
Birkett Dr *BOL* BL1...................20
Birley St *BOL* BL1....................20
  LEIGH WN7 52
Birtenshaw Crs *EDGW/EG* BL7....11
Birtle Dr *TYLD* M29..................54
Bishopbridge Cl *BOLS/LL* BL3......38
Bishop's Cl *BOLS/LL* BL3............39
Bishop's Rd *BOLS/LL* BL3...........39
Bispham Av *BOLE* BL2...............32
Bispham Cl *TOT/BURYW* BL8......23
Bispham St *BOLE* BL2 * 31
Blackbank St *BOL* BL1...............20
Blackburn Rd *EDGW/EG* BL7......10
  EDGW/EG BL7 4
Blackcap Cl *WALK* M28.............55
Blackcroft Cl *SWIN* M27.............57
Blackhorse Av *HOR/BR* BL6 * 15
Blackhorse Cl *HOR/BR* BL6.........15
Black Horse St *BOL* BL1............2
  FWTH BL4 48
  HOR/BR BL6 15
Blackleach Dr *WALK* M28...........47
Blackledge St *BOLS/LL* BL3........38
Black Moss Rd *RAD* M26 * 41
Blackrod Brow *HOR/BR* BL6........15

ckrod By-Pass Rd
IOR/BR BL6 26 B2
ckrod Dr TOT/BURYW BL8 33 H1
ckshaw La BOLS/LL BL3 30 A4
cksmiths Fold ATH M46 45 E5
ckthorne Cl BOL BL1 29 G1
ckwood St BOLS/LL BL3 39 E1
ir Av LHULT M38 47 F4
VGNE/HIN WN2 42 D5
ir La BOLE BL2 31 H1
irmore Dr BOLS/LL BL3 37 E1
ir St EDGW/EG BL7 10 D4
WTH BL4 48 C2
kefield Dr WALK M28 56 A2
ke Gdns BOL BL1 20 B5
kemore Pk ATH M46 44 B4
ke St BOL BL1 20 B5
DGW/EG BL7 11 E5
key Cl BOLS/LL BL3 37 F1
ndford Av WALK M28 56 C3
ndford Cl TYLD M29 53 G2
ndford Ri HOR/BR BL6 28 A1
ntyre Av WALK M28 56 A1
ntyre St SWIN M27 57 F3
VGNE/HIN WN2 42 A2
ydon Cl WGNE/HIN WN2 25 H5
akledge Gn WGNE/HIN WN2 42 B1
akledge Gv WGNE/HIN WN2 42 A2
ak St BOLE BL2 21 F5
asdale Cl HOR/BR BL6 27 H2
asdale Rd BOL BL1 19 F5
asedale Rd WGNE/HIN WN2 42 B3
nheim Dr LEIGH WN7 53 E4
nheim Rd BOLE BL2 32 A3
nheim St TYLD M29 53 F3
riot St BOLS/LL BL3 38 B2
thyn St BOLS/LL BL3 37 H3
wberry Cl LEIGH WN7 51 H4
h Rd WHTN BL5 35 G4
dsill Rd FWTH BL4 47 F1
omfield Dr WALK M28 55 E4
omfield Rd FWTH BL4 47 H2
omfield St BOL BL1 20 C4
ssom St TYLD M29 53 G2
ndell La HOR/BR BL6 15 E5
ndell St BOL BL1 2 D3
ardman Cl BOL BL1 20 C5
ardman St BOL BL1 20 C5
IOR/BR BL6 15 H5
ard St BOL BL1 2 A5
diam Rd TOT/BURYW BL8 13 H3
dmin Rd TYLD M29 53 H3
d St BOL BL1 2 E5
EIGH WN7 51 H5
WIN M27 57 H1
lin Cl FWTH BL4 48 C2
lings Yd BOL BL1 3 F5
ton House Rd
VGNE/HIN WN2 50 B4
ton Old Rd ATH M46 44 D5
ton Rd ATH M46 45 E4
OLE BL2 21 G2
HLYE PR6 7 G5
DGW/EG BL7 4 D5
WTH BL4 39 H3
WTH BL4 48 A1
AD M26 41 F1
OT/BURYW BL8 13 E2
VALK M28 47 H4
VGNE/HIN WN2 25 G5
VHTN BL5 35 H5
ton St RAD M26 41 H2
nd Cl HOR/BR BL6 17 E4
nd's La CHLY/EC PR7 6 D5
nd St ATH M46 53 F2
onfields EDGW/EG BL7 11 E4
othby Rd SWIN M27 57 G2
oth Hall Dr TOT/BURYW BL8 23 H2
oth Rd BOLS/LL BL3 40 D3
othsbank Av WALK M28 55 F5
oth's Hall WALK M28 55 F5
oth's Hall Gv WALK M28 55 F5
oth's Hall Rd WALK M28 55 F5
oth St BOL BL1 20 A4
OT/BURYW BL8 23 H2
oth Wy TOT/BURYW BL8 23 H2
ot La BOL BL1 28 D1
rder Brook La WALK M28 55 E4
res Hl WGN WN1 14 A3
rowdale Av BOL BL1 29 G2
rsdane Av WGNE/HIN WN2 42 A4
rsden St SWIN M27 57 F2
scobel Rd BOLS/LL BL3 39 F3
scombe Pl WGNE/HIN WN2 42 A4
scow Rd BOLS/LL BL3 40 C3
ston Gv LEIGH WN7 51 G2
ston St BOL BL1 * 20 C5
sworth St HOR/BR BL6 16 D3
esworth Cl WGNE/HIN WN2 42 D3
Bottom o' th' Knotts Brow
EDGW/EG BL7 12 B1
Bottom o' th' Moor BOLE BL2 21 H5
HOR/BR BL6 17 H4
Boundary Dr BOLE BL2 32 C5
Boundary Gdns BOL BL1 * 20 B5
Boundary Rd SWIN M27 57 H3
Boundary St BOL BL1 20 B5
BOLE BL2 32 D5
TYLD M29 53 G2
The Boundary SWIN M27 49 F4
Bournbrook Av LHULT M38 47 E2
Bourne Av SWIN M27 57 H4
Bourneville Dr TOT/BURYW BL8 23 H5
Bourton Ct TYLD M29 54 B2
Bowen St BOL BL1 29 H1
Bowgreave Av BOLE BL2 32 B3
Bowkers Rw BOL BL1 3 F4
Bowker St WALK M28 47 F5
Bowland Cl TOT/BURYW BL8 23 G4
Bowland Dr BOL BL1 19 E5
Bowness Rd BOLS/LL BL3 38 B1
BOLS/LL BL3 40 B1
Bowstone Hill Rd BOLE BL2 22 D2
Bow St BOL BL1 2 E3
Bowyer Gdns BOLS/LL BL3 37 F2
Boydell St LEIGH WN7 51 H5
Boyle St BOL BL1 29 G1
Brabham Ms SWIN M27 57 E4
Bracken Av WALK M28 48 A5
Bracken Cl BOL BL1 20 B1
Bracken Lea WHTN BL5 43 H3
Bracken Rd ATH M46 52 D1
Brackley Av TYLD M29 53 H2
Brackley Rd WHTN BL5 37 G5
Brackleys St FWTH BL4 39 H5
Brackley St FWTH BL4 39 H5
WALK M28 47 G4
Bracondale Av BOL BL1 19 H5
Bradbourne Cl BOLS/LL BL3 30 C5
Braddyll Rd WHTN BL5 37 F5
Bradford Av BOLS/LL BL3 39 F2
Bradford Crs BOLS/LL BL3 * 39 E1
Bradford Park Dr BOLE BL2 3 K5
Bradford Rd BOLS/LL BL3 39 E3
Bradford St BOLE BL2 3 H4
FWTH BL4 47 H1
Bradley Fold Rd BOLE BL2 32 D4
Bradley La RAD M26 32 D5
Bradshaw Brow BOLE BL2 21 G3
Bradshawgate BOL BL1 3 F4
Bradshaw Hall Dr BOLE BL2 21 G1
Bradshaw Hall Fold BOLE BL2 * 21 H1
Bradshaw Mdw BOLE BL2 21 H1
Bradshaw Rd BOLE BL2 11 H5
TOT/BURYW BL8 23 E1
Bradshaw St ATH M46 44 D5
FWTH BL4 47 H1
RAD M26 41 H2
Bradwell Pl BOLE BL2 31 F1
Brady St HOR/BR BL6 16 C2
Braemar La WALK M28 55 F5
Braeside Gv BOLS/LL BL3 29 E5
Brailsford Rd BOLE BL2 21 G4
Brakesmere Gv WALK M28 46 D4
Bramble Cft HOR/BR BL6 36 A2
Bramblewood WGNE/HIN WN2 42 B1
Brambling Dr WHTN BL5 43 F2
Bramcote Av BOLE BL2 3 J7
Bramdean Av BOLE BL2 22 A2
Bramford Cl WHTN BL5 43 G2
Bramhall Av BOLE BL2 22 C3
Bramhall St BOLS/LL BL3 39 F2
Bramley Cl SWIN M27 57 E5
Bramley Rd BOL BL1 20 D1
Brammay Dr TOT/BURYW BL8 23 G2
Brampton Rd BOLS/LL BL3 37 G2
Brampton St ATH M46 * 44 D5
Brancker St WHTN BL5 36 C5
Brandon St BOLS/LL BL3 38 B1
Brandwood Cl WALK M28 55 E3
Brandwood St BOLS/LL BL3 38 A1
Branscombe Gdns
BOLS/LL BL3 * 31 H5
Bransdale Cl BOLS/LL BL3 37 F1
Brantfell Gv BOLE BL2 32 B2
Brantwood Dr BOLE BL2 32 B2
Brathay Cl BOLE BL2 32 B1
Braybrook Dr BOL BL1 28 D3
Brayford Dr WGNE/HIN WN2 25 G5
Brazley Av BOLS/LL BL3 39 E2
HOR/BR BL6 27 G1
Breaktemper WHTN BL5 35 G4
Breckland Dr BOL BL1 28 D3
Breckles Pl BOLS/LL BL3 * 2 B7
Brecon Dr WGNE/HIN WN2 42 C5
Bredbury Dr FWTH BL4 40 A5
Breeze Hl ATH M46 45 F3
Breeze Hill Rd ATH M46 45 G3
Breightmet Dr BOLE BL2 32 A3
Breightmet Fold La
BOLE BL2 32 B3
Breightmet St BOLE BL2 3 F5
Brent Cl BOLE BL2 32 D5
Brentford Av BOL BL1 19 H5
Brentwood Av WALK M28 56 D5
Brentwood Dr FWTH BL4 39 F3
Brentwood Gv LEIGH WN7 51 H4
Brentwood Rd CHLYE PR6 7 F4
SWIN M27 57 F5
Brereton Dr WALK M28 56 B4
Brett Rd WALK M28 54 D5
Brian Rd FWTH BL4 39 E3
Briar Cl WGNE/HIN WN2 42 D4
Briarcroft Dr ATH M46 52 A2
Briarfield EDGW/EG BL7 10 B2
Briarfield Rd FWTH BL4 39 E4
WALK M28 56 B4
Briar Gv LEIGH WN7 51 G3
Briar Hill Av LHULT M38 46 C4
Briar Hill Cl LHULT M38 46 C4
Briar Hill Gv LHULT M38 46 C4
Briar St BOLE BL2 * 31 H3
Briary Dr TYLD M29 53 H3
Bride St BOL BL1 20 C5
Bridgeman Pl BOLE BL2 3 G5
Bridgeman St BOLS/LL BL3 2 E7
BOLS/LL BL3 38 C1
FWTH BL4 39 H4
Bridgemere Cl RAD M26 33 H5
Bridges Ct BOL BL1 * 2 E5
Bridge's St ATH M46 52 B1
Bridge St BOL BL1 2 E3
FWTH BL4 40 A4
HOR/BR BL6 17 E3
RAD M26 40 D5
Bridgewater Rd WALK M28 55 E4
WALK M28 55 G1
Bridgewater St BOL BL1 2 A5
FWTH BL4 39 H5
LHULT M38 47 F4
WGNE/HIN WN2 42 A2
Bridson La BOLE BL2 31 H1
Brief St BOLE BL2 31 G1
Briercliffe Rd BOLS/LL BL3 30 A5
Brierfield Av ATH M46 44 C4
Brierholme Av EDGW/EG BL7 10 C3
Brierley Rd East SWIN M27 57 G2
Brierley Rd West SWIN M27 57 G2
Brierwood BOLE BL2 31 F1
Briery Av BOLE BL2 21 H1
Brigade St BOL BL1 30 A3
Briggs Fold Cl EDGW/EG BL7 10 C2
Briggs Fold Rd EDGW/EG BL7 10 C2
Briggs St LEIGH WN7 51 G4
Brighton Av BOL BL1 29 G1
Bright St LEIGH WN7 51 G4
Briksdal Wy HOR/BR BL6 28 C3
Brimfield Av TYLD M29 54 A2
Brindlehurst Dr TYLD M29 54 B4
Brindle St TYLD M29 53 G2
WGNE/HIN WN2 42 B1
Brindley Av WALK M28 55 E5
Brindley Cl ATH M46 52 A1
FWTH BL4 39 F5
Brindley St HOR/BR BL6 * 17 E5
SWIN M27 57 H1
WALK M28 54 D5
WALK M28 55 H1
Brinks La BOLE BL2 32 C3
Brinks Rw HOR/BR BL6 * 17 F2
Brinksway BOL BL1 28 C3
Brinksworth Cl BOLE BL2 32 C2
Brinsop Hall La WHTN BL5 26 C5
Briscoe Ms BOLS/LL BL3 39 E1
Bristle Hall Wy WHTN BL5 35 H3
Bristol Av BOLE BL2 31 G1
Britannia Wy BOLE BL2 21 E5
Broach St BOLS/LL BL3 38 C1
Broadbent St SWIN M27 57 F4
Broadford Rd BOLS/LL BL3 29 F5
Broadgate Meadow
SWIN M27 * 57 H4
Broadgreen Gdns FWTH BL4 * 39 H3
Broadhead Rd EDGW/EG BL7 5 E2
Broadheath Cl WHTN BL5 36 A4
Broadhurst Av SWIN M27 49 H5
Broadhurst Ct BOLS/LL BL3 38 B1
Broadhurst St BOLS/LL BL3 * 38 B1
Broadlands Rd WALK M28 57 E5
Broadmeadow EDGW/EG BL7 11 F4
Broadoak Av WALK M28 54 D4
Broad Oak Cl CHLYE PR6 7 E4
Broad Oak Pk WALK M28 56 D5
Broad Oak Rd BOLS/LL BL3 39 E3
Broad o' th' La BOL BL1 20 C3
Broadstone Rd BOLE BL2 21 H2
Broad Wk WHTN BL5 43 G1
Broadway ATH M46 45 F3
FWTH BL4 39 E3
HOR/BR BL6 17 F4
WALK M28 55 H2
WGNE/HIN WN2 42 C3
Broadwood HOR/BR BL6 28 C3
Brock Av BOLE BL2 32 B3
Brockenhurst Dr BOLE BL2 22 B4
Brodick Dr BOLE BL2 32 B4
Bromley Cross Rd
EDGW/EG BL7 11 F5
Bromley Dr LEIGH WN7 51 F3
Bromwich St BOLE BL2 3 J6
Bronte Cl BOL BL1 30 B1
Brook Av SWIN M27 57 H4
Brook Bank BOLE BL2 * 21 H4
Brookbottom Rd RAD M26 33 H4
Brook Cl TYLD M29 53 G1
Brookdale ATH M46 45 F2
CHLYE PR6 7 E3
Brookdale Cl BOL BL1 20 D5
Brookdale Pk LHULT M38 * 47 F2
Brookdale Rd WGNE/HIN WN2 42 B3
Brookdean Cl BOL BL1 20 A4
Brook Dr TYLD M29 54 A5
Brookfield Av BOLE BL2 33 E1
Brookfield Dr SWIN M27 57 G2
WALK M28 54 D5
Brookfield St BOLE BL2 3 J3
LEIGH WN7 52 A5
Brookfold La BOLE BL2 22 B3
Brook Gdns BOLE BL2 22 A3
Brookhey Av BOLS/LL BL3 38 D2
Brookhouse Av FWTH BL4 47 G2
Brook House Cl BOLE BL2 22 A4
TOT/BURYW BL8 13 G4
Brookhouse Mill La
TOT/BURYW BL8 13 H4
Brookhurst La LHULT M38 46 C2
Brookland Av FWTH BL4 47 G1
Brookland Gv BOL BL1 19 G5
Brooklands HOR/BR BL6 17 E4
Brooklands Av ATH M46 44 D4
Brooklands Rd RAMS BL0 13 H2
SWIN M27 57 F5
Brooklyn St BOL BL1 30 C1
Brook Meadow WHTN BL5 * 36 A5
Brooks Av RAD M26 33 H4
Brooks Houses LEIGH WN7 51 G3
Brookside Av FWTH BL4 47 G1
Brookside Cl ATH M46 45 E4
BOLE BL2 21 H2
Brookside Crs TOT/BURYW BL8 13 H4
WALK M28 48 A5
Brookside Rd BOLE BL2 31 H2
Brook St ATH M46 44 B5
BOL BL1 2 E3
CHLYE PR6 7 E3
FWTH BL4 40 A4
RAD M26 48 C1
SWIN M27 57 F3
WHTN BL5 * 35 H4
Brookwater Cl TOT/BURYW BL8 23 H1
Brooky Moor EDGW/EG BL7 * 5 E3
Broom Av LEIGH WN7 51 G4
Broomfield Cl BOLE BL2 33 E2
Broomfield Rd BOLS/LL BL3 30 A5
Broomhey Av WGN WN1 24 A5
Broom St SWIN M27 57 H4
Broom Wy WHTN BL5 36 A3
Brougham St WALK M28 55 G1
Brough Cl WGNE/HIN WN2 42 A5
Broughton Av LHULT M38 47 E4
Broughton St BOL BL1 20 B5
Brow East BOLE BL2 21 G3
Browning Av ATH M46 44 D3
Browning Cl BOL BL1 30 B1
Browning Rd SWIN M27 57 G3
Browning St LEIGH WN7 51 F5
Brownlow Rd HOR/BR BL6 16 D3
Brownlow Wy BOL BL1 30 C1
Browns Rd BOLE BL2 32 D4
Brown St BOL BL1 3 F3
HOR/BR BL6 15 H5
RAD M26 33 H4
TYLD M29 * 53 F4
WGNE/HIN WN2 50 A2
Broxton Av BOLS/LL BL3 37 H2
Brunel St BOL BL1 20 B4
HOR/BR BL6 17 E5
Brunswick Av HOR/BR BL6 17 F5
Brunswick Ct BOL BL1 2 D2
Bryantsfield BOL BL1 28 D4
Bryngs Dr BOLE BL2 22 B3
Brynhall Cl RAD M26 33 G5
Brynheys Cl LHULT M38 47 E3
Bryn Lea Ter BOL BL1 19 F3
Bryn Wk BOL BL1 2 E1
Buchanan Dr WGNE/HIN WN2 42 D5

Buchanan St *SWIN* M27 ....57 H2
Buckingham Av *HOR/BR* BL6.....17 G5
Buckley La *FWTH* BL4 ....47 G1
Buckley Sq *FWTH* BL4 ....47 G1
Buckthorn Cl *WHTN* BL5 ....35 H3
Bude Av *TYLD* M29 ....54 A3
Buile Hill Av *LHULT* M38...............47 F4
Buile Hill Gv *LHULT* M38...............47 F4
Bullcroft Dr *TYLD* M29 ....54 A5
Buller St *BOLS/LL* BL3 ....39 G3
Bullough St *ATH* M46 ....52 C1
Bullows Rd *LHULT* M38 ....46 D2
Bulteel St *BOLS/LL* BL3 ....38 A3
   WALK M28.......................................54 C5
Bunting Ms *WALK* M28 ....55 F3
Burford Dr *BOLS/LL* BL3...................2 C7
   SWIN M27.......................................57 G1
Burghley Cl *RAD* M26 ....32 D5
Burghley Dr *RAD* M26 ....32 D5
Burgundy Dr *TOT/BURYW* BL8.....13 H5
Burke St *BOL* BL1 ....20 B5
Burlington St *WGNE/HIN* WN2.....42 A2
Burnaby St *BOLS/LL* BL3 ....30 B5
Burnden Rd *BOLS/LL* BL3 ....31 F5
Burnden Wy *HOR/BR* BL6..............27 E2
Burnet Cl *TYLD* M29 ....53 H4
Burnham Av *BOL* BL1 ....29 G1
Burnmoor Rd *BOLE* BL2 ....32 B2
Burns Av *ATH* M46.............................44 D3
   LEIGH WN7.....................................51 E3
   SWIN M27.......................................57 F3
Burnside Cl *RAD* M26 ....33 H4
   TYLD M29.......................................53 H4
Burnside Rd *BOL* BL1 ....19 H5
Burns Rd *LHULT* M38 ....47 F3
Burns St *BOLS/LL* BL3 ....2 E6
Burnt Edge La *HOR/BR* BL6.........18 B2
Burrington Dr *LEIGH* WN7 ....51 F4
Burton Av *TOT/BURYW* BL8 ....23 H3
Burton Gv *WALK* M28 ....57 E3
Burwell Cl *BOLS/LL* BL3 ....38 B1
Bury & Bolton Rd *RAD* M26............33 F3
Bury New Rd *BOL* BL1 ....3 G2
   BOLE BL2...32 D3
Bury Old Rd *BOLE* BL2 ....3 J3
   BOLE BL2...32 D1
Bury Rd *BOLE* BL2...............................31 H3
   EDGW/EG BL7...................................5 E3
   EDGW/EG BL7.................................12 E3
   TOT/BURYW BL8............................23 H1
Bushell St *BOLS/LL* BL3 ....37 H1
Bute St *BOL* BL1 ....29 H1
Buttercup Av *WALK* M28 *..............46 D5
Buttercup Cl *ATH* M46 ....44 D3
Butterfield Rd *WHTN* BL5 ....37 F5
Buttermere Av *SWIN* M27...............57 H5
Buttermere Cl *BOLS/LL* BL3 ....40 B1
Buttermere Rd *FWTH* BL4 ....38 C5
Butterwick Fld *HOR/BR* BL6........16 B4
Buxton Cl *ATH* M46 ....45 E4
Byland Cl *BOL* BL1 ....20 C5
Byng St *FWTH* BL4 ....39 H5
Byrness Cl *ATH* M46 ....45 E4
Byron Av *RAD* M26.............................41 F1
   SWIN M27.......................................57 G3
Byron Gv *LEIGH* WN7 ....51 G4
Byron Rd *TOT/BURYW* BL8 ....13 H2
Byron St *LEIGH* WN7 ....51 H5
Byron Wk *FWTH* BL4 ....47 F2

C

Cable St *BOL* BL1 ....3 F1
Caernarvon Cl *TOT/BURYW* BL8...13 H3
Caernarvon Rd *WGNE/HIN* WN2...42 C5
Cairngorm Dr *BOLS/LL* BL3...........29 E5
Caithness Dr *BOLS/LL* BL3 ....29 E5
Caldbeck Av *BOL* BL1........................29 F1
Caldbeck Dr *FWTH* BL4....................46 C1
Calder Av *WGNE/HIN* WN2.............43 E5
Calderburn Cl *HOR/BR* BL6...........27 F2
Calder Dr *FWTH* BL4..........................48 D3
   SWIN M27.......................................57 G2
   WALK M28.......................................55 E1
Calder Rd *BOLS/LL* BL3....................38 C2
Calderwood Cl *TOT/BURYW* BL8...23 H1
Caldew Cl *WGNE/HIN* WN2.............42 A4
Caldford Cl *WGNE/HIN* WN2.........25 G4
Caldwell St *WHTN* BL5 ....43 H3
Caleb Cl *TYLD* M29............................53 F2
Caledonia St *BOLS/LL* BL3..............30 A5
Caley St *BOL* BL1 ....19 F5
Calf Hey Cl *RAD* M26 ....41 G2
Callis Rd *BOLS/LL* BL3......................30 A4
Calver Hey Cl *WHTN* BL5 ....36 C5
Calverleigh Cl *BOLS/LL* BL3 ....37 G3
Calvert Rd *BOLS/LL* BL3..................38 D2

Calvin St *BOL* BL1 ....30 D1
Cambourne Dr *BOLS/LL* BL3...........29 G5
   WGNE/HIN WN2..........................51 E1
Cambria Sq *BOLS/LL* BL3 * 30 A5
Cambria St *BOLS/LL* BL3 ....30 A5
Cambridge Cl *FWTH* BL4 ....38 D4
Cambridge Dr *BOLS/LL* BL3 ....40 D1
Cambridge Rd *HOR/BR* BL6...........27 H2
Cambridge St *ATH* M46 ....52 C1
Camden Cl *BOLE* BL2 ....33 E1
Camellia Cl *BOL* BL1 ....29 H3
Cameron St *BOL* BL1 ....20 B2
   LEIGH WN7.....................................51 F4
Campbell Cl *TOT/BURYW* BL8.......23 G3
Campbell Ct *FWTH* BL4 ....39 G3
Campbell Rd *BOLS/LL* BL3 ....37 G3
   SWIN M27.......................................57 G5
Campbell St *FWTH* BL4 ....39 F4
Campbell Wy *WALK* M28 ....47 G5
Camrose Gdns *BOL* BL1...................30 C1
Cams Acre Cl *RAD* M26 ....41 G2
Cams La *RAD* M26 ....41 G3
Canada St *BOL* BL1 ....20 A5
   HOR/BR BL6...................................16 D4
Canal St *CHLY/EC* PR7 ....15 E1
Candahar St *BOLS/LL* BL3 ....39 E2
Canmore Cl *BOLS/LL* BL3 ....37 G2
Cannel Fold *WALK* M28 ....55 F4
Canning Dr *BOL* BL1 ....20 C5
Canning St *BOL* BL1 * 20 C5
Cannon Gv *BOLS/LL* BL3 ....2 A7
Cannon St *ATH* M46 ....44 D5
   BOLS/LL BL3 ....2 B7
   BOLS/LL BL3 ....30 B5
   RAD M26..33 H5
Cannon St North
   BOLS/LL BL3 * 2 B6
Cann St *TOT/BURYW* BL8 ....13 F5
Canons Cl *BOL* BL1 ....19 H5
Canonsway *SWIN* M27 ....57 G4
Cansfield Ct *FWTH* BL4....................48 C3
Canterbury Cl *ATH* M46...................45 E4
Canterbury Gv *BOLS/LL* BL3 ....38 B3
Canute Cl *BOLE* BL2 ....31 G1
   RAD M26..41 G2
Capitol Cl *BOL* BL1 ....19 G4
Cappadocia Wy *WHTN* BL5............43 F1
Captain Fold Rd *LHULT* M38..........47 H5
Captain Lees Gdns *WHTN* BL5......36 A5
Captain Lees Rd *WHTN* BL5 ....36 A5
Captain's Clough Rd *BOL* BL1 ......19 H5
Captain St *HOR/BR* BL6...................16 D3
Car Bank Av *ATH* M46.......................44 D4
Car Bank Sq *ATH* M46.......................44 D4
Car Bank St *ATH* M46........................44 B4
Carden Av *SWIN* M27 ....57 F4
Carder Cl *SWIN* M27..........................57 H4
Cardwell Gdns *BOL* BL1 * 20 C5
Carisbrooke Dr *BOL* BL1..................20 D4
Carisbrooke Rd *LEIGH* WN7..........52 D5
Carlisle Cl *BOLS/LL* BL3 ....40 C3
Carlisle Pl *EDGW/EG* BL7 ....11 E4
   SWIN M27.......................................57 H1
   WGNE/HIN WN2 * 42 A2
Carl St *BOL* BL1 * 20 B5
Carlton Av *BOLS/LL* BL3 ....37 G1
Carlton Cl *BOLE* BL2 ....22 A4
   HOR/BR BL6...................................15 H5
   WALK M28.......................................55 G2
Carlton Gv *HOR/BR* BL6 ....27 F1
   WGNE/HIN WN2..........................42 B5
Carlton Pl *FWTH* BL4 * 39 H4
Carlton Rd *BOL* BL1 ....29 G2
   WALK M28.......................................55 G2
Carlton St *BOLE* BL2 ....3 C5
   FWTH BL4.......................................39 H4
Carlyle Gv *LEIGH* WN7 ....51 E3
Carnation Rd *FWTH* BL4 ....39 E4
Carnforth Av *WGNE/HIN* WN2 ....42 C4
Carnoustie *BOLS/LL* BL3..................37 G2
Caroline St *BOLS/LL* BL3 ....38 B1
Carr Brook Dr *ATH* M46...................45 E4
Carr Common Rd
   WGNE/HIN WN2..........................43 F5
Carr Dr *FWTH* BL4..............................38 D4
Carrfield Av *LHULT* M38..................46 C4
Carrfield Gv *LHULT* M38..................46 C4
Carrie St *BOL* BL1 ....29 H2
Carrington Dr *BOLS/LL* BL3 ....38 D1
Carrington Gv *LEIGH* WN7 * 51 H4
Carrington Rd *CHLY/EC* PR7...........14 D1
Carrington St *LEIGH* WN7 ....51 H4
Carron Gv *BOLE* BL2 ....32 B3
Carr Rd *HOR/BR* BL6.........................16 D2
Carrslea Cl *RAD* M26 ....33 G5
Carr St *SWIN* M27 ....57 F4
Carslake Av *BOL* BL1 ....30 A2
Carswell Cl *TYLD* M29 ....54 A2

Carter St *BOLS/LL* BL3 ....39 E1
   FWTH BL4 * 48 A1
Cartleach Gv *WALK* M28 ....55 E1
Cartleach La *WALK* M28 ....54 D1
Cartmel Cl *BOLS/LL* BL3 ....36 D3
Cartmel Crs *BOLE* BL2......................21 G5
Cartmel Gv *WALK* M28 ....56 D4
Cartwright Gv *LEIGH* WN7............51 F2
Carville Gv *WGNE/HIN* WN2 ....42 D4
Carwood Gv *HOR/BR* BL6 ....27 F1
Castle Cen *HOR/BR* BL6...................17 E2
Castle Cft *BOLE* BL2 ....21 H4
Castlecroft Av *HOR/BR* BL6...........15 H5
Castle Dr *CHLY/EC* PR7 ....14 C1
Castleford Cl *BOL* BL1 * 2 B1
Castle Gv *LEIGH* WN7 ....52 D5
Castle Hill Pk *WGNE/HIN* WN2 ....42 B1
Castle Hill Rd *WGNE/HIN* WN2 ....42 A2
Castle Hill St *BOLE* BL2 ....21 F5
Castle House La *CHLY/EC* PR7........14 C1
Castle Ri *WGNE/HIN* WN2...............42 A3
Castle St *ATH* M46..............................53 F2
   BOLE BL2...3 J5
   FWTH BL4 * 47 H1
   WGNE/HIN WN2..........................42 A2
Castleton St *BOLE* BL2 ....21 F5
Castleway *WGNE/HIN* WN2 ....42 B3
Castlewood Sq *BOLE* BL2 ....31 G1
Caterham Av *BOLS/LL* BL3 ....37 F3
Catherine Rd *SWIN* M27 ....57 E4
Catherine St *BOLS/LL* BL3 ....37 H3
   LEIGH WN7.....................................51 H5
Catherine St East *HOR/BR* BL6.....16 D3
Catherine St West *HOR/BR* BL6....16 C3
Caton Dr *ATH* M46.............................52 A3
Catterall Crs *BOLE* BL2.....................21 H1
Catterick Dr *BOLS/LL* BL3................40 C1
Cavendish Gdns *BOLS/LL* BL3.......38 A2
Cavendish Rd *WALK* M28 ....56 D5
Cavendish St *LEIGH* WN7 ....51 H4
Cavenham Gv *BOL* BL1.....................30 A2
Cawdor Ct *FWTH* BL4 ....39 G3
Cawdor St *FWTH* BL4 ....39 F3
   SWIN M27.......................................57 F3
   WALK M28.......................................56 A1
   WGNE/HIN WN2..........................42 A3
Cecilia St *BOLS/LL* BL3 ....39 E1
Cecil St *BOLE* BL2 ....3 J4
   WALK M28.......................................47 H5
Cedar Av *ATH* M46.............................44 B4
   BOLS/LL BL3 ....40 D3
   HOR/BR BL6...................................27 G1
   WGNE/HIN WN2..........................42 B5
Cedar Dr *SWIN* M27..........................49 F4
Cedar Gv *FWTH* BL4 ....39 F5
   WHTN BL5.......................................43 G1
Cedar Rd *LEIGH* WN7.......................51 G3
Cedar Wood Ct *BOL* BL1 * 29 F2
Cellini Sq *BOL* BL1..............................30 B1
Cemetery Rd *BOLE* BL2 ....3 K3
   FWTH BL4.......................................40 B4
   RAD M26..41 H1
   SWIN M27.......................................57 G2
Cemetery Rd North *SWIN* M27......57 G1
Cemetery St *WHTN* BL5...................35 G4
Cemetery Vw *CHLY/EC* PR7............14 D1
Centaur Cl *SWIN* M27.......................57 H1
Centenary Ct *BOLS/LL* BL3..............38 D1
Central Av *ATH* M46 ....45 E4
   FWTH BL4.......................................39 E5
   WALK M28.......................................47 G3
Central Dr *WHTN* BL5 ....35 G4
Central St *BOL* BL1 ....2 D3
Centre Gdns *BOL* BL1 ....30 B1
Centre Park Rd *BOL* BL1 ....30 B1
Century Ldg *FWTH* BL4 ....39 G5
Cestrian St *BOLS/LL* BL3..................38 D2
Chadbury Cl *HOR/BR* BL6...............36 C2
Chaddock La *TYLD* M29 ....54 B5
Chadwick St *BOLE* BL2 ....3 H5
   BOLS/LL BL3 ....40 D2
   LEIGH WN7.....................................51 H5
   SWIN M27.......................................57 H3
   WGNE/HIN WN2..........................42 A2
Chale Gn *BOLE* BL2............................22 A4
Chalfont Dr *TYLD* M29 ....53 G4
   WALK M28.......................................56 A3
Chalfont St *BOL* BL1 ....20 D5
Chamberlain St *BOLS/LL* BL3.........2 B6
Chancery Cl *TYLD* M29 ....53 H3
Chancery La *BOL* BL1 ....3 F4
Chanters Av *ATH* M46 ....45 E5
The Chanters *WALK* M28.................55 G4
Chantry Cl *WHTN* BL5 ....43 H3
Chapel Aly *BOL* BL1 * 2 E3
Chapelfield Dr *WALK* M28 ....47 F5
Chapel Flds *EDGW/EG* BL7...............4 C5
Chapel Fields La
   WGNE/HIN WN2..........................42 A3

Chapelfield St *BOL* BL1 20
Chapel Gdns *TOT/BURYW* BL8.....13
Chapel Gra *EDGW/EG* BL7 4
Chapel Green Rd
   WGNE/HIN WN2..........................42
Chapel Meadow *WALK* M28 55
Chapel Pl *BOLS/LL* BL3 31
Chapel Rd *SWIN* M27 57
Chapelstead *WHTN* BL5...................43
Chapel St *ATH* M46 44
   BOL BL1..3
   BOLS/LL BL3 * 40
   CHLY/EC PR7..................................14
   EDGW/EG BL7...................................7
   FWTH BL4 * 40
   HOR/BR BL6.....................................6
   HOR/BR BL6...................................17
   TOT/BURYW BL8............................13
   TYLD M29 * 53
   WALK M28.......................................54
   WGNE/HIN WN2..........................50
Chapeltown Rd
   EDGW/EG BL7.................................11
Chapman St *BOL* BL1........................29
Chappeltown Rd *RAD* M26.............41
Charles Ct *BOL* BL1 * 3
Charles Holden St *BOL* BL1................2
Charles St *BOL* BL1...............................3
   EDGW/EG BL7.................................10
   FWTH BL4.......................................40
   FWTH BL4.......................................48
   LEIGH WN7.....................................51
   SWIN M27.......................................57
   TYLD M29.......................................53
   WGNE/HIN WN2..........................42
Charlesworth Av *BOLS/LL* BL3......39
   WGNE/HIN WN2..........................42
Charlock Av *WHTN* BL5....................43
Charlotte St *BOL* BL1 20
   EDGW/EG BL7...................................4
Charlton Dr *SWIN* M27.....................57
Charlton Fold *WALK* M28 47
Charnock Dr *BOL* BL1 30
Charnwood Cl *TYLD* M29 53
   WALK M28.......................................55
Chassen Rd *BOL* BL1 29
Chatburn Rd *BOL* BL1.......................19
Chatham Gdns *BOLS/LL* BL3............2
Chatham Pl *BOLS/LL* BL3 * 2
Chatham St *LEIGH* WN7 51
Chatsworth Av *BOL* BL1...................20
Chatsworth Dr *LEIGH* WN7............52
Chatsworth Rd *RAD* M26.................33
Chatteris Cl *WGNE/HIN* WN2........42
Chatton Cl *TOT/BURYW* BL8..........33
Chaucer Gv *LEIGH* WN7 51
Chaucer St *BOL* BL1...........................30
Cheadle Sq *BOL* BL1 * 2
Cheapside Sq *BOL* BL1 * 2
Chedworth Crs *LHULT* M38.............47
Chedworth Gv *BOLS/LL* BL3 * 2
The Cheethams *HOR/BR* BL6..........26
Chelburn Cl *WGNE/HIN* WN2........50
Chelford Av *BOL* BL1.........................20
Chelford Dr *SWIN* M27 57
   TYLD M29.......................................54
Chelmer Cl *WHTN* BL5......................35
Chelsea Av *RAD* M26.........................41
Chelsea Cl *WHTN* BL5 43
Chelsea Ct *WHTN* BL5 * 43
Chelsea Rd *BOLS/LL* BL3 38
Chelwood Cl *BOL* BL1 10
Chelwood Ms *HOR/BR* BL6 * 28
Chepstow Av *LEIGH* WN7................53
Cherington Dr *TYLD* M29................54
Cheriton Dr *BOLE* BL2 32
Cherry Gv *LEIGH* WN7 51
Cherry Tree Av *FWTH* BL4 51
Cherry Tree Gv *LEIGH* WN7 51
   ATH M46..46
Cherry Tree Wy *BOLE* BL2...............21
   HOR/BR BL6..................................
Cherrywood Av *WHTN* BL5.............45
Cherrywood Cl *WALK* M28..............25
Cherwell Cl *WGNE/HIN* WN2.........25
Cherwell Rd *WHTN* BL5....................35
Chesham Av *BOL* BL1 20
Chester Av *BOLS/LL* BL3...................20
Chester Cl *BOLS/LL* BL3 40
Chester Pl *CHLYE* PR6...........................7
Chester Rd *TYLD* M29 54
Chester St *ATH* M46 53
   SWIN M27.......................................57
Chesterton Gv *BOLS/LL* BL3...........29
Chester Wk *BOL* BL1..........................20
Chestnut Av *ATH* M46 * 44
   WALK M28.......................................55
Chestnut Cl *BOLS/LL* BL3.................37
Chestnut Dr *WHTN* BL5....................35

estnut Gv RAD M26 41 H5
VGNE/HIN WN2 42 C4
etwyn Av EDGW/EG BL7 11 E5
eviot Cl BOL BL1 20 B2
IOR/BR BL6 17 E2
ew Moor La WHTN BL5 36 A3
chester Av ATH M46 52 A1
dwall Cl BOLS/LL BL3 38 C3
grove Av HOR/BR BL6 25 H1
ham Rd WALK M28 56 A1
ham St BOLS/LL BL3 37 H3
WIN M27 57 G5
tern Av ATH M46 45 F3
tern Cl HOR/BR BL6 17 E2
VALK M28 56 A3
tern Dr BOLE BL2 31 G3
WIN M27 57 H5
tern Wy TYLD M29 53 H3
ton Cl LEIGH WN7 51 H4
na La BOL BL1 2 E1
nnor Cl LEIGH WN7 51 H4
o Hill Rd BOLS/LL BL3 37 G1
pping Rd BOL BL1 19 F5
sholme Cl TOT/BURYW BL8 13 H2
swick Dr RAD M26 32 D5
sworth Cl LEIGH WN7 51 G4
sworth St BOLE BL2 21 F4
rley Cl TOT/BURYW BL8 33 H1
rley New Rd BOL BL1 29 E3
OR/BR BL6 16 D4
OR/BR BL6 28 A2
rley Old Rd BOL BL1 2 A1
OL BL1 19 E5
OR/BR BL6 17 G4
rley Rd CHLYE PR6 7 F4
OR/BR BL6 15 E2
WIN M27 57 F2
VGN WN1 14 A2
VHTN BL5 35 E1
rley St BOL BL1 2 C2
HLYE PR6 7 F4
wbent Cl ATH M46 45 E5
ist Church Cl BOLE BL2 * 22 B5
ist Church La BOLE BL2 22 B4
onnell Dr BOLE BL2 32 A2
lsey Gate La HOR/BR BL6 36 A1
lsey St BOLS/LL BL3 37 H2
rch Av BOLS/LL BL3 38 A1
VGNE/HIN WN2 50 B3
rch Bank BOL BL1 3 F3
rch Cl RAD M26 40 D5
rchfield Cl RAD M26 41 H4
rchgate BOL BL1 3 F3
rchill Av BOLE BL2 33 F1
rchill Dr BOLS/LL BL3 41 E2
WTH BL4 38 D3
rchill St BOLE BL2 31 G3
rch La WHTN BL5 35 G2
rch Mdw BOLE BL2 22 B4
rch Rd BOL BL1 19 H5
WTH BL4 40 A5
AD M26 40 C5
YLD M29 54 A5
VALK M28 47 H5
rchside FWTH BL4 47 F1
rch St BOLE BL2 21 H2
OLE BL2 33 F1
OLS/LL BL3 40 B2
HLY/EC PR7 7 E5
WTH BL4 40 A5
WTH BL4 48 A1
OR/BR BL6 15 G5
OR/BR BL6 17 E4
WIN M27 57 G3
OT/BURYW BL8 23 H2
VGNE/HIN WN2 25 F4
VHTN BL5 35 G4
rchtown Av BOLE BL2 32 B3
rch Wk FWTH BL4 * 39 G5
WIN M27 49 H4
OT/BURYW BL8 * 13 F3
rchward Sq HOR/BR BL6 17 E5
rnett Cl WHTN BL5 35 H3
namon Av WGNE/HIN WN2 42 C4
ncester Cl LHULT M38 47 E2
Rd WALK M28 55 E3
nmerclough Rd FWTH BL4 40 B5
ebank BOL BL1 29 F3
emont Av WGNE/HIN WN2 42 B3
emont Ct BOL BL1 * 30 C1
emont Dr LHULT M38 47 F3
ence Ct BOL BL1 * 2 C2
ence Rd SWIN M27 57 E4
ence St ATH M46 53 E2
OL BL1 2 E2
WTH BL4 40 A4
endon Gv BOLE BL2 3 J6
endon Rd BOLE BL2 31 G3
WIN M27 57 H3
Clarendon St BOLS/LL BL3 38 C1
Clarke Crs LHULT M38 46 B2
Clarke St BOL BL1 30 A2
Claude Av SWIN M27 57 F3
Claude St SWIN M27 57 F3
Claughton Av BOLE BL2 32 B3
WALK M28 55 G3
Claughton Rd TOT/BURYW BL8 23 H2
Claybank Dr TOT/BURYW BL8 13 G5
Claybrook Cl ATH M46 52 A1
Claydon Dr RAD M26 32 D5
Claymore St BOLS/LL BL3 38 D2
Claypool Rd HOR/BR BL6 27 G1
Clay St EDGW/EG BL7 11 E5
Clayton Av BOLE BL2 31 F5
Clayton Cl TOT/BURYW BL8 33 H1
Clayton St BOLE BL2 31 G5
Clegg's Buildings BOL BL1 * 2 C2
Clegg's La LHULT M38 47 E3
Clegg St BOLE BL2 31 G3
TYLD M29 53 G5
Clelland St FWTH BL4 48 A1
Clement Av ATH M46 52 A1
Cleveland Gdns BOLS/LL BL3 37 H1
Cleveland St BOLS/LL BL3 * 37 H1
Cleveleys Av BOLE BL2 31 G2
Cliff Av TOT/BURYW BL8 13 G5
Clifford Rd BOLS/LL BL3 * 37 G3
Clifton Av TYLD M29 54 A5
Clifton Ct FWTH BL4 39 F3
Clifton Dr HOR/BR BL6 15 F4
SWIN M27 57 F1
Clifton Gv SWIN M27 57 F1
Clifton House Rd SWIN M27 49 G4
Clifton St BOL BL1 2 C2
FWTH BL4 39 F3
FWTH BL4 48 B1
TYLD M29 54 C3
Clifton Vw SWIN M27 49 G4
Clitheroe Dr TOT/BURYW BL8 23 H5
Clivedale Pl BOL BL1 3 F4
Clive Rd WHTN BL5 43 G2
Clive St BOL BL1 3 F4
Clock Tower Cl WALK M28 46 D5
Cloister Av LEIGH WN7 51 F2
The Cloisters WHTN BL5 43 G3
Cloister St BOL BL1 20 A5
Clondberry Cl TYLD M29 54 C2
Close La WGNE/HIN WN2 42 B5
WGNE/HIN WN2 50 D2
Closes Farm BOLS/LL BL3 37 H3
Close St WGNE/HIN WN2 42 B2
The Close ATH M46 45 F3
BOLE BL2 21 F4
Cloudstock Gv LHULT M38 46 C3
Clough Av WHTN BL5 35 H5
Cloughbank RAD M26 49 E1
Cloughfold RAD M26 48 D1
Clough Meadow BOL BL1 28 D4
Clough Meadow Rd RAD M26 41 G2
Clough St FWTH BL4 48 B1
The Clough BOL BL1 * 29 E2
Clovelly Av LEIGH WN7 51 H3
Clovelly Rd SWIN M27 57 E4
Cloverdale Sq BOL BL1 29 G1
Clunton Av BOLS/LL BL3 37 H1
Clyde Rd RAD M26 33 H5
TYLD M29 54 A4
Clyde St BOL BL1 * 20 C5
Clyde Ter RAD M26 * 33 H5
Coach Rd TYLD M29 54 A5
Coach St ATH M46 44 D5
Coal Pit La ATH M46 44 B5
LEIGH WN7 51 G3
WGNE/HIN WN2 50 D2
Coal Pit Rd BOL BL1 19 F1
Cobden St BOL BL1 20 B4
EDGW/EG BL7 * 10 B2
RAD M26 33 H4
TYLD M29 53 G2
Cobham Av BOLS/LL BL3 38 B2
Cochrane St BOLS/LL BL3 30 D5
Cockerell Springs BOLE BL2 * 3 G5
Cocker St LHULT M38 47 E4
Cockey Moor Rd BOLE BL2 33 F1
Codale Dr BOLE BL2 32 B2
Code La WHTN BL5 34 D1
Coe St BOLS/LL BL3 2 E7
Colchester Av BOLE BL2 32 A2
Colchester Dr FWTH BL4 38 D4
Coleford Gv BOL BL1 2 C5
Colenso Ct BOLE BL2 * 31 G3
Coleridge Av RAD M26 41 G2
Coleridge Rd TOT/BURYW BL8 13 H2
Colesbourne Cl LHULT M38 47 E2
Colindale Cl BOLS/LL BL3 * 30 A5
Colinton Cl BOL BL1 30 B1
Collard St ATH M46 44 B4
College Cl BOLS/LL BL3 2 D6
College Wy BOLS/LL BL3 2 C6
Collegiate Wy SWIN M27 49 H5
Colliers Row Rd BOL BL1 18 D2
Collier St SWIN M27 57 G4
Colliery La ATH M46 44 A4
Collingwood Wy WHTN BL5 35 G4
Collins La WHTN BL5 43 H2
Collins St TOT/BURYW BL8 23 H3
Collyhurst Av WALK M28 56 A1
Colmore Gv BOLE BL2 21 F3
Colmore St BOLE BL2 21 F4
Columbia Rd BOL BL1 30 A2
Colwith Av BOLE BL2 32 A1
Colwyn Dr WGNE/HIN WN2 51 E1
Colwyn Gv ATH M46 44 C3
Colwyn Rd SWIN M27 57 E5
Combermere Cl TYLD M29 53 H2
Common End CHLY/EC PR7 14 C3
Common La TYLD M29 53 G2
Common Side Rd WALK M28 54 D4
Common St WHTN BL5 42 D1
The Common CHLY/EC PR7 14 C2
Como St BOLS/LL BL3 * 38 A1
Congresbury Rd LEIGH WN7 51 F4
Conisber Cl EDGW/EG BL7 10 C3
Coniston BOL BL1 * 20 D4
Coniston Av ATH M46 44 D3
CHLYE PR6 7 F4
FWTH BL4 46 C1
LHULT M38 47 E4
Coniston Cl BOLS/LL BL3 40 C1
Coniston Gv LHULT M38 47 E4
Coniston Rd HOR/BR BL6 15 H4
SWIN M27 57 H5
TYLD M29 53 G4
WGNE/HIN WN2 42 A4
Connaught Sq BOLE BL2 31 F1
Connel Cl BOLE BL2 32 B4
Conningsby Cl EDGW/EG BL7 10 D4
Constable Cl BOL BL1 30 B1
Constance Rd BOLS/LL BL3 30 A5
Conway Av BOL BL1 29 G1
Conway Cl LEIGH WN7 53 E4
Conway Crs TOT/BURYW BL8 13 H2
Conway Rd WGNE/HIN WN2 42 B4
Conway St FWTH BL4 47 H1
Cooke St FWTH BL4 48 A1
HOR/BR BL6 17 F3
Cooling La TYLD M29 52 D3
Coombe Cl TYLD M29 53 H3
Co-operative St LHULT M38 * 46 C3
Cooper St HOR/BR BL6 16 D3
Coop St BOL BL1 20 C3
Cope Bank BOL BL1 30 A1
Cope Bank West BOL BL1 * 19 H5
Copeland Ms BOL BL1 29 G3
Copesthorne Cl
WGNE/HIN WN2 25 G4
Cope St BOL BL1 30 A1
Coplow Dl WGNE/HIN WN2 42 A5
Copperas La WGNE/HIN WN2 25 E4
Copperfields HOR/BR BL6 36 B2
Coppice Cl HOR/BR BL6 36 A2
The Coppice BOLE BL2 21 H2
WALK M28 56 B3
Coppull Hall La CHLY/EC PR7 6 A5
The Copse EDGW/EG BL7 11 G2
Copthorne Dr BOLE BL2 32 A4
Copthorn Wk TOT/BURYW BL8 23 H2
Corfe Cl WGNE/HIN WN2 25 H5
Corhampton Crs ATH M46 45 E3
Cormorant Cl LHULT M38 47 G5
Cornbrook Cl WHTN BL5 43 F2
Corner Brook HOR/BR BL6 36 A2
Cornergate WHTN BL5 43 G3
Corner La LEIGH WN7 51 F1
Cornlea Dr WALK M28 55 G4
Cornwall Av TYLD M29 45 G5
WHTN BL5 37 F5
Cornwall Dr WGNE/HIN WN2 42 B2
Coronation Av ATH M46 44 C3
Coronation Dr LEIGH WN7 52 D5
Coronation Gdns RAD M26 41 G1
Coronation Rd RAD M26 41 G1
Coronation St BOL BL1 2 E4
Corporation St BOL BL1 2 E3
Corranstone Cl HOR/BR BL6 16 D4
Corrie Crs FWTH BL4 49 F4
Corrie Dr FWTH BL4 49 F4
Corrie St LHULT M38 47 E4
Corring Wy BOL BL1 21 F3
Corrin Rd BOLE BL2 3 K7
Corsey Rd WGNE/HIN WN2 42 A4
Corson St BOLS/LL BL3 39 H3
Corston Gv HOR/BR BL6 25 H1
Cotefield Av BOLS/LL BL3 38 D2
Cotford Rd BOL BL1 20 D2
Cotswold Dr HOR/BR BL6 17 E2
Cottage Cft BOLE BL2 21 H2
Cottingley Cl BOL BL1 20 B2
Cottonfields EDGW/EG BL7 10 D5
Cotton St BOL BL1 20 B5
Coucill Sq FWTH BL4 40 A5
Countess La RAD M26 33 F5
County Rd LHULT M38 47 E4
Coupes Gn WHTN BL5 43 G2
Coupland Rd WGNE/HIN WN2 42 D4
WGNE/HIN WN2 43 F5
Court St BOLE BL2 3 H4
Courtyard Dr WALK M28 46 D5
The Courtyard BOL BL1 * 30 D1
Cousin Flds EDGW/EG BL7 11 G5
Coventry Rd RAD M26 33 H5
Coverdale Av BOL BL1 29 G2
Coverdale Rd WHTN BL5 35 F5
Cowburn St WGNE/HIN WN2 42 B1
Cowdals Rd HOR/BR BL6 36 B1
Cow La BOLS/LL BL3 37 H3
Cow Lees WHTN BL5 36 A4
Cowley Rd BOL BL1 20 D2
Cox Green Cl EDGW/EG BL7 10 B1
Cox Green Rd EDGW/EG BL7 10 D3
Cox Wy ATH M46 44 D5
Crab Tree La ATH M46 52 D1
Craighall Rd BOL BL1 20 C1
Cramond Cl BOL BL1 30 B1
Cramond Wk BOL BL1 30 B1
Cranark Cl BOL BL1 29 G3
Cranberry Dr BOLS/LL BL3 37 F1
Cranborne Cl HOR/BR BL6 27 H1
Crane St BOLS/LL BL3 * 37 H2
Cranfield Rd HOR/BR BL6 27 F3
Cranford St BOLS/LL BL3 38 A3
Cranham Close Crs
LHULT M38 * 47 E2
Cranleigh Cl HOR/BR BL6 25 H1
Cranleigh Dr TYLD M29 53 H3
WALK M28 56 A3
Cranshaw St TYLD M29 54 B3
Cranstal Dr WGNE/HIN WN2 42 C3
Cranworth Av TYLD M29 53 G5
Crathie Ct BOL BL1 29 H1
Craven Pl BOL BL1 19 E5
Craven St East HOR/BR BL6 17 F5
Crawford Av BOLE BL2 3 J5
CHLY/EC PR7 14 C2
TYLD M29 53 F1
WALK M28 56 B3
WGNE/HIN WN2 25 G5
Crawford St BOLE BL2 3 H4
Crawley Cl TYLD M29 54 A2
Crediton Dr BOLE BL2 32 C3
Crescent Av BOL BL1 2 B2
FWTH BL4 47 G2
WHTN BL5 37 G5
Crescent Dr LHULT M38 47 F3
Crescent Rd BOLS/LL BL3 39 F2
FWTH BL4 48 B2
HOR/BR BL6 27 G2
The Crescent BOLE BL2 22 B3
BOLS/LL BL3 40 D3
EDGW/EG BL7 11 E4
HOR/BR BL6 27 F1
RAD M26 33 F5
WHTN BL5 43 G1
Cressingham Rd BOLS/LL BL3 37 G2
Crestfold LHULT M38 47 E4
Cricketers Wy WHTN BL5 35 G5
Cricketfield La WALK M28 47 G5
Cricket St BOLS/LL BL3 30 C5
Cringle Cl BOLS/LL BL3 37 E1
Crippen St ATH M46 52 A2
Croal St BOL BL1 2 A5
Croasdale St BOL BL1 30 D1
Crocus St BOL BL1 20 D3
Croft Av ATH M46 52 D1
Croft Dr TOT/BURYW BL8 23 G1
Crofters Wk BOLE BL2 21 G1
Croft Ga BOLE BL2 22 A3
Croft Gv LHULT M38 46 D3
Croft La BOLS/LL BL3 31 F5
Croft Pl TYLD M29 53 F3
Croftside Av WALK M28 48 A5
Croftside Cl WALK M28 48 A5
Croftside Gv WALK M28 48 A5
Croft St BOLS/LL BL3 39 F1
LHULT M38 46 D3
WHTN BL5 35 G2
Croichbank TOT/BURYW BL8 12 D2
Crombouke Dr LEIGH WN7 51 G2
Crombouke Fold WALK M28 55 F4
Cromdale Av BOL BL1 29 H2
Cromer Av BOLE BL2 31 G1
Cromer Dr ATH M46 52 A1
Cromford Cl BOL BL1 30 C1
Cromford Gdns BOL BL1 20 D5
Crompton Av BOLE BL2 32 A2
Crompton Cl BOL BL1 21 E3

Crompton Pl *BOL* BL1 *...............3 F4
Crompton Rd *HOR/BR* BL6.........27 H2
   RAD M26............................40 C5
Crompton St *BOL* BL1...................3 G2
   FWTH BL4............................48 A1
   SWIN M27............................57 G3
   WALK M28............................56 B1
Crompton V *BOLE* BL2................31 H2
Crompton Wy *BOLE* BL2.............21 G4
Cromwell Rd *SWIN* M27..............57 G3
Cromwell St *BOL* BL1...................2 C5
Crook St *BOLS/LL* BL3..................2 E6
   CHLY/EC PR7.........................6 D5
Cropton Wy *WGNE/HIN* WN2......42 B5
Crosby Av *WALK* M28..................56 B1
Crosby Rd *BOL* BL1......................29 H2
   RAD M26............................33 G3
Crosby St *ATH* M46.....................45 E4
Crossdale Rd *BOLE* BL2...............32 B2
   WGNE/HIN WN2...................42 C4
Crossen St *BOLS/LL* BL3..............31 G5
Crossfield Dr *RAD* M26................41 G2
   SWIN M27............................57 G2
   WALK M28............................56 B4
   WGNE/HIN WN2...................43 E5
Crossfields *EDGW/EG* BL7..........11 F4
Crossford Dr *BOLS/LL* BL3...........29 F5
Crosslands Rd *WALK* M28............54 D5
Crossley St *BOLS/LL* BL3.............40 C1
Crossmoor Dr *BOLE* BL2................3 K1
Cross Ormrod St
   BOLS/LL BL3..........................2 B6
Cross St *ATH* M46.......................44 B4
   BOL BL1...............................3 F1
   BOLS/LL BL3........................40 D2
   EDGW/EG BL7.....................10 D5
   FWTH BL4............................39 H4
   FWTH BL4............................48 D3
   TYLD M29 *.........................53 F3
   WALK M28............................56 D5
The Cross *TOT/BURYW* BL8 *.....23 H1
Croston Av *CHLYE* PR6..................7 E4
Croston St *BOLS/LL* BL3...............38 A1
Crowborough Cl *HOR/BR* BL6.....27 H1
Crowland Rd *BOLE* BL2...............21 G5
Crowndale *EDGW/EG* BL7.............4 D2
Crown Gdns *EDGW/EG* BL7...........4 D3
Crown Gv *LEIGH* WN7..................52 D5
Crown La *HOR/BR* BL6.................16 B4
Crown St *ATH* M46......................44 C5
   BOL BL1...............................3 F3
Crow's Nest *BOLS/LL* BL3...........32 B5
Crow Trees La *EDGW/EG* BL7.......4 C2
Croyde Cl *BOLE* BL2....................22 B5
Croydon Av *LEIGH* WN7..............51 H3
Crummock Cl *BOLS/LL* BL3..........40 B2
Crummock Rd *FWTH* BL4.............46 C1
Crumpsall St *BOL* BL1.................20 C5
Crundale Rd *BOL* BL1..................20 D1
Culham Cl *BOL* BL1 *.....................2 D1
Culraven *WGNE/HIN* WN2 *........25 F3
Culross Av *BOLS/LL* BL3..............29 E4
Cumberland Av *SWIN* M27...........57 H1
   TYLD M29............................53 F1
Cumberland Rd *ATH* M46............45 E4
Cundey St *BOL* BL1 *...................30 A1
Cunliffe Brow *BOL* BL1................29 H1
Cunningham Rd *WHTN* BL5..........43 E1
Curteis St *HOR/BR* BL6...............16 D3
Curtels Cl *WALK* M28...................57 E4
Curtis St *BOLS/LL* BL3.................38 A3
Curzon Rd *BOL* BL1.....................30 A3
Cutacre Cl *TYLD* M29..................53 H2
Cutacre La *WHTN* BL5.................46 B2
Cuthbert St *BOL* BL1...................37 G3
Cypress Gv *FWTH* BL4 *..............48 B1
Cyril St *BOLS/LL* BL3...................31 E5

D

Daccamill Dr *SWIN* M27..............57 H5
Daffodil Rd *FWTH* BL4.................39 E4
Daffodil St *BOL* BL1.....................20 D2
Dagmar St *WALK* M28.................47 G4
Daisy Av *FWTH* BL4.....................39 E4
Daisyfield *HOR/BR* BL6 *.............27 F1
Daisy Hall Dr *WHTN* BL5.............43 G3
Daisyhill Ct *WHTN* BL5................43 H3
Daisy Hill Dr *CHLYE* PR6...............7 E4
Daisy St *BOLS/LL* BL3..................38 A1
Dalby Av *SWIN* M27.....................55 H2
Dalby Rd *WGNE/HIN* WN2...........42 D3
Dalebank *ATH* M46......................44 C3
Dalebank Ms *SWIN* M27 *...........49 F3
Dalegarth Av *BOL* BL1.................28 C3
Dale Lee *WHTN* BL5.....................36 A5
Dalesbrook Cl *BOLS/LL* BL3.........40 C1

Dales Brow *BOL* BL1...................20 D1
   SWIN M27 *.........................57 F5
Dales Gv *WALK* M28...................56 B2
Dales Park Dr *SWIN* M27 *..........57 F5
Dale St *FWTH* BL4 *....................40 A4
   SWIN M27............................57 G5
   WHTN BL5............................43 H3
Dale St East *HOR/BR* BL6............27 F1
Dale St West *HOR/BR* BL6...........17 F5
Dalkeith Gv *BOLS/LL* BL3............29 F5
Dalkeith Rd *WGNE/HIN* WN2.......42 C3
Dalton Fold *WHTN* BL5................35 H5
Dalwood Cl *WGNE/HIN* WN2........42 B4
Dalymount Cl *BOLE* BL2..............21 F5
Dams Head Fold *WHTN* BL5.........35 H4
Danby Rd *BOLS/LL* BL3................38 C2
Danebridge Cl *FWTH* BL4............40 A5
Danes Av *WGNE/HIN* WN2...........42 A2
Danes Brook Cl
   WGNE/HIN WN2...................42 A2
Danesbury Rd *BOLE* BL2..............21 F3
Danes Gn *WGNE/HIN* WN2...........42 A1
Dane St *BOLS/LL* BL3 *................38 A1
Danesway *CHLY/EC* PR7.................6 D3
Danesway Ct *BOL* BL1.................20 B5
Darbishire St *BOL* BL1.................31 E1
Darbyshire Cl *BOL* BL1................30 A3
Darcy St *BOL* BL1........................31 G5
Dark La *HOR/BR* BL6...................15 F4
Darley Av *FWTH* BL4...................40 A4
Darley Gv *FWTH* BL4...................40 A4
Darley St *BOL* BL1.......................30 B1
   FWTH BL4............................40 A5
   HOR/BR BL6.........................16 D2
Darley Ter *BOL* BL1 *..................30 B1
Darlington St *TYLD* M29...............53 G2
Darlington St East
   TYLD M29.............................53 H2
Darnley Av *WALK* M28.................55 G2
Darvel Cl *BOLE* BL2.....................32 B4
Darwen Rd *EDGW/EG* BL7...........10 D4
Darwin St *BOL* BL1......................20 B5
Davenport Fold Rd *BOLE* BL2 *....22 C3
Davenport Gdns *BOL* BL1..............2 D2
Davenport St *BOL* BL1...................2 C2
David Brow *BOLS/LL* BL3.............37 G3
Davies St *FWTH* BL4....................48 C1
Dawson La *BOL* BL1......................2 C3
Dawson St *ATH* M46 *.................44 C5
Dealey Rd *BOLS/LL* BL3...............37 G1
Deal St *BOLS/LL* BL3....................38 D2
Dean Cl *FWTH* BL4......................38 D5
Dean Ct *BOL* BL1...........................3 F1
Deane Av *BOLS/LL* BL3................29 H5
Deane Church La *BOLS/LL* BL3.....37 H1
Deane Rd *BOLS/LL* BL3................30 A5
Deane Wk *BOLS/LL* BL3.................2 C6
Deanscourt Av *SWIN* M27...........57 G4
Deansgate *BOL* BL1.......................2 E3
   WGNE/HIN WN2...................42 A2
Deans Rd *SWIN* M27....................57 G4
Dean St *RAD* M26........................41 H2
Deansway *SWIN* M27...................57 G4
Dearden Av *LHULT* M38...............47 E3
Dearden St *BOLS/LL* BL3..............40 C1
Debenham St *FWTH* BL4 *...........47 H1
Dee Dr *FWTH* BL4........................48 C3
Deepdale Rd *BOLE* BL2................32 B1
Dee Rd *TYLD* M29........................54 A4
Defence St *BOLS/LL* BL3................2 B6
Defiance St *ATH* M46...................44 C5
Delaford Av *WALK* M28................56 A4
Dellside Av *WALK* M28.................48 A5
The Dell *BOLE* BL2.......................21 G2
Delph Av *EDGW/EG* BL7..............10 B1
Delph Brook Wy *EDGW/EG* BL7...10 B2
Delph Gv *LEIGH* WN7..................51 F2
Delph Hl *BOL* BL1........................19 E5
Delph Hill Cl *BOL* BL1..................19 E5
Delphi Av *WALK* M28...................55 H1
Delph La *BOLE* BL2......................33 E1
Delph St *BOLS/LL* BL3..................30 B5
The Delph *WALK* M28 *................56 B5
Denbigh Gv *ATH* M46...................44 C3
Denbigh Rd *BOLE* BL2....................3 J7
Dene Bank *BOLE* BL2...................21 G2
Dene St *BOLE* BL2........................21 G2
Denham Cl *BOL* BL1.....................21 E2
Denstone Crs *BOLE* BL2...............21 H5
Dentdale Cl *BOL* BL1...................28 D4
Denton Rd *BOLE* BL2...................32 D4
Derby Pl *CHLYE* PR6......................7 E4
Derby Rd *RAD* M26.....................40 C5
Derbyshire Rw *BOL* BL1..............20 C4
Derby St *ATH* M46.......................44 C4
   BOLS/LL BL3..........................2 C7
   BOLS/LL BL3........................30 B5
   HOR/BR BL6.........................27 F1
   WHTN BL5............................35 H4

Derwent Cl *BOLS/LL* BL3.............40 B2
   WALK M28............................55 F1
Derwent Dr *FWTH* BL4................48 D3
Derwent Rd *FWTH* BL4................46 D1
   WGNE/HIN WN2...................42 A3
Derwent St *TYLD* M29.................53 G4
Design St *BOLS/LL* BL3................37 H2
Desmond St *ATH* M46.................52 A1
Devoke Av *WALK* M28..................56 A1
Devoke Gv *FWTH* BL4.................38 C5
Devon Cl *BOLS/LL* BL3................40 D1
   WGNE/HIN WN2...................25 H5
Devon Dr *BOLE* BL2.....................33 E1
Devon Rd *TYLD* M29....................53 F1
Devonshire Dr *WALK* M28...........54 C5
Devonshire Rd *ATH* M46.............44 C3
   BOL BL1.............................29 H2
   WALK M28............................47 G2
Devon St *BOLE* BL2.......................3 H4
   FWTH BL4............................39 H3
   SWIN M27............................57 H1
   WGNE/HIN WN2...................42 A3
Dewberry Cl *TYLD* M29................54 C2
Dewham Cl *WHTN* BL5................35 H4
Dewhurst Clough Rd
   EDGW/EG BL7.....................10 B2
Dewhurst Ct *EDGW/EG* BL7.........10 B1
Dewhurst Rd *BOLE* BL2...............22 A4
Dial Ct *FWTH* BL4 *.....................39 H5
Dicconson La *WHTN* BL5.............34 C1
Dickenson St *WGNE/HIN* WN2.....42 A4
Dickinson Cl *BOL* BL1 *................30 C1
Dickinson St *BOL* BL1..................30 C1
Dickson St West *HOR/BR* BL6......16 C3
Dijon St *BOLS/LL* BL3...................38 A1
Dilham Ct *BOL* BL1......................30 A2
Dimple Pk *EDGW/EG* BL7............10 B1
Dingle Wk *BOL* BL1.......................2 E1
Dinsdale Dr *BOLS/LL* BL3...............2 A7
Ditton Brook *WHTN* BL5..............35 H4
Division St *BOLS/LL* BL3..............38 D2
Dixey St *HOR/BR* BL6..................16 C4
Dixon Dr *SWIN* M27....................49 G4
Dixon Green Dr *FWTH* BL4..........39 G5
Dixon St *HOR/BR* BL6..................16 C4
   WHTN BL5............................35 G2
Dobb Brow Rd *WHTN* BL5...........43 F1
Dobhill St *FWTH* BL4...................39 H5
Dobson Rd *BOL* BL1....................30 A3
Dobson St *BOL* BL1.....................20 B5
Dodd La *WHTN* BL5.....................34 D2
Dodd's Farm La
   WGNE/HIN WN2...................34 A2
Dodhurst Rd *WGNE/HIN* WN2.....42 B2
Doe Brow *SWIN* M27...................49 G4
Doefield Av *WALK* M28................55 H3
Doe Hey Gv *FWTH* BL4................39 F3
Doe Hey Rd *BOLS/LL* BL3............39 F3
Doffcocker Brow *BOL* BL1...........29 F1
Doffcocker La *BOL* BL1................29 F1
Doman St *BOLS/LL* BL3................30 D5
Doncaster Cl *BOLS/LL* BL3...........40 B2
Donnington Gdns *WALK* M28 *....47 H5
Donnington Rd *RAD* M26.............33 E5
Don St *BOLS/LL* BL3.....................38 D2
Doodson Sq *FWTH* BL4................39 H5
Dootson St *WGNE/HIN* WN2........42 C2
Dorchester Av *BOLE* BL2.............32 A1
Dorchester Rd *SWIN* M27............57 H5
Doris Av *BOLE* BL2.......................31 H3
Dorket Gv *WHTN* BL5..................43 F2
Dorking Cl *BOL* BL1.....................20 D5
Dormer St *BOL* BL1......................20 D4
Dorning St *ATH* M46....................53 F2
   FWTH BL4............................40 B5
   HOR/BR BL6.........................26 A3
Dorris Av *BOLS/LL* BL3 *.............38 A2
Dorset Av *FWTH* BL4...................39 G5
   TYLD M29............................45 F5
Dorset Cl *FWTH* BL4....................39 G5
Dorset Rd *ATH* M46.....................44 C4
Dorset St *BOLE* BL2.......................3 H4
   SWIN M27............................57 H1
   WGNE/HIN WN2...................42 A3
Dorstone Cl *WGNE/HIN* WN2......42 D3
Dotterel Cl *LEIGH* WN7................52 A5
Douglas Av *HOR/BR* BL6.............17 E3
Douglas Cl *HOR/BR* BL6..............17 E5
Douglas Pk *ATH* M46..................46 A5
Douglas Rd *ATH* M46..................53 E1
   LEIGH WN7..........................51 E4
   WALK M28............................57 E4
Douglas St *ATH* M46...................45 E5
   BOL BL1 *............................20 C2
Douglas Vw *HOR/BR* BL6............15 E1
Dove Bank Rd *BOLS/LL* BL3.........40 B1
Dovecote Cl *EDGW/EG* BL7.........11 F4
Dovecote La *LHULT* M38..............46 C5
Dovedale Rd *BOLE* BL2................32 B1

Dover Gv *BOLS/LL* BL3..................2 B1
Dove Rd *BOLS/LL* BL3..................37 H3
Dover St *FWTH* BL4.....................39 H4
Dove St *BOL* BL1..........................20 C5
Dovey Cl *TYLD* M29.....................54 C2
Dow Fold *TOT/BURYW* BL8..........23 H1
Dow La *TOT/BURYW* BL8.............23 H1
Downgreen Rd *BOLE* BL2............22 B4
Downhall Gn *BOL* BL1....................2 A5
Downham Av *BOLE* BL2...............31 H2
Dowson St *BOL* BL1.......................3 F3
Doyle Cl *BOLS/LL* BL3..................37 H2
Drake Av *FWTH* BL4....................47 E1
Drake Hall *WHTN* BL5..................43 E3
Drake St *ATH* M46.......................52 A1
Draycott Cl *WGNE/HIN* WN2........20 A3
Draycott St *BOL* BL1....................20 A5
Draycott St East *BOL* BL1............20 A5
Drayton Cl *BOL* BL1.....................20 A5
The Drive *ATH* M46 *...................44 C5
Droxford Gv *ATH* M46..................45 E5
Druids Cl *EDGW/EG* BL7..............10 A1
Drummond St *BOL* BL1 *.............20 B1
Dryad Cl *SWIN* M27.....................57 H1
Dryburgh Av *BOL* BL1..................20 A1
Dryden Av *SWIN* M27...................57 G4
Dryfield La *HOR/BR* BL6...............16 A2
Drysdale Vw *BOL* BL1..................30 C1
Duchess Wk *BOLS/LL* BL3............37 G2
Duchy Av *WALK* M28....................55 F1
   WHTN BL5............................37 H2
Ducie Av *BOL* BL1........................30 A1
Ducie St *RAD* M26.......................33 H2
Duckshaw La *FWTH* BL4..............39 F5
Duddon Av *BOLE* BL2...................32 B2
Dudley Av *BOL* BL1......................31 E1
Dudley Rd *SWIN* M27...................57 G4
Dudwell Cl *BOL* BL1.....................30 A3
Duerden St *BOLS/LL* BL3 *...........37 H2
Duke Rd *BOLE* BL2.......................33 E1
Duke St *BOL* BL1............................2 A5
   LHULT M38.........................47 G5
   TYLD M29............................54 B3
   WALK M28............................56 D5
Duke St North *BOL* BL1.................2 A5
Dulverton Gdns *BOLS/LL* BL3 *....40 C1
Dumbell St *SWIN* M27.................57 H1
Dunbar Dr *BOLS/LL* BL3...............38 D2
Dunblane Av *BOLS/LL* BL3...........29 F5
Duncan St *HOR/BR* BL6...............17 E4
Dunchurch Cl *HOR/BR* BL6..........26 A3
Duncombe Rd *BOLS/LL* BL3.........38 A4
Dunedin Rd *TOT/BURYW* BL8......13 H1
Dunham Cl *WHTN* BL5.................43 E3
Dunlin Cl *BOLE* BL2........................3 K1
Dunmail Cl *TYLD* M29..................54 C2
Dunoon Cl *BOL* BL1.....................20 A1
Dunoon Rd *WGNE/HIN* WN2........25 H5
Dunsop Dr *BOL* BL1.....................19 E5
Dunstan St *BOLE* BL2...................31 G1
Dunster Pl *WALK* M28..................54 C5
Dunster Rd *WALK* M28.................54 C5
Durban Rd *BOL* BL1.....................20 A4
Durban St *ATH* M46.....................52 B1
Durham Cl *BOLS/LL* BL3..............40 C1
   TYLD M29............................45 F5
Durham Rd *WGNE/HIN* WN2.......20 A3
Durham St *BOL* BL1.....................20 C2
Durrington Pl *WHTN* BL5.............35 H4
Duty St *BOL* BL1..........................20 B1
Duxbury Av *BOLE* BL2.................22 A5
   BOLS/LL BL3........................32 B5
Duxbury Hall Rd *CHLY/EC* PR7......6 A1
Duxbury St *BOL* BL1....................20 B1
Dymchurch Av *RAD* M26..............49 G4
Dyson Av *FWTH* BL4....................39 H4
Dyson St *FWTH* BL4 *..................47 H1

E

Eagle St *BOLE* BL2.........................3 K3
Eagley Brook Wy *BOL* BL1...........20 C3
Eagley Brow *BOL* BL1..................10 D5
Eagley Wy *BOL* BL1......................20 C3
Ealand Cha *HOR/BR* BL6..............16 D3
Ealinger Wy *SWIN* M27................57 H5
Eames Av *RAD* M26.....................40 D4
Earlesdon Crs *LHULT* M38...........47 G4
Earl St *ATH* M46..........................52 B1
Earlswood Wk *BOLS/LL* BL3........38 A1
Earnshaw St *BOLS/LL* BL3 *........38 C2
Easedale Rd *BOL* BL1...................20 A1
Eastbank St *BOL* BL1...................20 A5
Eastbourne Gv *BOL* BL1...............20 A3
Eastchurch Cl *FWTH* BL4.............47 G1
Eastfields *RAD* M26....................33 H1
Eastgrove Av *BOL* BL1.................20 A1

tham Wy *LHULT* M38 ....47 F3
t Lancashire Rd *SWIN* M27 .....57 H5
t Lancashire Rd *WALK* M28 ....54 D4
t Meade *BOLS/LL* BL3 ....38 C3
t Lynn Dr *WALK* M28 ....56 C1
WIN M27 ....57 G5
t Moor *WALK* M28 ....55 E4
tmoor Gv *BOLS/LL* BL3 ....37 H3
t Rd *BOL* BL1 ....20 C3
t St *ATH* M46 ....53 F2
GNE/HIN WN2 ....42 D5
t Wk *EDGW/EG* BL7 ....10 B2
t Wy *BOL* BL1 ....21 F4
twood Av *WALK* M28 ....47 E5
twood Cl *BOLS/LL* BL3 ....37 G2
twood Ter *BOL* BL1 ....29 F2
ock Wy *WHTN* BL5 ....43 F2
on St *WGNE/HIN* WN2 ....42 A2
ry St *RAD* M26 ....41 H2
es Rd *SWIN* M27 ....57 H5
eston Av *BOLE* BL2 ....31 F1
WIN M27 ....57 F4
ersley Fold La *ATH* M46 ....52 A2
ersley Rd *BOL* BL1 ....20 C4
ersley St *BOLS/LL* BL3 ....38 A1
le Cl *ATH* M46 ....44 C5
itch Gv *BOL* BL1 ....20 C4
le Fold *FWTH* BL4 * 38 A4
le Fold Crs *WALK* M28 ....55 H3
le Fold Rd *WALK* M28 ....55 H2
e Gn *WALK* M28 * 55 G3
le Hill Rd *BOLS/LL* BL3 ....37 H2
le La *EDGW/EG* BL7 ....4 A1
OR/BR BL6 ....18 C2
emoor Cl *RAD* M26 ....33 G5
eworth Av *BOLE* BL2 ....33 F1
eworth Rd *WGNE/HIN* WN2 .....42 C5
eworth V *EDGW/EG* BL7 ....5 E3
mont Av *BOLS/LL* BL3 ....38 B1
aburgh Dr *WGNE/HIN* WN2 ......42 D5
aburgh Rd *BOLS/LL* BL3 ....40 C3
h St *BOLE* BL2 ....30 A4
WTH BL4 ....47 H1
aunds Rd *BOLS/LL* BL3 ....2 B6
a Rd *LEIGH* WN7 ....51 E4
tone Cl *BOLS/LL* BL3 ....37 F1
ard St *BOLS/LL* BL3 ....2 A7
WTH BL4 ....39 F3
OR/BR BL6 ....16 C4
AD M26 ....40 D5
HTN BL5 ....35 G5
rton Ct *WALK* M28 * 56 C3
rton Gv *WALK* M28 ....47 H5
rton Ldg *EDGW/EG* BL7 ....10 C5
rton Pk *WALK* M28 ....56 D4
rton Rd *WALK* M28 ....55 H2
rton St *FWTH* BL4 ....39 G4
rton V *EDGW/EG* BL7 ....10 B2
ar Cl *TYLD* M29 ....53 H4
am Ct *BOLE* BL2 * 31 F1
ptian St *BOL* BL1 ....30 D1
r Cl *TOT/BURYW* BL8 ....23 H2
rcot Gv *BOLS/LL* BL3 ....37 G1
rcot Rd *BOLS/LL* BL3 ....37 G1
r Dr *BOLS/LL* BL3 ....32 A5
n St *BOLE* BL2 ....31 F1
EIGH WN7 ....51 F5
nor St *BOL* BL1 ....21 E2
n St *BOL* BL1 ....20 A5
l Dr *BOLS/LL* BL3 ....29 E5
m Cl *RAD* M26 ....49 E1
abeth Av *WGNE/HIN* WN2 ....50 A2
abeth St *ATH* M46 ....44 D5
WIN M27 ....57 H1
tone Av *LHULT* M38 ....47 E2
nd Cl *WHTN* BL5 ....35 F2
nbrook Rd *WALK* M28 ....55 F3
ndale Gra *WALK* M28 ....55 F3
n Gv *FWTH* BL4 ....49 F3
nor Dr *TYLD* M29 ....54 A4
n St *BOL* BL1 ....20 A4
ray Cl *BOLS/LL* BL3 ....41 E2
rbeck Cl *BOLE* BL2 ....21 G1
rbeck Crs *WALK* M28 ....55 G4
r Brook Cl *CHLYE* PR6 ....6 D3
smere Av *WALK* M28 ....47 G5
smere Gdns *BOLS/LL* BL3 ......38 B2
smere Rd *BOLS/LL* BL3 ....38 A2

Ellesmere St *BOLS/LL* BL3 ....2 A6
FWTH BL4 ....39 H5
LHULT M38 ....47 G5
SWIN M27 ....57 F4
TYLD M29 ....53 G2
Elliot St *BOL* BL1 ....20 A4
Elliott St *FWTH* BL4 ....47 G1
TYLD M29 ....53 E3
Ellis Crs *WALK* M28 ....47 F5
Ellis St *BOLS/LL* BL3 ....30 B5
Ellonby Ri *HOR/BR* BL6 ....28 C5
Elm Av *HOR/BR* BL6 ....27 G1
RAD M26 ....41 H5
Elmbridge Wk *BOLS/LL* BL3 ....2 A7
Elm Crs *WALK* M28 ....56 C4
Elmfield Av *ATH* M46 ....44 B4
Elmfield Cl *BOLS/LL* BL3 ....20 D5
Elm Gv *EDGW/EG* BL7 ....11 G4
FWTH BL4 ....39 F5
SWIN M27 ....56 D2
Elmridge *LEIGH* WN7 ....52 B5
Elm Rd *BOLS/LL* BL3 ....40 D3
FWTH BL4 ....48 B3
WHTN BL5 ....43 G1
Elmstone Gv *BOL* BL1 * 30 D1
Elmwood Cl *WHTN* BL5 ....45 G2
Elmwood Gv *BOL* BL1 ....30 A2
WALK M28 ....47 G2
Elsdon Dr *ATH* M46 ....45 E4
Elsdon Gdns *BOLE* BL2 ....31 F1
Elsfield Cl *BOL* BL1 * 28 B5
Elsham Cl *BOL* BL1 ....20 C2
Elsham Dr *WALK* M28 ....47 H5
Elsie St *FWTH* BL4 ....47 G1
Elsinore St *BOLE* BL2 ....21 F4
Elswick Av *BOLS/LL* BL3 ....29 H5
Elsworth Dr *BOL* BL1 ....20 D3
Elterwater Rd *FWTH* BL4 ....46 C1
Elton Av *FWTH* BL4 ....38 D5
Elton St *BOLE* BL2 ....3 H3
Elvington Crs *WALK* M28 ....55 G3
Ely Cl *WALK* M28 ....55 F3
Ely Dr *TYLD* M29 ....54 A4
Ely Gv *BOL* BL1 ....30 C1
Embankment Rd *EDGW/EG* BL7 ....4 C4
Embla Wk *BOLS/LL* BL3 ....39 E1
Embleton Cl *BOLS/LL* BL3 ....2 B7
Embleton Cl *BOLE* BL2 ....22 A3
Embsay Cl *BOL* BL1 ....29 H1
Emerald St *BOL* BL1 ....20 D4
Emlyn St *FWTH* BL4 ....39 G4
SWIN M27 ....57 F3
WALK M28 ....47 H5
Emmanuel Cl *BOLS/LL* BL3 * 2 B2
Emmanuel Pl *BOLS/LL* BL3 ....2 B7
Emmerson St *SWIN* M27 ....57 H2
Emmett St *HOR/BR* BL6 ....16 D4
Empire Rd *BOLE* BL2 ....31 H2
Empress Dr *LEIGH* WN7 ....53 E5
Empress St *BOL* BL1 ....29 H1
Ena Crs *LEIGH* WN7 ....51 E4
Ena St *BOLS/LL* BL3 ....39 E2
Endon St *BOL* BL1 ....29 H1
Endsley Av *WALK* M28 ....55 G2
Enfield Av *WALK* M28 ....30 C1
Enfield Cl *LEIGH* WN7 ....52 A5
Enfield Rd *SWIN* M27 ....57 G5
Enfield St *WALK* M28 ....47 H3
Engine Fold Rd *WALK* M28 ....47 E5
Engine La *ATH* M46 ....45 C4
Engledene *BOL* BL1 ....20 B1
Ennerdale Av *BOLE* BL2 ....32 B1
SWIN M27 ....57 H5
Ennerdale Cl *BOLS/LL* BL3 ....40 B2
Ennerdale Gv *FWTH* BL4 ....38 C5
Ennerdale Rd *TYLD* M29 ....53 H4
WGNE/HIN WN2 ....42 A3
Enstone Wy *WGNE/HIN* WN2 ......54 A2
Enterprise Pk *HOR/BR* BL6 ....27 E2
Entwisle Rw *FWTH* BL4 ....39 H5
Entwisle St *FWTH* BL4 ....39 H4
SWIN M27 ....57 F2
Entwistle Hall La *EDGW/EG* BL7 ...4 B2
Entwistle St *BOLE* BL2 ....3 K1
Ephraim's Fold *WGNE/HIN* WN2 ...25 H4
Epsom Cft *CHLYE* PR6 ....7 G5
Era St *BOLE* BL2 ....31 H3
Ernest St *BOL* BL1 ....2 A1
BOL BL1 ....30 A4
Erniouen Av *BOL* BL1 ....29 G2
Errington Cl *BOLS/LL* BL3 ....29 F5
Erskine St *BOLS/LL* BL3 ....29 E5
Eskdale Av *BOLE* BL2 ....22 B5
HOR/BR BL6 ....26 A3
Eskdale Gv *FWTH* BL4 ....38 D5

Eskdale Rd *WGNE/HIN* WN2 ......42 A3
Eskrick St *BOL* BL1 ....20 B5
Essex Pl *TYLD* M29 ....45 F5
Essex St *HOR/BR* BL6 ....27 F1
Essingdon St *BOLS/LL* BL3 ....38 B1
Esthwaite Dr *TYLD* M29 ....53 G4
Ethel St *BOLS/LL* BL3 ....2 A6
Europa Wy *RAD* M26 ....48 C1
Eustace St *BOLS/LL* BL3 ....39 E2
Evanstone Cl *HOR/BR* BL6 ....16 D4
Eva St *LEIGH* WN7 ....51 E4
Everard St *WALK* M28 ....55 F3
Everbrom Rd *BOLS/LL* BL3 ....37 G3
Everest Rd *ATH* M46 ....44 C3
The Evergreens *HOR/BR* BL6 .....27 G1
Everleigh Cl *BOLE* BL2 ....22 A2
Everton St *SWIN* M27 ....57 G3
Evesham Cl *BOLS/LL* BL3 ....2 B6
Evesham Dr *FWTH* BL4 * 39 F3
Evesham Wk *BOLS/LL* BL3 ....2 B7
Ewart St *BOL* BL1 ....20 C5
Ewhurst Av *SWIN* M27 ....57 F5
Exchange St *BOL* BL1 * 2 E4
Exeter Av *BOLE* BL2 ....21 F5
FWTH BL4 ....38 D4
RAD M26 ....33 F5
Exeter Dr *WGNE/HIN* WN2 ....25 H5
Exeter Rd *WGNE/HIN* WN2 ....42 A3
Exford Dr *BOLE* BL2 ....32 C4

F

Factory Brow *HOR/BR* BL6 ....15 H4
Factory Hl *HOR/BR* BL6 ....17 F3
Factory La *CHLYE* PR6 ....7 F4
Factory St *TYLD* M29 ....53 F2
Factory St East *ATH* M46 ....44 C5
Factory St West *ATH* M46 ....44 C5
Fair Acres *BOLE* BL2 ....22 A4
Fairbairn St *BOL* BL1 ....16 D5
Fairclough St *BOLS/LL* BL3 ....38 D1
Fairfield Rd *FWTH* BL4 ....47 G1
Fairfields *EDGW/EG* BL7 ....10 D4
Fairford Dr *BOLS/LL* BL3 ....30 C5
Fairhaven Av *WHTN* BL5 ....36 B5
Fairhurst Dr *WALK* M28 ....55 F2
Fairlie Av *BOLS/LL* BL3 ....29 F5
Fairlyn Cl *WHTN* BL5 ....45 G1
Fairlyn Dr *WHTN* BL5 ....45 G1
Fairman Dr *WGNE/HIN* WN2 ......42 A2
Fairoak Ct *BOLS/LL* BL3 ....2 A7
Fairstead Cl *WHTN* BL5 ....45 G1
Fair St *BOLS/LL* BL3 * 38 A3
Fairview Dr *CHLYE* PR6 ....6 C4
Fairway Av *BOLE* BL2 ....22 C3
Fairway Rd *BOLE* BL2 ....17 E4
The Fairways *WHTN* BL5 ....35 G5
Faith St *BOL* BL1 ....29 G1
Falcon Dr *LHULT* M38 ....47 E5
Falconwood Cha *WALK* M28 ......55 F5
Falkirk Gv *BOLE* BL2 ....32 B4
Falkland Rd *BOL* BL1 ....32 C3
Fall Birch Rd *HOR/BR* BL6 ....27 H2
Fallons Rd *WALK* M28 ....55 G3
Fallow Cl *WHTN* BL5 ....35 G3
Fallowfield Wy *ATH* M46 ....53 E2
Faraday Dr *BOL* BL1 ....30 C1
Far Hey Cl *RAD* M26 ....41 G2
Faringdon Wk *BOLS/LL* BL3 ....2 C7
Farland Pl *BOLS/LL* BL3 ....29 F5
Farliegh Cl *WHTN* BL5 ....36 A3
Farman St *BOLS/LL* BL3 * 38 B2
Farm Av *CHLYE* PR6 ....7 E4
Farm Cl *TOT/BURYW* BL8 ....23 H1
Farnborough Rd *BOL* BL1 ....30 A1
Farndale Sq *LHULT* M38 ....47 G5
Farnham Cl *BOL* BL1 ....30 C1
LEIGH WN7 ....51 H5
Farnworth St *BOLS/LL* BL3 * 38 A1
Faulkner St *BOLS/LL* BL3 ....30 C5
Fawcetts Fold *WHTN* BL5 ....35 G1
Fawcett St *BOLE* BL2 ....3 K3
Fearney Side *BOLS/LL* BL3 ....40 B2
Fearnhead Cl *FWTH* BL4 ....40 A3
Fearnhead St *BOLS/LL* BL3 ....38 A1
Fellbridge Cl *WHTN* BL5 ....36 B4
Fells Gv *WALK* M28 ....56 B2
Fellside *BOL* BL1 ....22 C4
Fellside Cl *TOT/BURYW* BL8 * 13 H5
Felsted *BOL* BL1 ....29 E2
Felton Wk *BOL* BL1 ....20 C5
Fenners Cl *BOLS/LL* BL3 ....38 B2
Fenton Wy *WGNE/HIN* WN2 ......42 B4
Fenwick Cl *WHTN* BL5 ....43 H2

Fereday St *WALK* M28 ....47 G4
Fernbray Rd *WGNE/HIN* WN2 .....42 B3
Fern Cl *ATH* M46 ....52 D1
Fern Clough *BOL* BL1 ....29 F3
Ferndown Rd *BOLE* BL2 ....22 A4
Fernhill Av *BOLS/LL* BL3 ....37 G1
Fernhills *EDGW/EG* BL7 ....10 C2
Fernlea Crs *SWIN* M27 ....57 G4
Fern Lea Gv *LHULT* M38 ....46 D4
Fernleigh *HOR/BR* BL6 * 27 F1
Ferns Gv *BOL* BL1 ....29 H3
Fernside *RAD* M26 ....48 D2
Fernside Gv *WALK* M28 * 48 A4
Fernstead *BOLS/LL* BL3 ....30 A4
Fernstone Cl *HOR/BR* BL6 ....16 C4
Fern St *BOLS/LL* BL3 ....30 A4
FWTH BL4 ....38 D4
Fettler Cl *SWIN* M27 ....57 G5
Fewston Cl *BOL* BL1 ....20 C2
Fielders Wy *SWIN* M27 ....49 G4
Fielding Pl *CHLYE* PR6 ....7 F4
Field St *WGNE/HIN* WN2 ....42 A4
Fifth Av *BOL* BL1 ....29 H3
BOLS/LL BL3 ....40 B1
Fifth St *BOL* BL1 ....19 F3
Filton Av *BOLS/LL* BL3 * 2 B7
Finger Post *BOLS/LL* BL3 ....40 C1
Finlay St *FWTH* BL4 * 39 H5
Finney St *BOLS/LL* BL3 * 38 D1
Firecrest Cl *WALK* M28 ....55 F3
Firethorn Cl *WHTN* BL5 ....35 H3
Firfield Gv *WALK* M28 ....48 B5
Fir Rd *FWTH* BL4 ....39 F5
SWIN M27 ....57 G5
Firs Rd *WHTN* BL5 ....45 F2
First Av *ATH* M46 ....44 D4
BOLS/LL BL3 ....40 B1
TOT/BURYW BL8 ....23 H1
Fir St *BOL* BL1 ....20 D5
First St *BOL* BL1 ....19 F3
Firswood Dr *SWIN* M27 ....57 G5
Fir Tree Av *WALK* M28 ....55 F5
Firtree Cl *CHLYE/EC* PR7 ....6 A1
Fir Tree Wy *HOR/BR* BL6 ....27 G1
Firwood Av *FWTH* BL4 ....47 G2
Firwood Gv *BOLE* BL2 ....21 F4
Firwood La *BOLE* BL2 ....21 G4
Fitton Crs *SWIN* M27 ....49 H5
Fitzhugh St *BOL* BL1 * 21 E2
Five Quarters *RAD* M26 ....33 G5
Flapper Fold La *ATH* M46 ....44 C4
Fleet St *HOR/BR* BL6 ....17 F4
Fleetwood Rd *WALK* M28 ....47 E5
Fletcher Av *ATH* M46 ....44 D3
Fletcher St *ATH* M46 * 44 C5
BOLS/LL BL3 ....2 D7
BOLS/LL BL3 ....40 D2
FWTH BL4 ....39 H5
Flitcroft Ct *BOLS/LL* BL3 * 38 D1
Florence Av *BOL* BL1 ....20 D3
Florence St *BOLS/LL* BL3 ....38 B1
Fogg La *BOLS/LL* BL3 ....40 A2
Fold Rd *RAD* M26 ....49 E1
Folds *HOR/BR* BL6 ....15 G4
Folds Rd *BOL* BL1 ....3 G2
Fold St *BOL* BL1 * 3 F4
Fold Vw *EDGW/EG* BL7 ....10 C3
Fontwell Rd *BOLS/LL* BL3 ....40 C3
Footman Cl *TYLD* M29 ....53 H4
Forbes Cl *WGNE/HIN* WN2 ....42 A1
Fordham Gv *BOL* BL1 ....30 A2
Ford St *RAD* M26 ....40 C5
Forest Dr *WHTN* BL5 ....36 A5
Forester Hill Av *BOLS/LL* BL3 ....38 D2
Forester Hill Cl *BOLS/LL* BL3 ....38 D2
Forest Rd *BOL* BL1 ....19 H4
Forest Wy *EDGW/EG* BL7 ....21 G1
Forfar St *BOL* BL1 ....20 C2
Formby Av *ATH* M46 ....44 D4
Forresters Cl *WGNE/HIN* WN2 ....50 C3
Forrester St *WALK* M28 ....56 C3
Forth Pl *RAD* M26 ....33 H5
Forth Rd *RAD* M26 ....33 H5
Forton Av *BOLE* BL2 ....32 A3
Fortune St *BOLS/LL* BL3 ....31 F5
Fossgill Av *BOLE* BL2 ....21 G2
Foster La *BOLE* BL2 ....32 B1
Foster St *RAD* M26 ....41 H2
Foundry St *BOLS/LL* BL3 ....3 F7
BOLS/LL BL3 ....40 C2
Fountain Pk *WHTN* BL5 ....43 E3
Fountains Av *BOLE* BL2 ....31 G1
Fountains Cl *TYLD* M29 ....54 A4
Fourth Av *BOL* BL1 ....29 H3
BOLS/LL BL3 ....40 B1
Fourth St *BOL* BL1 ....19 F3
Foxdale Cl *EDGW/EG* BL7 ....5 E3
Foxendale Wk *BOLS/LL* BL3 * 30 C5
Foxfold Cl *WALK* M28 ....54 D4

Foxholes Rd HOR/BR BL6 17 F3
Foxley Gv BOLS/LL BL3 2 B5
Fox St HOR/BR BL6 17 E5
Frances Pl ATH M46 52 A2
Frances St BOL BL1 20 B5
France St WHTN BL5 43 G2
Francis Av WALK M28 56 B1
Francis St FWTH BL4 39 G4
LEIGH WN7 51 G4
TYLD M29 54 B3
Frankford Av BOL BL1 20 A5
Frankford Sq BOL BL1 * 20 A5
Frank St BOL BL1 30 B1
Freckleton Dr TOT/BURYW BL8 33 H2
Frederick St FWTH BL4 39 H5
Freelands TYLD M29 54 A2
Freesia Av WALK M28 46 D5
French Gv BOLS/LL BL3 31 H5
Freshfield Av ATH M46 44 C4
BOLS/LL BL3 38 B3
Freshfield Gv BOLS/LL BL3 38 D3
Freshfield Rd WGNE/HIN WN2 42 B3
Freshfields RAD M26 33 F5
Friars Cl TYLD M29 54 B2
Frinton Rd BOLS/LL BL3 37 H2
Frogley St BOLE BL2 * 21 F4
Frome Cl TYLD M29 53 H5
Fryent Cl HOR/BR BL6 15 H5
Fulbrook Wy TYLD M29 54 A2
Fulmar Cl WHTN BL5 43 F2
Fulmere Ct SWIN M27 57 F5
Fulwell Av TYLD M29 53 E3
Fulwood Cl TOT/BURYW BL8 33 H1
Furness Av BOLE BL2 21 F5
Furness Crs LEIGH WN7 51 F2
Furness Rd BOL BL1 29 H3
Furness Sq BOLE BL2 21 F5
Furnival St LEIGH WN7 51 H4
Furze Av WHTN BL5 43 H1
Futura Pk HOR/BR BL6 27 E1
Fylde Av BOLE BL2 32 A3
Fylde St BOLS/LL BL3 39 H3
Fylde St East BOLS/LL BL3 39 H3

G

Gabbot St CHLY/EC PR7 6 D5
Gable St BOLE BL2 * 21 H2
Gadbury Av ATH M46 44 B5
Gadbury Fold ATH M46 52 A1
Gadfield Gv ATH M46 44 A5
Gadwall Cl WALK M28 55 H3
Gainford Wk BOLS/LL BL3 * 38 C1
Gainsborough Av BOLS/LL BL3 38 A2
Galgate Cl TOT/BURYW BL8 33 H1
Galindo St BOLE BL2 21 G3
Galloway Cl BOLS/LL BL3 29 E5
Galloway Dr SWIN M27 49 H4
Galloway Rd SWIN M27 * 57 F5
Gambleside Cl WALK M28 55 F3
Garden Av SWIN M27 57 F4
Garden La WALK M28 55 E5
The Gardens BOL BL1 20 D1
EDGW/EG BL7 5 E5
Garden St FWTH BL4 40 A5
TOT/BURYW BL8 13 H5
TYLD M29 53 G3
Garfield Gv BOLS/LL BL3 2 B6
Garfield St BOLS/LL BL3 38 A2
Garforth Ri BOL BL1 29 G3
Gargrave Av BOL BL1 19 F5
Garnett St BOL BL1 20 C4
Garrett Hall Rd WALK M28 54 C4
Garrett La TYLD M29 54 B4
Garsdale La BOL BL1 28 D3
Garside Gv BOL BL1 20 A5
Garside St BOL BL1 2 C4
Garstang Av BOLE BL2 32 A4
Garstang Dr TOT/BURYW BL8 33 H1
Garston Av ATH M46 44 B3
Garston Cl LEIGH WN7 51 G2
Garswood Rd BOLS/LL BL3 38 C3
Garthmere Rd ATH M46 45 F3
Garwick Rd BOL BL1 19 H4
Gaskell St BOL BL1 2 C1
SWIN M27 57 H1
WGNE/HIN WN2 42 A1
Gas St BOL BL1 2 C4
CHLY/EC PR7 14 D1
FWTH BL4 39 H4
Gate Field Cl RAD M26 41 G2
Gatehouse Rd WALK M28 47 E4
Gatemere Cl WALK M28 55 F3
The Gateways SWIN M27 57 H2
Gatley Cl TYLD M29 53 H2
Gaythorne St BOL BL1 20 D4
Gellert Pl WHTN BL5 43 G2
Gellert Rd WHTN BL5 43 G2
Gencoyne Dr BOL BL1 20 B1
Gendre Rd EDGW/EG BL7 10 C4
Geoffrey St WHTN BL5 37 F5
George Barton St BOLE BL2 * 31 F1
George's La HOR/BR BL6 9 F5
George St ATH M46 44 D5
FWTH BL4 47 F1
HOR/BR BL6 17 E4
RAD M26 41 H2
WGNE/HIN WN2 42 A4
WHTN BL5 35 H5
Georgiana St FWTH BL4 39 F4
Georgina Ct BOLS/LL BL3 37 H3
Georgina St BOLS/LL BL3 37 H3
Gerrard St FWTH BL4 40 A5
WHTN BL5 35 G4
Ghyll Gv WALK M28 56 A1
Gibbon St BOLS/LL BL3 30 B5
Gibb Rd WALK M28 56 D4
Gibfield Dr ATH M46 52 A1
Gibraltar St BOLS/LL BL3 2 A6
Gibson Gv WALK M28 47 E5
Gibson La WALK M28 47 E5
Gibson St BOLE BL2 31 G1
Gidlow Av CHLYE PR6 7 E5
Gifford Pl WGNE/HIN WN2 42 B4
Gilbertson Rd CHLY/EC PR7 6 C2
Gilbert St WALK M28 55 G2
Gilda Rd WALK M28 54 C4
Gilderdale St BOLS/LL BL3 31 E5
Gillers Gn WALK M28 55 G1
Gilnow Gdns BOL BL1 30 A4
Gilnow Gv BOL BL1 2 A5
Gilnow La BOLS/LL BL3 30 A4
Gilnow Rd BOL BL1 30 A4
Gingham Brow HOR/BR BL6 17 F3
Gingham Pk RAD M26 33 G5
Girvan Cl BOLS/LL BL3 38 A2
Gisburn Av BOL BL1 19 E5
Gisburn Dr TOT/BURYW BL8 23 G4
Glabyn Av HOR/BR BL6 27 H2
Glade St BOL BL1 30 A3
The Glade BOL BL1 30 B1
Gladstone Cl BOL BL1 * 20 C5
Gladstone Pl FWTH BL4 39 G4
Gladstone Rd FWTH BL4 39 G4
Gladstone St BOL BL1 20 C5
WHTN BL5 35 G4
Gladys St BOLS/LL BL3 39 H3
Glaisdale Cl BOLE BL2 21 G5
Glaisdale St BOLE BL2 21 F5
Glaister La BOLE BL2 31 H1
Glamis Cl LEIGH WN7 52 D5
Glass St FWTH BL4 * 48 A1
Glastonbury Rd TYLD M29 53 H4
Glazebury Dr WHTN BL5 35 H3
Gleaves Av BOLE BL2 22 C3
Gleave St BOL BL1 * 3 F2
Glebeland Rd BOLS/LL BL3 29 G5
Glebe St BOLE BL2 3 G5
LEIGH WN7 51 H5
WGNE/HIN WN2 51 E1
WHTN BL5 35 G4
Gledhill Wy EDGW/EG BL7 11 E4
Glen Av BOLS/LL BL3 29 H5
FWTH BL4 48 D2
SWIN M27 57 F3
WALK M28 56 C3
Glenbeck Cl HOR/BR BL6 27 F1
Glen Bott St BOL BL1 20 B5
Glenbrook Gdns FWTH BL4 39 H3
Glenburn St BOLS/LL BL3 38 B2
Glencar WHTN BL5 43 F1
Glencoe Dr BOLE BL2 32 B4
Glen Cottages BOL BL1 * 19 E5
Glendale Dr BOLS/LL BL3 29 F4
Glendale Rd WALK M28 54 D4
Glendevon Cl BOLS/LL BL3 37 F1
Gleneagles BOLS/LL BL3 37 F2
Glenfield Sq FWTH BL4 39 F3
Glengarth Dr HOR/BR BL6 28 C4
Glenilla Av WALK M28 56 A4
Glenmaye Gv WGNE/HIN WN2 42 C3
Glenmore Av FWTH BL4 39 E3
Glenmore Cl BOLS/LL BL3 29 E5
Glenmore Rd TOT/BURYW BL8 13 H2
Glenpark LEIGH WN7 52 A5
Glenridge Cl BOL BL1 20 D5
Glenshee Dr BOLS/LL BL3 29 F5
Glenside Dr BOLS/LL BL3 38 D3
Glenside Gv WALK M28 48 A5
The Glen BOL BL1 29 E3
Glenthorne St BOL BL1 30 C1
Glentrool Ms BOL BL1 29 G3
Glenview Rd TYLD M29 53 F1
Globe La EDGW/EG BL7 10 B1
Glossop Wy WGNE/HIN WN2 42 A4
Gloster St BOLE BL2 3 H4
Gloucester Av HOR/BR BL6 17 F5
Gloucester Crs
WGNE/HIN WN2 42 A2
Gloucester Pl ATH M46 44 D4
Gloucester St ATH M46 44 C5
Glover St HOR/BR BL6 16 D3
LEIGH WN7 51 E3
Glynne St FWTH BL4 39 G5
Glynrene Dr SWIN M27 57 E1
Glynwood Pk FWTH BL4 39 G4
Godlee Dr SWIN M27 57 G4
Goldcrest Cl WALK M28 55 F4
Goldrill Av BOLE BL2 32 B2
Goldrill Gdns BOLE BL2 32 B2
Goldsmith St BOLS/LL BL3 38 B1
Gooch St HOR/BR BL6 16 D5
Goodshaw Rd WALK M28 55 G3
Goodwill Cl SWIN M27 57 H4
Goodwin St BOL BL1 3 G2
Goodwood Cl BOLS/LL BL3 40 B2
Goose Cote Hl EDGW/EG BL7 10 C3
Gordon Av BOLS/LL BL3 30 A5
Gordon Rd SWIN M27 57 E5
Gordon St LEIGH WN7 51 H5
Gorse Dr LHULT M38 46 D2
Gorsefield Dr SWIN M27 57 H4
Gorse Rd SWIN M27 57 G5
WALK M28 56 A1
Gorses Dr WGNE/HIN WN2 25 G4
Gorses Mt BOLE BL2 31 G5
Gorses Rd BOLS/LL BL3 31 H5
Gorsey Clough Wk
TOT/BURYW BL8 23 H2
Gorsey Gv WHTN BL5 43 F1
Gorsey Hey WHTN BL5 43 G1
Gorton Gv WALK M28 47 G3
Gorton St BOLE BL2 3 G5
FWTH BL4 47 F1
Gowanlock's St BOL BL1 20 C5
Gower St BOL BL1 2 A2
FWTH BL4 39 G4
Grace St HOR/BR BL6 16 D3
Grafton St ATH M46 52 A2
BOL BL1 2 A2
CHLY/EC PR7 14 D1
Graham St BOL BL1 * 2 E1
Granby Rd SWIN M27 57 E4
Granby St TOT/BURYW BL8 23 H3
Grange Av BOLS/LL BL3 41 E2
SWIN M27 57 F1
Grange Park Rd EDGW/EG BL7 21 G1
Grange Rd BOLS/LL BL3 29 H5
EDGW/EG BL7 11 G5
FWTH BL4 39 E4
WALK M28 54 C4
WGNE/HIN WN2 50 A2
The Grange WHTN BL5 35 E5
Grangewood EDGW/EG BL7 11 G5
Grantchester Pl FWTH BL4 38 D4
Grantchester Wy BOLE BL2 32 A1
Grantham Cl BOL BL1 * 30 C1
Grant St FWTH BL4 39 F3
Granville Rd BOLS/LL BL3 38 A2
Granville St CHLYE PR6 7 E5
FWTH BL4 39 H4
LEIGH WN7 51 H4
WALK M28 47 G5
WGNE/HIN WN2 * 42 A3
Grasmere Av BOLS/LL BL3 40 C1
FWTH BL4 46 D1
SWIN M27 57 E1
WGNE/HIN WN2 42 A4
Grasmere Rd SWIN M27 57 H5
Grasmere St BOL BL1 20 D5
Grasscroft Rd WGNE/HIN WN2 42 C4
Grassington Ct
TOT/BURYW BL8 23 G3
Grassington Pl BOLE BL2 31 E1
Gratten Ct WALK M28 47 G4
Graymar Rd LHULT M38 47 E4
Grayson Rd LHULT M38 47 F4
Gray St BOL BL1 2 D1
Gray St North BOL BL1 2 E1
Graythwaite Rd BOL BL1 19 F5
Great Bank Rd WHTN BL5 35 F3
Great Boys Cl TYLD M29 54 C2
Great Holme BOLS/LL BL3 38 D2
Great Marld Cl BOL BL1 19 F5
Great Moor St BOL BL1 2 E5
Great Stone Cl RAD M26 * 41 F2
Great Stones Cl EDGW/EG BL7 10 C2
Grecian Crs BOLS/LL BL3 38 D1
Green Acre WHTN BL5 43 H1
Green Acre Pk BOL BL1 * 30 D1
Greenacres EDGW/EG BL7 5 E3
Green Av BOLS/LL BL3 39 F2
LHULT M38 46 C3
SWIN M27 57 H4
Green Bank BOLE BL2 22 A4
Greenbank FWTH BL4 39
WGNE/HIN WN2 42
Greenbank Av SWIN M27 * 57
Greenbank Rd BOLS/LL BL3 * 37
RAD M26 33
Greenbarn Wy HOR/BR BL6 25
Greenburn Dr BOLE BL2 22
Green Cl ATH M46 53
Green Common La ATH M46 44
Greencourt Dr LHULT M38 46
Greendale ATH M46 45
Green Dr HOR/BR BL6 28
Greenfield Cl WHTN BL5 36
Greenfield Rd ATH M46 45
CHLYE PR6 7
Greenfields Cl WGNE/HIN WN2 42
Greenfold Av FWTH BL4 47
Green Fold La WHTN BL5 43
Greengate La BOLE BL2 32
Greenhalgh La CHLYE PR6 7
Green Hall Cl ATH M46 45
Greenhaven Cl WALK M28 48
Greenheys BOLE BL2 22
Greenheys Crs TOT/BURYW BL8 13
Greenheys Rd LHULT M38 46
Greenhill Av BOLS/LL BL3 29
FWTH BL4 47
Greenhill La BOLS/LL BL3 37
Greenhill Rd TOT/BURYW BL8 33
Greenland Cl TYLD M29 53
Greenland La CHLYE PR6 15
Greenland Rd BOLS/LL BL3 38
TYLD M29 53
Green La BOLS/LL BL3 38
FWTH BL4 48
HOR/BR BL6 16
LEIGH WN7 52
WGNE/HIN WN2 42
Greenleach La WALK M28 56
Greenleaf Cl WALK M28 54
Greenleas HOR/BR BL6 28
Greenleigh Cl BOL BL1 20
Green Mdw WHTN BL5 43
Greenmount Cl
TOT/BURYW BL8 13
Greenmount Ct BOL BL1 29
Greenmount Dr
TOT/BURYW BL8 13
Greenmount La BOL BL1 29
Greenmount Pk FWTH BL4 48
Greenoak RAD M26 49
Greenoak Dr WALK M28 47
Greenock Cl BOLS/LL BL3 29
Greenough St ATH M46 52
Greenpark Cl TOT/BURYW BL8 13
Green Pine Rd HOR/BR BL6 27
Greenroyd Av BOLE BL2 22
Greensbridge Gdns WHTN BL5 35
Greenside BOLE BL2 33
Greenside Av FWTH BL4 48
Greenside Cl TOT/BURYW BL8 12
Greenside Dr TOT/BURYW BL8 13
Greensmith Wy WHTN BL5 35
Greenstone Av HOR/BR BL6 16
Green St ATH M46 53
BOL BL1 3
CHLYE PR6 7
FWTH BL4 39
TOT/BURYW BL8 23
TYLD M29 53
The Green CHLYE PR6 6
TOT/BURYW BL8 13
Greenthorne Cl EDGW/EG BL7 5
Green Wy BOL BL1 21
Greenway HOR/BR BL6 17
Green Way Cl BOL BL1 21
Greenways LEIGH WN7 52
Greenwood Av HOR/BR BL6 27
WALK M28 47
Greenwood Cl WALK M28 54
Greenwood La HOR/BR BL6 27
Greenwoods La BOLE BL2 22
Greenwood St FWTH BL4 39
Greenwood V BOL BL1 20
Greenwood V South BOL BL1 * 20
Gregory Av ATH M46 44
BOLE BL2 32
Gregory St WHTN BL5 42
Gregson Fld BOLS/LL BL3 38
Grenaby Av WGNE/HIN WN2 42
Grendon St BOLS/LL BL3 38
Gresham St BOL BL1 20
Gresley Av HOR/BR BL6 16
Gretna Rd ATH M46 52
Greylag Crs WALK M28 55
Greystoke Dr BOL BL1 20
Greystone Av WGNE/HIN WN2 25
Grierson St BOL BL1 20
Grimeford La CHLYE PR6 15

ndrod St RAD M26 41 H1
ndsbrook Rd RAD M26 33 H3
sdale Rd BOLS/LL BL3 30 A5
zedale Cl BOL BL1 19 F5
osvenor Cl WALK M28 47 G3
osvenor Dr WALK M28 47 G3
osvenor Rd LEIGH WN7 51 F5
WALK M28 47 G3
osvenor St BOLE BL2 3 G6
OLS/LL BL3 40 C1
WTH BL4 40 B5
RAD M26 41 H2
WIN M27 57 H1
ove Av CHLYE PR6 7 E5
ove Crs CHLYE PR6 7 E5
ove Hl WALK M28 54 D5
ovehurst SWIN M27 56 D5
ove Ms WALK M28 * 47 H5
ove St BOL BL1 20 B5
WTH BL4 40 A5
Grove BOLE BL2 3 K7
OLS/LL BL3 40 D2
ndy Rd FWTH BL4 48 A1
ndy's La CHLY/EC PR7 6 A3
ndy St BOLS/LL BL3 38 B1
ALK M28 48 B5
HTN BL5 35 G4
do St BOL BL1 20 B5
ld Av WALK M28 55 H1
ldford Rd BOL BL1 19 H5
ld St EDGW/EG BL7 21 F1
nters Av WHTN BL5 43 G2

H

bergham Cl WALK M28 55 G4
ken Bridge Rd BOLS/LL BL3 39 H1
ken La BOLS/LL BL3 39 G1
kford Cl BOL BL1 30 A2
dleigh Cl BOL BL1 21 E1
dwin St BOL BL1 30 D1
gh Rd WGNE/HIN WN2 25 G5
gh St BOL BL1 2 E1
le Dr WALK M28 54 D5
bury Wk BOL BL1 * 20 D5
e Bank WHTN BL5 35 H3
esfield WGNE/HIN WN2 50 D1
f Acre RAD M26 33 H4
f Acre La HOR/BR BL6 25 G1
bridge Gdns BOL BL1 21 E4
Hall Coppice EDGW/EG BL7 10 B3
gate WHTN BL5 43 G3
lington Cl BOLS/LL BL3 38 D1
i' th' Wood La BOL BL1 21 E3
liwell Rd BOL BL1 20 B5
liwell St BOL BL1 * 20 B5
La FWTH BL4 39 H3
WTH BL4 40 A2
OR/BR BL6 8 C2
OR/BR BL6 27 G3
Lee Dr WHTN BL5 36 A4
stead Av LHULT M38 46 C4
stead Gv LHULT M38 46 C4
St BOLS/LL BL3 39 H3
AD M26 33 H4
WIN M27 57 H1
OT/BURYW BL8 23 G2
view Wy WALK M28 46 D5
sall Dr BOLS/LL BL3 38 C3
shaw La FWTH BL4 48 B1
stead St BOLE BL2 3 H4
ton St BOLE BL2 3 K4
nbleden Cl BOLS/LL BL3 29 F5
nbledon Cl ATH M46 45 E3
nbleton Cl TOT/BURYW BL8 33 H1
nel St BOLS/LL BL3 38 B2
ner St BOLE BL2 31 F1
nilton Rd TYLD M29 54 B5
GNE/HIN WN2 42 B4
nilton St ATH M46 52 C1
OL BL1 20 C3
EIGH WN7 51 F5
WIN M27 57 F2
Hamlet CHLY/EC PR7 * 6 D3
OR/BR BL6 28 B2
nnet Cl BOL BL1 21 E2
npson Fold RAD M26 41 H1
npson St ATH M46 * 44 C5
OR/BR BL6 16 D3
npton Gv LEIGH WN7 53 E4
npton Rd BOLS/LL BL3 39 E2
borough Ct TYLD M29 53 E3
del St BOL BL1 20 B4
dley Gdns BOL BL1 29 H3
over Ct WALK M28 * 56 D5
over St BOL BL1 2 C4
EIGH WN7 52 A5
Hansom Dr ATH M46 52 A3
Hanson St CHLY/EC PR7 14 D2
Harbern Dr LEIGH WN7 51 F1
Harbour La EDGW/EG BL7 4 D4
Harbourne Av WALK M28 55 G3
Harbourne Cl WALK M28 55 G3
Harbury Cl BOLS/LL BL3 37 G2
Harcourt St WALK M28 47 H3
Hardcastle Cl BOLE BL2 21 G1
Hardcastle Gdns BOLE BL2 21 G1
Hardcastle St BOL BL1 20 D5
Harden Dr BOLE BL2 21 H5
Hardie Av FWTH BL4 47 F1
Harding St CHLYE PR6 7 F4
Hardman Cl RAD M26 33 H4
Hardmans EDGW/EG BL7 10 D5
Hardmans La EDGW/EG BL7 10 D4
Hardman St FWTH BL4 48 A1
RAD M26 33 H4
Hardwick Cl RAD M26 32 D5
Hardy Cl WHTN BL5 35 G2
Hardy Gv WALK M28 56 B3
Hardy Mill Rd BOLE BL2 22 B4
Harebell Av WALK M28 * 46 D5
Harewood Wy SWIN M27 57 H1
Hargreaves St BOL BL1 * 20 C5
Harlea Av WGNE/HIN WN2 42 C5
Harlech Av WGNE/HIN WN2 42 C4
Harlesden Crs BOLS/LL BL3 * 29 H5
Harley Av BOLE BL2 22 A4
BOLE BL2 33 F1
Haroldene St BOLE BL2 21 F5
Harold St BOL BL1 20 B5
WGNE/HIN WN2 25 H5
Harper Fold Rd RAD M26 41 G2
Harper Green Rd FWTH BL4 39 F4
Harpers La BOL BL1 19 H5
Harper St FWTH BL4 39 F3
Harpford Cl BOLE BL2 32 C5
Harpford Dr BOLE BL2 32 C5
Harptree Gv LEIGH WN7 51 F4
Harrier Cl WALK M28 55 H3
Harriet St WALK M28 47 H5
Harrison Crs HOR/BR BL6 15 G4
Harrison Rd CHLY/EC PR7 15 E1
Harrison St HOR/BR BL6 16 D3
LHULT M38 47 E4
WGNE/HIN WN2 42 D5
Harris St BOLS/LL BL3 2 C6
Harrop St BOLS/LL BL3 37 G1
WALK M28 47 F5
Harrowby Fold FWTH BL4 39 G5
Harrowby La FWTH BL4 39 G5
Harrowby Rd BOL BL1 19 F5
BOLS/LL BL3 * 37 G2
SWIN M27 57 G5
Harrowby St FWTH BL4 39 F5
Harrow Rd BOL BL1 29 H3
Hartford Rd WHTN BL5 43 H3
Hartington Rd BOL BL1 30 A2
Hartland Cl TYLD M29 53 H3
Hartley St HOR/BR BL6 16 D5
Harts Farm Ms LEIGH WN7 51 H4
Hart St TYLD M29 54 A3
WHTN BL5 42 D1
Hartwell Cl BOLE BL2 21 G5
Harvest Pk BOL BL1 30 A2
Harvey St BOL BL1 20 B4
Harwood Crs TOT/BURYW BL8 13 G5
Harwood Gv BOLE BL2 * 31 F1
Harwood Meadow BOLE BL2 22 B4
Harwood Rd BOLE BL2 22 D3
Harwood V BOLE BL2 22 A4
Haseley Cl RAD M26 32 D5
TYLD M29 53 G3
Hasguard Cl BOL BL1 29 F3
Haskoll St HOR/BR BL6 27 F1
Haslam Hall Ms BOL BL1 29 E3
Haslam Hey Cl BOLE BL2 * 33 E1
TOT/BURYW BL8 23 H5
Haslam St BOLS/LL BL3 30 B5
Hastings Rd BOL BL1 29 H2
Hatfield Rd BOL BL1 30 A1
Hatford Cl TYLD M29 54 A2
Hathaway Ct LEIGH WN7 52 B5
Hathaway Dr BOL BL1 21 E2
Hatton Av ATH M46 44 D3
Hatton Fold ATH M46 52 B1
Hatton Gv BOL BL1 21 E2
Hatton St CHLY/EC PR7 14 D1
Haven Cl RAD M26 33 F5
Haverhill Gv BOLE BL2 21 F5
Havisham Cl HOR/BR BL6 36 B1
Hawarden St BOL BL1 20 C3
Hawes Av FWTH BL4 46 C1
SWIN M27 * 57 H5
Haweswater Av TYLD M29 53 H4
Hawfinch Gv WALK M28 55 H3
Hawker Av BOLS/LL BL3 38 B2
Hawkridge Cl WHTN BL5 43 H2
Hawkshaw Cl TOT/BURYW BL8 12 D1
Hawkshaw La TOT/BURYW BL8 5 H3
Hawkshaw St HOR/BR BL6 16 D5
Hawkshead Dr BOLS/LL BL3 37 G2
Hawksheath Cl EDGW/EG BL7 10 D3
Hawksley St HOR/BR BL6 17 F5
Hawkstone Cl BOLE BL2 22 A4
Haworth St EDGW/EG BL7 4 D4
TOT/BURYW BL8 23 H3
Hawthorn Av WALK M28 56 A2
WGNE/HIN WN2 42 C5
Hawthorn Cl TYLD M29 54 B2
Hawthorn Crs TOT/BURYW BL8 13 H5
Hawthorne Av FWTH BL4 39 F5
HOR/BR BL6 27 G1
Hawthorne Dr WALK M28 56 D4
Hawthorne Gv LEIGH WN7 * 51 G4
Hawthorne Rd BOLS/LL BL3 37 H1
Hawthorne St BOLS/LL BL3 29 H5
Hawthorn Rd FWTH BL4 48 D3
WHTN BL5 43 H1
Haxey Wk HOR/BR BL6 16 B4
Haydock Dr WALK M28 55 F5
Haydock La EDGW/EG BL7 11 F4
Haydock St BOL BL1 2 E1
Hayes St LEIGH WN7 51 G4
Hayfield Av TYLD M29 54 A5
Hayfield Cl TOT/BURYW BL8 13 H3
Haymill Av LHULT M38 47 E2
Haynes St BOLS/LL BL3 37 H2
Haysbrook Av LHULT M38 46 D4
WALK M28 * 47 E4
Hayward Av BOLS/LL BL3 41 E2
Hazel Av LHULT M38 46 C3
RAD M26 40 C5
TOT/BURYW BL8 23 H2
WHTN BL5 43 H1
Hazeldene WHTN BL5 43 F3
Hazelfields WALK M28 56 D4
Hazel Gv FWTH BL4 39 F5
LEIGH WN7 51 G4
RAD M26 41 H5
Hazelhurst Cl BOL BL1 20 C5
Hazelhurst Fold WALK M28 57 E4
Hazelhurst Rd WALK M28 56 D4
Hazelmere Gdns
WGNE/HIN WN2 42 A4
Hazel Mt EDGW/EG BL7 10 C2
Hazel Rd ATH M46 44 C4
Hazelwood Av BOLE BL2 22 A4
Hazelwood Rd BOL BL1 19 H5
Hazlemere FWTH BL4 48 C1
Headingley Wy BOLS/LL BL3 38 B2
Heaplands TOT/BURYW BL8 13 H3
Heap St BOLS/LL BL3 38 C1
Heapy Cl TOT/BURYW BL8 23 H5
Heath Cl BOLS/LL BL3 37 H3
Heather Bank
TOT/BURYW BL8 * 13 G5
Heather Cl HOR/BR BL6 16 D3
Heatherfield BOL BL1 20 B2
EDGW/EG BL7 5 E3
Heather Gv LEIGH WN7 51 G4
Heathfield BOLE BL2 22 B3
CHLYE PR6 6 D3
FWTH BL4 40 A4
Heathfield Dr BOLS/LL BL3 37 H3
TYLD M29 54 B2
Heath Gdns WGNE/HIN WN2 43 E5
Heathlea WGNE/HIN WN2 51 E1
Heathlea Cl BOL BL1 20 C1
Heathside Gv WALK M28 47 H5
Heaton Av BOL BL1 29 F1
BOLE BL2 22 A2
BOLS/LL BL3 40 C1
FWTH BL4 39 G5
Heaton Grange Dr BOL BL1 29 G3
Heaton Mt BOL BL1 29 F1
Heaton Rd BOLE BL2 32 D5
HOR/BR BL6 28 D4
Heatons Gv WHTN BL5 36 A3
Heaton St WGNE/HIN WN2 25 H4
Heaviley Gv HOR/BR BL6 16 C2
Hebble Cl BOLE BL2 21 F2
Hedley St BOL BL1 20 A5
The Heights HOR/BR BL6 27 F1
Helen St FWTH BL4 39 H5
Helias Cl WALK M28 46 D5
Helmclough Wy WALK M28 55 G3
Helmsdale WALK M28 55 G1
Helmsdale Av BOLS/LL BL3 29 F4
Helsby Gdns BOL BL1 20 D3
Helston Wy TYLD M29 54 A3
Hemley Cl WHTN BL5 43 F2
Hemsworth Rd BOL BL1 2 B1
Henderson Av SWIN M27 57 H2
Hendon Gv LEIGH WN7 51 H3
Hendon St LEIGH WN7 51 H3
Hen Fold Rd TYLD M29 54 A4
Hengist St BOLE BL2 31 G3
Henley Gv BOLS/LL BL3 38 A2
Henley St WGNE/HIN WN2 25 F4
Henniker Rd BOLS/LL BL3 37 G3
Henniker St SWIN M27 57 G5
WALK M28 55 H2
Hennon St BOL BL1 30 B1
Henrietta St BOLS/LL BL3 37 H1
Henry Herman St BOLS/LL BL3 37 G2
Henry Lee St BOLS/LL BL3 * 38 A2
Henry St BOLE BL2 3 G6
TYLD M29 53 G2
Henshaw Wk BOL BL1 20 C5
Herbert St BOLS/LL BL3 40 D2
HOR/BR BL6 16 C3
RAD M26 33 H5
WHTN BL5 35 G3
Hereford Crs BOLS/LL BL3 40 D1
Hereford Dr SWIN M27 57 H5
Hereford Rd BOL BL1 29 H2
WGNE/HIN WN2 42 B2
Hereford St BOL BL1 20 D5
Herevale Gra WALK M28 55 F4
Heron's Wy BOLE BL2 3 G7
Hertford Dr TYLD M29 45 G5
Hesketh Av BOL BL1 20 D2
Hesketh Ct ATH M46 44 C5
Hesketh St ATH M46 44 D4
Heswall Dr TOT/BURYW BL8 23 G2
Hewlett St BOLE BL2 3 G4
WHTN BL5 42 D1
Hexham Av BOL BL1 29 F1
Hexham Cl ATH M46 45 E4
Heys Av SWIN M27 57 F1
Heys Cl North SWIN M27 57 E1
Heywood Gdns BOLS/LL BL3 38 C1
Heywood Park Vw
BOLS/LL BL3 30 C5
Heywoods Hollow BOL BL1 20 D4
Heywood St BOL BL1 2 E1
BOLS/LL BL3 40 D2
SWIN M27 57 G3
Hibbert St BOL BL1 20 D5
Hibernia St BOLS/LL BL3 30 A5
High Av BOLE BL2 * 32 A3
High Bank ATH M46 45 G2
EDGW/EG BL7 10 D5
Highbank Gra HOR/BR BL6 28 B2
High Bank La HOR/BR BL6 28 B3
High Bank St BOLE BL2 31 G3
High Beeches BOLE BL2 32 D5
Highbridge Cl BOLE BL2 32 C4
Highbury Cl WHTN BL5 43 F2
Highcrest Gv TYLD M29 54 B2
Highcroft BOL BL1 21 E4
Higher Ainsworth Rd RAD M26 33 G3
Higher Barn HOR/BR BL6 17 H4
Higher Bridge St BOL BL1 2 E1
Higherbrook Cl HOR/BR BL6 27 F1
Higher Damshead WHTN BL5 35 H5
Higher Darcy St BOLE BL2 31 G5
Higher Dean St RAD M26 41 G2
Higher Drake Meadow
WHTN BL5 43 F3
Higher Dunscar EDGW/EG BL7 10 C3
Higher Green La TYLD M29 54 A5
Higher Highfield Ct
WGNE/HIN WN2 * 25 F4
Higher Knowles HOR/BR BL6 17 G5
Higher Market St FWTH BL4 40 A5
Higher Pit La BOLE BL2 33 G2
Higher Ridings EDGW/EG BL7 10 D5
Higher Shady La EDGW/EG BL7 11 G5
Higher Southfield WHTN BL5 43 G1
Higher Swan La BOLS/LL BL3 38 B1
Highfield Av ATH M46 45 E3
BOLE BL2 22 C4
WALK M28 54 C3
Highfield Cl CHLYE PR6 7 E5
Highfield Dr FWTH BL4 47 E1
Highfield Gv WGNE/HIN WN2 25 G5
Highfield Rd BOL BL1 19 H5
CHLYE PR6 7 E5
FWTH BL4 38 C5
HOR/BR BL6 26 A1
LHULT M38 46 D3
Highfield Rd North CHLYE PR6 7 E4
Highfield St FWTH BL4 48 C2
Highgate BOLS/LL BL3 36 C3
Highgate Dr LHULT M38 46 C3
Highgate La LHULT M38 46 C3
Highgrove Cl BOL BL1 20 D4
The Highgrove BOL BL1 28 D1
High Houses BOL BL1 * 20 B1
Highland Rd EDGW/EG BL7 11 G4
HOR/BR BL6 27 G1
High Lea CHLYE PR6 7 E4
Highmeadow RAD M26 41 H4

High Mdw *EDGW/EG* BL7 ....11 F4
High Mt *BOLE* BL2 ....22 A4
High Rid La *HOR/BR* BL6 ....28 B1
High Stile St *FWTH* BL4 ....48 A1
High St *ATH* M46 ....44 D5
  BOLS/LL BL3 ....38 C1
  BOLS/LL BL3 ....40 D2
  EDGW/EG BL7 ....4 C5
  HOR/BR BL6 ....16 D3
  TOT/BURYW BL8 ....23 H4
  TYLD M29 ....53 F2
  WALK M28 ....47 G5
High View St *BOL* BL1 ....20 C2
  BOLS/LL BL3 * 38 A1
Highwood Cl *BOLE* BL2 * 32 B1
Highworth Cl *BOLS/LL* BL3 * 30 C5
Hilary Av *ATH* M46 ....44 C3
Hilary Gv *FWTH* BL4 ....47 G1
Hilda Av *TOT/BURYW* BL8 ....23 H1
Hilda St *BOLS/LL* BL3 ....39 E1
  LEIGH WN7 ....51 E5
Hilden St *BOLE* BL2 ....3 H5
Hillbank Cl *BOL* BL1 ....20 A4
Hill Cot Rd *BOL* BL1 ....20 D2
Hill Crs *LEIGH* WN7 ....51 E3
Hill Crest *ATH* M46 ....45 F3
Hill Crest Av *LEIGH* WN7 ....51 E3
Hillcrest Rd *TYLD* M29 ....54 B3
Hillfield Dr *BOLE* BL2 ....31 F1
  WALK M28 ....55 E4
Hillfield Wk *BOLE* BL2 ....31 F1
Hill La *BOLE* BL2 ....3 H1
  HOR/BR BL6 ....15 F4
Hillsdale Gv *BOLE* BL2 ....22 A4
Hill Side *BOL* BL1 ....29 F3
Hillside Av *ATH* M46 ....45 F4
  EDGW/EG BL7 ....11 F5
  FWTH BL4 ....47 G1
  HOR/BR BL6 ....17 E3
  HOR/BR BL6 ....26 A1
  WALK M28 ....47 G4
Hillside Cl *BOLE* BL2 ....22 A2
  BOLS/LL BL3 ....36 D3
Hillside Crs *HOR/BR* BL6 ....17 E3
Hillside St *BOLS/LL* BL3 ....30 B5
Hillstone Cl *TOT/BURYW* BL8 ......13 H2
Hill St *RAD* M26 ....41 H1
  TOT/BURYW BL8 ....23 H3
Hill Top *ATH* M46 ....45 F3
  BOLS/LL BL3 ....40 C1
Hilltop Dr *TOT/BURYW* BL8 ....23 C3
Hill Top Rd *WALK* M28 ....47 H4
Hillview Rd *BOL* BL1 * 20 C3
Hilly Cft *EDGW/EG* BL7 ....10 D4
Hilmarton Cl *BOLE* BL2 ....22 A2
Hilton Av *HOR/BR* BL6 ....28 B1
Hilton Crs *WALK* M28 ....55 F5
Hilton Gv *WALK* M28 ....55 F5
Hilton La *WALK* M28 ....55 F1
Hilton Pl *WGNE/HIN* WN2 ....25 G3
Hilton St *BOLE* BL2 ....31 G3
  LHULT M38 ....47 E4
Hinchcombe Cl *LHULT* M38 * 47 F4
Hinchley Wy *SWIN* M27 ....57 H1
Hindburn Dr *WALK* M28 ....55 E3
Hindles Cl *ATH* M46 ....52 B1
Hindley Mill La *WGNE/HIN* WN2...42 A1
Hindley Rd *WHTN* BL5 ....43 F3
Hindsford St *ATH* M46 ....53 F2
Hind St *BOLE* BL2 ....31 H3
Hinkler Av *BOLS/LL* BL3 ....38 C2
Hirst Av *WALK* M28 ....47 H3
Hoade St *WGNE/HIN* WN2 ....42 A1
Hobart St *BOL* BL1 ....20 B5
Hob La *EDGW/EG* BL7 ....4 C2
Hodge Rd *WALK* M28 ....55 H1
Hodson Rd *SWIN* M27 ....57 G1
Holbeach Cl *WGNE/HIN* WN2.......42 A4
Holbeck Cl *HOR/BR* BL6 ....27 F2
Holborn Av *LEIGH* WN7 ....51 H3
  RAD M26 ....41 G1
Holbrook Av *LHULT* M38 ....47 E2
Holcombe Cl *FWTH* BL4 ....48 C3
Holcombe Ct *RAMS* BL0 ....13 H2
Holcombe Crs *FWTH* BL4 ....48 C2
Holcombe Old Rd
  TOT/BURYW BL8 ....13 H1
Holcombe Rd *BOLS/LL* BL3 ....40 B2
  TOT/BURYW BL8 ....13 H2
Holden Av *BOL* BL1 ....20 C1
Holden Lea *WHTN* BL5 ....35 G2
Holden St *CHLY/EC* PR7 ....9 D5
Holder Av *BOLS/LL* BL3 ....32 C5
Holdsworth St *SWIN* M27 ....57 G1
Holhouse La *TOT/BURYW* BL8 ....13 H2
Holkar Mdw *EDGW/EG* BL7 ....11 F4
Holland St *BOL* BL1 ....20 D3
The Hollies *ATH* M46 * 44 D5
  WGNE/HIN WN2 * 25 G5

Hollin Acre *WHTN* BL5 ....35 H5
Hollin Hey Rd *BOL* BL1 ....19 E4
Hollinhurst Dr *HOR/BR* BL6 ....28 C3
Hollins *FWTH* BL4 * 38 B5
Hollins Cl *TYLD* M29 ....53 G3
Hollins Rd *WGNE/HIN* WN2 ....42 C3
Hollins St *BOLE* BL2 ....3 J6
Hollinswood Rd *BOLE* BL2 ....3 K5
  WALK M28 ....55 F5
Holloway Dr *WALK* M28 ....57 E2
Hollowell La *HOR/BR* BL6 ....27 F1
Hollow Mdw *RAD* M26 ....49 E2
Holly Av *WALK* M28 ....56 A1
Hollybank St *RAD* M26 ....41 H2
Hollycroft Av *BOLE* BL2 ....32 A5
Hollydene *WGNE/HIN* WN2 * 25 F5
Holly Dene Dr *HOR/BR* BL6 ....28 B3
Holly Gv *BOL* BL1 ....30 A1
  FWTH BL4 ....39 E5
  HOR/BR BL6 ....28 B3
  LEIGH WN7 ....51 G4
Hollyhurst *WALK* M28 ....56 D5
Holly Mill Crs *BOL* BL1 ....20 D3
Holly Rd *SWIN* M27 ....57 F5
  WGNE/HIN WN2 ....25 F5
Holly St *BOL* BL1 ....20 D3
  TOT/BURYW BL8 ....23 H1
Hollywood Rd *BOL* BL1 ....19 H5
Holmbrook *TYLD* M29 ....54 A2
Holmebrook Dr *HOR/BR* BL6 ....27 F2
Holmes Cottages *BOL* BL1 * 20 A4
Holmes St *BOLS/LL* BL3 ....38 D1
Holmeswood Rd *BOLS/LL* BL3 ......38 B3
Holmfield Gn *BOLS/LL* BL3 * 37 F2
Holthouse Rd *TOT/BURYW* BL8 ...23 C2
Holt St *BOLS/LL* BL3 ....2 A7
  LEIGH WN7 ....51 H4
  SWIN M27 ....57 H1
  TYLD M29 ....53 G2
Holy Harbour St *BOL* BL1 * 20 C5
Holyhurst Wk *BOL* BL1 * 20 A5
Holyoake Rd *WALK* M28 ....55 H1
Holyrood Dr *SWIN* M27 ....57 E4
Hondwith Cl *BOLE* BL2 ....21 F2
Honeybourne Cl *TYLD* M29 ....54 A2
Honiton Cl *LEIGH* WN7 ....51 F1
Honiton Dr *BOLE* BL2 ....32 C4
Honiton Gv *RAD* M26 ....33 F5
Hood Cl *TYLD* M29 ....54 B2
Hooton St *BOLS/LL* BL3 ....38 A2
Hope Av *BOLE* BL2 ....3 K6
  BOLE BL2 ....22 A2
  LHULT M38 ....47 F4
Hopefield St *BOLS/LL* BL3 ....38 B1
Hope Fold Av *ATH* M46 ....52 B1
Hopefold Dr *WALK* M28 ....56 A1
Hope Hey La *LHULT* M38 ....46 D3
Hope St *CHLYE* PR6 ....7 F5
  HOR/BR BL6 ....16 D3
  HOR/BR BL6 ....26 A2
  LEIGH WN7 ....51 H5
  LHULT M38 ....47 E4
  WGNE/HIN WN2 ....34 B2
  WGNE/HIN WN2 ....42 B2
Hope St North *HOR/BR* BL6 ....16 D2
Hopwood Av *HOR/BR* BL6 ....17 E3
Horace St *BOL* BL1 ....20 B5
Horeb St *BOLS/LL* BL3 ....30 B5
Horkers Nook *WHTN* BL5 ....43 H1
Hornby Dr *BOLS/LL* BL3 ....36 D3
Hornby Gv *LEIGH* WN7 ....52 D4
Hornsea Cl *TOT/BURYW* BL8 ....23 H5
Horridge Fold *EDGW/EG* BL7 ......10 C1
Horridge Fold Av *WHTN* BL5 ....37 F3
Horrobin Fold *EDGW/EG* BL7 * 11 G2
Horrobin La *CHLYE* PR6 ....7 H3
  EDGW/EG BL7 ....11 G2
Horrocks Fold Av *BOL* BL1 ....20 B1
Horrocks Rd *EDGW/EG* BL7 ....4 D2
Horrocks St *ATH* M46 ....53 E2
  BOLS/LL BL3 ....29 G5
Horsa St *BOLE* BL2 ....31 F1
Horseshoe La *EDGW/EG* BL7 ....11 E4
Horsfield St *BOLS/LL* BL3 ....37 G1
Horsham Cl *WHTN* BL5 ....43 H2
Horton Av *BOL* BL1 ....20 C1
The Hoskers *WHTN* BL5 ....43 F1
Hospital Rd *EDGW/EG* BL7 ....11 E4
Hotel St *BOL* BL1 ....2 E4
Hough Fold Wy *BOLE* BL2 ....21 H3
Hough La *EDGW/EG* BL7 ....10 D5
  TYLD M29 ....54 A3
Hough St *BOLS/LL* BL3 ....37 G1
  TYLD M29 ....54 B3
Houghton St *BOLS/LL* BL3 ....2 C7
  LEIGH WN7 ....51 H5
Houldsworth St *RAD* M26 ....33 H5
Hove Cl *TOT/BURYW* BL8 ....13 H3
Hove St *BOLS/LL* BL3 ....30 A5

Hove St North *BOLS/LL* BL3 * 30 A5
Howard Av *BOLS/LL* BL3 ....37 G1
  FWTH BL4 ....48 B1
Howard St *BOL* BL1 ....30 D1
Howarth Av *WALK* M28 ....57 E4
Howarth Fold *EDGW/EG* BL7 * 10 D3
Howarth St *FWTH* BL4 ....47 H1
  WHTN BL5 ....35 H5
Howbridge Cl *WALK* M28 ....55 G3
How Clough Cl *WALK* M28 ....56 B1
How Clough Dr *WALK* M28 ....56 B1
Howcroft Cl *BOL* BL1 ....2 C2
Howcroft St *BOLS/LL* BL3 ....30 B5
Howe Bridge Cl *ATH* M46 ....52 A2
Howell Cft North *BOL* BL1 ....2 E4
Howell Cft South *BOL* BL1 * 2 E4
Howsin Av *BOLE* BL2 ....21 F3
Hudson Rd *BOLS/LL* BL3 ....37 H2
Hughenden Ct
  TOT/BURYW BL8 * 13 H5
Hughes Av *HOR/BR* BL6 ....16 C3
Hughes St *BOL* BL1 ....20 B5
Hugh Lupus St *BOL* BL1 ....21 E2
Hugo St *FWTH* BL4 ....39 F3
Hulme Gv *LEIGH* WN7 ....51 E5
Hulme Rd *BOLE* BL2 ....22 A1
  LEIGH WN7 ....51 E5
  RAD M26 ....49 E2
Hulme St *BOL* BL1 ....3 F2
Hulton Av *WALK* M28 ....47 F5
Hulton Cl *BOLS/LL* BL3 ....37 G1
Hulton Dr *BOLS/LL* BL3 ....37 G2
Hulton La *BOLS/LL* BL3 ....37 G2
Humber Rd *TYLD* M29 ....54 A4
Hunger Hill Av *BOLS/LL* BL3 ....37 E3
Hunters Gn *RAMS* BL0 ....2 A1
Hunt Fold Dr *TOT/BURYW* BL8.....13 H3
Huntingdon Wk *BOL* BL1 ....20 C5
Huntroyde Av *BOLE* BL2 ....31 G2
Hunt St *ATH* M46 ....44 D5
Hurlston Rd *BOLS/LL* BL3 ....38 B3
Hurst Cl *WHTN* BL5 ....45 F1
Hurstfield Rd *WALK* M28 ....55 F3
Hurst Green Cl *RAD* M26 ....33 H2
Hurst St *BOLS/LL* BL3 ....38 A2
  WALK M28 ....47 G2
Hurstwood *BOL* BL1 ....20 B3
Hurstwood Ct *BOLS/LL* BL3 ....39 G1
Hutton Av *WALK* M28 ....54 D5
Huxley St *BOL* BL1 ....20 A5
Huyton Rd *CHLY/EC* PR7 ....15 E1
Hyde Dr *WALK* M28 ....55 G1
Hyde Gv *WALK* M28 ....55 G1
Hyde Rd *WALK* M28 ....55 G1
Hyde St *BOLS/LL* BL3 * 38 A2
Hypatia St *BOLE* BL2 ....3 K3
Hythe St *BOLS/LL* BL3 * 37 G1

I

Ice House Cl *WALK* M28 ....46 D5
Idonia St *BOL* BL1 ....20 B4
Ilkeston Dr *WGNE/HIN* WN2 ....34 B2
Imperial Dr *LEIGH* WN7 ....52 D5
Ina Av *BOL* BL1 ....29 F1
Independent St *BOLS/LL* BL3 ....40 C1
Industrial St *WHTN* BL5 ....43 H1
Infirmary St *BOL* BL1 ....3 F4
Ingersol Rd *HOR/BR* BL6 ....27 G2
Ingham St *LEIGH* WN7 ....51 G3
Ingleby Cl *WHTN* BL5 ....35 H3
Ingledene Gv *BOL* BL1 * 19 G5
Ingles Fold *WALK* M28 ....55 F3
Ingleton Cl *BOLE* BL2 ....21 H3
Institute St *BOL* BL1 ....3 G4
Invar Rd *WALK* M28 ....57 E3
Inverbeg Dr *BOLE* BL2 ....32 C3
Inverlael Av *BOL* BL1 ....29 H2
Inworth Cl *WHTN* BL5 ....43 H2
Iona Pl *BOLE* BL2 ....21 G5
Iris Av *FWTH* BL4 ....39 E4
  FWTH BL4 ....48 A1
Irlam St *BOL* BL1 ....20 C4
Irma St *BOL* BL1 ....20 D4
Iron St *HOR/BR* BL6 ....17 E5
Irvine Av *WALK* M28 ....55 G1
Irvine St *LEIGH* WN7 ....51 H5
Irving St *BOL* BL1 ....20 C5
Irwell Av *LHULT* M38 ....47 F4
Irwell Pl *RAD* M26 ....40 D5
Irwell St *RAD* M26 ....48 C1
Isaac St *BOL* BL1 ....30 A2
Isabel Wk *BOLS/LL* BL3 ....30 B5
Isherwood Fold *EDGW/EG* BL7 .....4 D2
Isherwood St *LEIGH* WN7 ....51 H3
Ivanhoe Ct *BOLS/LL* BL3 ....39 G3
Ivanhoe St *BOLS/LL* BL3 ....39 G3

Ivy Bank Cl *BOL* BL1 20
Ivy Bank Rd *BOL* BL1 20
Ivy Gv *FWTH* BL4 39
  FWTH BL4 * 48
  LHULT M38 46
Ivy Rd *BOL* BL1 30
  WHTN BL5 43
Ivy St *BOLS/LL* BL3 38

J

Jackdaw Rd *TOT/BURYW* BL8 13
Jack's La *WHTN* BL5 42
Jackson St *FWTH* BL4 48
  FWTH BL4 48
  WALK M28 48
Jack St *BOLE* BL2 31
James St *ATH* M46 53
  BOLS/LL BL3 40
  EDGW/EG BL7 10
  FWTH BL4 40
  HOR/BR BL6 16
  TYLD M29 53
  WHTN BL5 35
Jasmine Ct *BOLS/LL* BL3 38
Jauncey St *BOLS/LL* BL3 30
Jedburgh Av *BOL* BL1 29
Jennaby Wk *BOL* BL1 20
Jenny Lind Cl *BOLS/LL* BL3 39
Jesmond Rd *BOL* BL1 19
Jessie St *BOLS/LL* BL3 30
Jessop Forge *BOLS/LL* BL3 40
Jethro St *BOLE* BL2 21
  BOLE BL2 31
John Brown St *BOL* BL1 * 2
John Cross St *BOLS/LL* BL3 38
Johnson Av *WGNE/HIN* WN2 50
Johnson Fold Av *BOL* BL1 19
Johnson St *ATH* M46 52
  BOL BL1 3
  TYLD M29 53
John St *BOLS/LL* BL3 * 40
  EDGW/EG BL7 11
  FWTH BL4 40
  TYLD M29 53
  WALK M28 47
  WGNE/HIN WN2 42
Jolly Brows *BOLE* BL2 21
Jolly Tar La *CHLY/EC* PR7 6
Jones St *BOL* BL1 2
  HOR/BR BL6 16
Jonquil Dr *WALK* M28 54
Joseph St *FWTH* BL4 39
Jubilee Houses *WALK* M28 * 47
Julia St *HOR/BR* BL6 16
Junction Rd *BOLS/LL* BL3 38
Junction Rd West *HOR/BR* BL6.....28
June Av *LEIGH* WN7 51
Juniper Cl *BOL* BL1 30
Juniper Dr *WGNE/HIN* WN2 42
Jury St *LEIGH* WN7 51
Jutland Gv *WHTN* BL5 35

K

Kayfields *BOLE* BL2 22
Kay St *ATH* M46 52
  BOL BL1 3
  BOL BL1 30
  BOLS/LL BL3 40
  RAMS BL0 6
Kearsley Dr *BOLS/LL* BL3 39
Kearsley Hall Rd *RAD* M26 49
Kearsley Rd *RAD* M26 41
Kearsley V *RAD* M26 40
Keats Crs *RAD* M26 41
Keats Rd *TOT/BURYW* BL8 13
Keats St *LEIGH* WN7 51
Keble Gv *LEIGH* WN7 51
The Keep *BOL* BL1 20
Keighley Cl *TOT/BURYW* BL8 23
Keighley St *BOL* BL1 20
Keilder Ms *BOL* BL1 20
Kellets Rw *WALK* M28 * 47
Kellett St *BOL* BL1 30
Kempnough Hall Rd *WALK* M28...56
Kempston Gdns *BOL* BL1 20
Kempton Av *BOLS/LL* BL3 40
Kendal Gv *WALK* M28 56
Kendal Rd *BOL* BL1 18
  RAMS BL0 13
  WALK M28 54
  WGNE/HIN WN2 50
Kendal Rd West *RAMS* BL0 13
Kendrew Rd *BOLS/LL* BL3 37

ilworth Cl RAD M26 .....33 H4
ilworth Dr LEIGH WN7 .....53 E4
GNE/HIN WN2 .....42 B4
imay Av BOLS/LL BL3 .....29 F4
nedy Rd TYLD M29 .....54 B4
net Cl WHTN BL5 .....35 H4
neth Av LEIGH WN7 .....51 F5
neth Gv LEIGH WN7 .....51 F5
net Wy LEIGH WN7 .....51 H4
nington Fold
OLS/LL BL3 .....38 B2
sington Av RAD M26 .....41 F1
nsington Ct BOL BL1 * 2 B2
nsington Dr HOR/BR BL6 .....17 E4
EIGH WN7 .....53 E4
sington St BOL BL1 .....2 C3
sworth Cl BOL BL1 * 30 B1
sworth Dr BOL BL1 .....30 B1
et Cl WALK M28 .....55 E1
et Ct BOL BL1 .....2 D2
et Dr FWTH BL4 .....48 D2
tford Rd BOL BL1 .....30 C1
tmere Dr TYLD M29 .....53 H4
tmere Gv FWTH BL4 .....46 D1
tmere Rd BOLE BL2 .....32 B1
ton Cl BOL BL1 .....30 B1
t Rd ATH M46 .....44 C4
YLD M29 .....53 F1
tsford Dr RAD M26 .....32 D5
at St BOL BL1 .....2 D1
WIN M27 .....57 H1
awood Rd BOL BL1 .....19 H4
yon Gv LHULT M38 .....46 C4
yon Rd BOLE BL2 .....32 D5
yon St LEIGH WN7 .....51 F3
yon Ter LHULT M38 .....46 C5
yon Wy LHULT M38 .....46 D5
OT/BURYW BL8 .....23 H2
ans Dr WHTN BL5 .....35 G4
mishaw Nook TYLD M29 .....53 G5
moor Av BOL BL1 .....20 C1
ry Gv BOLE BL2 .....3 K1
OLE BL2 .....31 G2
sal Av LHULT M38 .....47 F4
shaw Av BOLS/LL BL3 .....40 C1
shaw St BOLE BL2 .....21 G2
OLS/LL BL3 .....2 B7
YLD M29 .....53 G2
tor St BOLE BL2 .....3 J3
trel Av FWTH BL4 * 46 D1
trel St BOL BL1 * 3 G2
wick Av WALK M28 .....56 B1
wick St BOL BL1 .....20 D5
bles Brow EDGW/EG BL7 .....11 F4
rs Ct HOR/BR BL6 .....17 G3
ride Av BOLE BL2 .....32 B4
urn Clqse LEIGH WN7 .....51 F2
urn Rd RAD M26 .....41 F1
ale Cl BOLS/LL BL3 .....37 E1
are Rd SWIN M27 .....57 G4
are St FWTH BL4 .....47 G1
onan Dr BOLS/LL BL3 .....29 F4
ngworth Ms HOR/BR BL6 * 27 F1
naine Dr BOLS/LL BL3 .....29 E5
nory Dr BOLE BL2 .....32 B4
Brow EDGW/EG BL7 .....11 G4
Fld EDGW/EG BL7 .....10 D4
hurst Wk BOL BL1 * 2 B2
by Cl FWTH BL4 .....39 F3
OR/BR BL6 .....28 C4
vorth Dr HOR/BR BL6 .....28 D4
aberley Rd BOL BL1 .....20 C2
able Cl TOT/BURYW BL8 .....13 H2
craig Cl BOLS/LL BL3 .....37 E1
gfisher Dr FWTH BL4 .....46 D1
gholm Gdns BOL BL1 * 30 B1
gsbridge Rd BOLE BL2 .....33 F1
gsbury Av BOL BL1 .....29 G1
gscourt Av BOL BL1 .....20 A5
g's Crs TYLD M29 .....53 E3
gsdown Dr BOL BL1 .....30 D1
gsdown Gdns BOL BL1 .....30 D1
gsfield Wy TYLD M29 .....53 H3
gs Fold ATH M46 .....45 G5
gsgate BOL BL1 .....2 D3
gsland Rd FWTH BL4 .....38 D4
gslea CHLY/EC PR7 .....6 D4
gsley Rd SWIN M27 .....57 F2
VALK M28 .....47 G5
/GNE/HIN WN2 * 42 B3
gsley St BOL BL1 .....20 B5
EIGH WN7 .....51 H4
gs Pk ATH M46 .....52 A3
gs St WHTN BL5 .....35 H4
gston Av BOLE BL2 .....31 G4

King St BOL BL1 .....2 D3
BOLE BL2 .....21 H2
EDGW/EG BL7 .....10 D4
FWTH BL4 .....39 H5
HOR/BR BL6 .....16 C3
Kingsway FWTH BL4 .....48 B2
WALK M28 .....55 H3
Kingswear Dr BOL BL1 .....30 A1
Kingthorpe Gdns
BOLS/LL BL3 * 38 C1
King William St TYLD M29 .....53 F2
Kingwood Av BOL BL1 .....29 F2
Kinlay Rd FWTH BL4 .....38 D4
Kinloch Dr BOL BL1 .....29 H3
Kinnerly Gv WALK M28 .....55 E2
Kinross Dr BOLS/LL BL3 .....29 F5
Kinsley Dr WALK M28 .....55 G1
Kintyre Dr BOLS/LL BL3 .....29 E5
Kipling Gv LEIGH WN7 .....51 F4
Kirby Av ATH M46 .....44 C3
Kiribati Wy LEIGH WN7 .....51 G5
Kirkby Rd BOL BL1 .....29 H2
Kirkebrok Rd BOLS/LL BL3 .....37 G1
Kirkfell Dr TYLD M29 .....53 H4
Kirkhall La BOL BL1 .....30 A2
LEIGH WN7 .....51 G5
Kirkham St BOLE BL2 .....31 G1
LHULT M38 .....47 E3
Kirkhill Gra WHTN BL5 .....36 A3
Kirkhope Dr BOL BL1 .....30 B1
Kirkhope Wk BOL BL1 .....30 B1
Kirklands BOLE BL2 .....21 H5
Kirklees St TOT/BURYW BL8 .....13 H5
Kirkpatrick St WGNE/HIN WN2 .....42 D5
Kirkstile Pl SWIN M27 .....49 G4
Kirkstone Av WALK M28 .....56 B2
Kirkwall Dr BOLE BL2 .....3 K7
Kitchener St BOLS/LL BL3 .....39 F2
Kitchener Wy FWTH BL4 .....38 D4
Kittiwake Cl TYLD M29 .....53 G4
Kiveton Cl WALK M28 .....55 F1
Knaresborough Rd
WGNE/HIN WN2 .....42 A4
Knight St BOL BL1 .....2 E1
Knightswood BOLS/LL BL3 .....37 F2
Knott La BOL BL1 .....19 F5
Knowles Edge St BOL BL1 .....20 A5
Knowsley Av ATH M46 .....44 C4
Knowsley Dr SWIN M27 .....57 F5
Knowsley Gra BOL BL1 .....28 D3
Knowsley Gv HOR/BR BL6 .....27 F1
Knowsley Rd BOL BL1 .....19 H5
BOLE BL2 .....33 E1
Knowsley St BOL BL1 .....2 E1
Knutshaw Crs BOLS/LL BL3 .....36 D3
Kylemore Cl BOLS/LL BL3 .....29 H5

L

Laburnum Av ATH M46 .....45 E5
LEIGH WN7 .....51 G3
SWIN M27 .....57 G5
TOT/BURYW BL8 .....13 H5
Laburnum Gv HOR/BR BL6 .....27 G1
TYLD M29 .....54 B2
Laburnum Pk BOLE BL2 .....21 G2
Laburnum Rd FWTH BL4 .....39 H5
WALK M28 .....56 A1
Laburnum St ATH M46 .....45 G5
BOL BL1 .....2 A2
Ladybridge Av WALK M28 .....55 G3
Lady Bridge La BOL BL1 .....29 F3
Ladyhill Vw WALK M28 .....55 G3
Ladymere Dr WALK M28 .....55 F3
Ladyshore Rd BOLS/LL BL3 .....41 G3
Ladywell Av LHULT M38 .....47 E4
Ladywell Gv LHULT M38 .....47 E3
Lakelands Dr BOLS/LL BL3 .....29 F5
Lakenheath Cl BOL BL1 .....20 D1
Lakenheath Dr BOL BL1 .....20 D1
Lake Side LEIGH WN7 .....51 F5
Lakeside Av BOLS/LL BL3 .....39 E3
WALK M28 .....47 H3
Lake St BOLS/LL BL3 * 30 C5
LEIGH WN7 .....52 A5
Lambeth Cl HOR/BR BL6 .....17 F4
Lambeth St ATH M46 .....44 B5
Lambley Cl LEIGH WN7 .....51 F3
Lambourn Cl BOLS/LL BL3 .....30 C5
Lambton Rd WALK M28 .....57 E5
Lambton St BOLS/LL BL3 .....38 A3
Lamphey Cl BOL BL1 .....28 D2
Lancaster Av ATH M46 .....44 D5
FWTH BL4 .....38 D5
HOR/BR BL6 .....17 F5
TYLD M29 .....45 G5

Lancaster Cl BOL BL1 .....3 G4
CHLYE PR6 .....7 F5
Lancaster Dr BOLS/LL BL3 .....40 D1
Lancaster Pl CHLYE PR6 .....7 E4
Lancaster Rd WGNE/HIN WN2 .....42 B3
Lancaster St RAD M26 .....41 G2
Lancaster Wk BOL BL1 * 20 C5
Lanchester Dr BOLS/LL BL3 .....2 A7
Landau Dr WALK M28 .....46 D5
Landedmans WHTN BL5 .....43 H1
Landmark Ct BOL BL1 .....29 F1
Landrace Dr WALK M28 .....55 F5
Lane North BOLS/LL BL3 * 37 H1
The Lane BOL BL1 .....28 D3
Langdale Dr WALK M28 .....56 B2
Langdale Rd WGNE/HIN WN2 .....42 A3
Langdale St BOLS/LL BL3 .....38 C2
FWTH BL4 .....47 G1
Langdon Cl BOL BL1 .....2 B1
Langford Gdns BOLS/LL BL3 .....38 C1
Langham Cl BOL BL1 .....21 E1
Langholm Dr BOLE BL2 .....32 B4
Langley Dr WALK M28 .....54 C5
Langley Platt La TYLD M29 .....52 D3
Langshaw Rd BOLS/LL BL3 .....30 A5
Langshaw Wk BOLS/LL BL3 * 30 A5
Langside Dr BOLS/LL BL3 .....37 E1
Langstone Cl HOR/BR BL6 .....16 D4
Langthorne Wk BOLS/LL BL3 .....2 A6
Langtree Cl WALK M28 .....55 F3
Langworthy Av LHULT M38 .....47 H4
Lansdowne Cl BOLE BL2 * 31 F1
Lansdowne Dr WALK M28 .....55 G5
Lansdowne Rd ATH M46 .....45 F3
BOLE BL2 .....31 F1
Larch Av BOLS/LL BL3 .....32 A5
Larch Gv ATH M46 .....44 C4
SWIN M27 .....56 D1
Larch Rd LEIGH WN7 .....51 G3
Larchwood St BOL BL1 .....20 D5
Larkfield Av LHULT M38 .....46 D3
Larkfield Cl TOT/BURYW BL8 .....13 G2
Larkfield Gv BOLS/LL BL3 .....3 K1
Larkfield Ms LHULT M38 .....46 D3
Lark Hi FWTH BL4 .....47 H1
Larkside Av WALK M28 .....48 A5
Larkspur Cl BOL BL1 .....21 E4
Lark St BOL BL1 .....3 F2
FWTH BL4 .....47 H1
Latham Av HOR/BR BL6 .....15 G4
Latham St BOL BL1 .....20 D5
Launceston Rd RAD M26 .....33 F5
WGNE/HIN WN2 .....43 E5
Laurel Av BOLS/LL BL3 .....32 A5
Laurel Ct BOL BL1 .....2 E1
Laurel Crs WGNE/HIN WN2 .....42 C5
Laurel Dr LHULT M38 .....47 E4
Laurel Gv LEIGH WN7 .....51 G3
Laurel St BOL BL1 .....30 A3
TOT/BURYW BL8 .....23 H5
Lauria Ter BOLE BL2 .....33 F1
Lavender Rd FWTH BL4 .....39 E4
Lavender St RAD M26 .....41 F2
Lawefield Crs SWIN M27 .....49 F5
Lawn Dr SWIN M27 .....57 G4
Lawn St BOL BL1 .....30 A1
Lawnswood Dr TYLD M29 .....54 B2
Lawson Av LEIGH WN7 .....51 G2
Lawson Cl WALK M28 .....57 E4
Lawson Rd BOL BL1 .....20 A5
Lawson St BOL BL1 .....20 C3
Laxey Av ATH M46 .....53 E1
Laxey Crs LEIGH WN7 .....51 E4
Laxford Gv BOLS/LL BL3 .....29 E4
Laycock Av BOLE BL2 .....21 F4
Layfield Cl TOT/BURYW BL8 .....13 F4
Layton Dr FWTH BL4 .....48 B2
Lazonby Av WGNE/HIN WN2 .....34 B2
Leach St BOLS/LL BL3 .....30 C5
FWTH BL4 .....40 A4
Leaconfield Dr WALK M28 .....56 B4
Leacroft Av BOLE BL2 .....31 H5
Leafield TYLD M29 .....54 A2
Leafield Cl RAD M26 .....41 G2
Leafield Dr WALK M28 .....55 E5
Lea Gate Cl BOLE BL2 .....21 H2
Leaside Gv WALK M28 .....48 A5
Leavale Cl LHULT M38 .....46 D4
Leckenby Cl WALK M28 .....55 E5
Lecturers Cl BOLS/LL BL3 .....2 E7
Ledbury St LEIGH WN7 .....51 H5
Lee Av BOLS/LL BL3 .....38 B2
Lee Bank WHTN BL5 .....36 A5
Lee Fold TYLD M29 .....54 A3
Lee Ga BOLE BL2 .....21 H2
Lee Gv FWTH BL4 .....38 D5
Leek St RAD M26 .....41 G2
Lee La HOR/BR BL6 .....16 C3

Lees Rd CHLYE PR6 .....7 F4
Lees St SWIN M27 .....57 H2
Lee St ATH M46 .....52 D1
Leewood SWIN M27 .....49 F4
Le Gendre St BOLE BL2 .....31 G1
Leicester Av HOR/BR BL6 .....16 C4
WGNE/HIN WN2 .....42 B3
Leicester Rd TYLD M29 .....53 G1
Leigh Cl TOT/BURYW BL8 .....13 G5
Leigh Rd ATH M46 .....51 G5
WALK M28 .....55 G1
WGNE/HIN WN2 .....50 D2
WHTN BL5 .....35 H5
WHTN BL5 .....43 H1
Leigh St FWTH BL4 .....39 H5
TOT/BURYW BL8 .....23 H3
WGNE/HIN WN2 .....34 B2
WGNE/HIN WN2 .....50 D2
Leighton Av ATH M46 .....44 B5
BOL BL1 .....29 H2
Leighton St ATH M46 .....44 B5
Leinster Rd SWIN M27 .....57 G4
Leinster St FWTH BL4 .....39 G5
Le Mans Crs BOL BL1 .....2 E4
Lemon St TYLD M29 .....53 F3
Lena St BOL BL1 .....20 D5
Lenham Gdns BOLE BL2 .....32 A4
Lennox Gdns BOLS/LL BL3 .....29 F5
Lenora St BOLS/LL BL3 .....37 H1
Lentworth Dr WALK M28 .....47 G3
Leonard St BOLS/LL BL3 .....38 C2
Leslie St BOLE BL2 .....31 F1
Lester Rd LHULT M38 .....46 C5
Letitia St HOR/BR BL6 .....16 C4
Leven Cl FWTH BL4 .....48 D3
Levengreave Cl
WGNE/HIN WN2 .....43 E5
Levens Dr BOLE BL2 .....32 A1
Lever Bridge Pl BOLS/LL BL3 .....30 C5
Lever Dr BOLS/LL BL3 .....30 C5
Lever Edge La BOLS/LL BL3 .....38 A3
Lever Gv BOLE BL2 .....3 H7
Lever Hall Rd BOLE BL2 .....31 H3
Leverhulme Av BOLS/LL BL3 .....39 E2
Lever Park Av HOR/BR BL6 .....16 C2
Lever St BOLE BL2 .....3 G7
BOLS/LL BL3 .....38 D1
BOLS/LL BL3 .....40 C1
RAD M26 .....33 H5
TYLD M29 .....53 F2
WHTN BL5 .....35 G2
Levi St BOL BL1 .....29 F1
Lewis Cl CHLY/EC PR7 .....14 C1
Leybourne St BOL BL1 .....20 C5
Ley Crs TYLD M29 .....53 H5
Ley Rd TYLD M29 .....53 H5
Leyton Cl FWTH BL4 .....38 D4
Library St WHTN BL5 .....35 H5
Libra St BOL BL1 .....20 B5
Lichfield Av BOLE BL2 .....21 F5
TYLD M29 .....54 A4
Lichfield Cl FWTH BL4 .....39 E5
Lichfield Dr SWIN M27 .....57 H5
Lichfield Rd RAD M26 .....33 F5
Lidgett Cl LHULT M38 .....47 G3
Lightbounds Rd BOL BL1 .....19 F4
Lightbourne Av SWIN M27 .....57 H4
Lightburne Av BOL BL1 .....29 H3
Lightwood WALK M28 .....55 F3
Lightwood Cl FWTH BL4 .....40 A4
Lilac Av LEIGH WN7 .....51 G4
Lilford St ATH M46 .....52 B1
Lilly St BOL BL1 .....2 A1
Lily Av FWTH BL4 .....39 H5
Lime Av LEIGH WN7 .....51 G3
SWIN M27 .....57 E5
Limefield Av FWTH BL4 .....39 H4
Limefield Cl BOL BL1 .....19 H3
Limefield Rd BOL BL1 .....19 H3
RAD M26 .....41 F2
Lime Gv WALK M28 .....55 H2
WGNE/HIN WN2 .....42 B5
Limesdale Cl BOLE BL2 .....32 D5
Lime St ATH M46 .....43 H5
FWTH BL4 .....40 A5
TYLD M29 .....53 F2
Limewood Meadow TYLD M29 .....54 A3
Linacre Av BOLS/LL BL3 .....38 C3
Lincoln Av BOLS/LL BL3 .....40 C2
Lincoln Cl TYLD M29 .....53 H5
Lincoln Dr WGNE/HIN WN2 .....25 H5
Lincoln Gv BOLE BL2 .....22 B3
Lincoln Rd BOL BL1 .....29 H2
WGNE/HIN WN2 .....42 A3
Lincroft Rd WGNE/HIN WN2 .....42 C5
Lindale Av BOL BL1 .....29 F2
Lindale Cl WALK M28 .....54 C4
Lindale Rd WALK M28 .....54 C4

Linden Av *ATH* M46 ....52 B1
  BOLS/LL BL3 ....32 C5
  SWIN M27 ....57 F4
Linden Crs *TOT/BURYW* BL8 ..23 H2
Linden Gv *LEIGH* WN7 ....51 G4
Linden Ms *WALK* M28 ....54 D5
Linden Rd *WALK* M28 ....54 D5
  WGNE/HIN WN2 ....42 A1
Linden Wk *BOLE* BL2 ....21 F2
Lindfield Dr *BOL* BL1 ....30 C1
Lindisfarne Pl *BOLE* BL2 ....21 G5
Lindley St *BOLS/LL* BL3 * 40 D2
  FWTH BL4 ....48 D2
Lindrick Ter *BOLS/LL* BL3 ....30 B5
Lindsay Av *SWIN* M27 ....57 G4
Lindsay St *HOR/BR* BL6 ....27 F1
Lindsay Ter *WGNE/HIN* WN2 ....25 F5
Linfield Cl *BOLE* BL2 ....21 H3
Ling Dr *ATH* M46 ....52 D1
Lingfield Cl *FWTH* BL4 ....47 G1
Lingmell Cl *BOL* BL1 ....29 F2
Lingmoor Dr *TYLD* M29 ....53 H4
Lingmoor Rd *BOL* BL1 ....29 F1
Linkfield Dr *WALK* M28 ....54 D5
Links Dr *HOR/BR* BL6 ....28 B3
Links Rd *BOLE* BL2 ....22 C4
  HOR/BR BL6 ....28 B3
The Linkway *HOR/BR* BL6 ....27 E2
Linnet's Wood Ms *WALK* M28 ..48 A5
Linslade Gdns *BOLS/LL* BL3 * 2 C7
Linstock Wy *ATH* M46 ....44 A5
Linthorpe Wk *BOLS/LL* BL3 ....37 H1
Lion La *HOR/BR* BL6 ....15 G5
Lions Dr *SWIN* M27 ....57 H4
Liscard St *ATH* M46 ....44 B5
Lismore Av *BOLS/LL* BL3 ....37 G2
Lister St *BOLS/LL* BL3 ....37 H2
Litchfield Gv *WALK* M28 ....56 D4
Litherland Rd *BOLS/LL* BL3 ....38 C3
Littlebourne Wk *BOL* BL1 ....21 E1
Little Brow *EDGW/EG* BL7 ....11 E5
Little Factory St *TYLD* M29 ....53 F2
Littlegate *WHTN* BL5 ....43 G3
Little Harwood Lee *BOLE* BL2 ....21 H4
Little Holme Wk *BOLS/LL* BL3 * ..38 D1
Little Mdw *EDGW/EG* BL7 * 10 D5
Little Moor Clough
  EDGW/EG BL7 ....10 C2
Little Moss La *SWIN* M27 ....57 H1
Little Pasture *LEIGH* WN7 ....51 F4
Little Scotland *HOR/BR* BL6 ....15 F5
Little Stones Rd
  EDGW/EG BL7 ....10 C2
Livsey Cl *BOL* BL1 ....30 A2
Liza St *LEIGH* WN7 ....51 G3
Lloyd Ct *SWIN* M27 * 57 G4
Lobelia Av *FWTH* BL4 ....39 E4
Lock La *HOR/BR* BL6 ....36 C1
Lodge Bank *HOR/BR* BL6 ....16 B4
Lodge Dr *TYLD* M29 ....53 H5
Lodge Gv *ATH* M46 ....53 E2
Lodge La *ATH* M46 ....52 D2
Lodge Rd *ATH* M46 ....53 E2
Loen Crs *BOL* BL1 ....20 A4
Logan St *BOL* BL1 ....20 C2
Lomax's Buildings *BOLE* BL2 ....3 F5
Lombard St *ATH* M46 ....44 B5
Lomond Pl *BOLS/LL* BL3 ....29 E4
London St *BOLS/LL* BL3 ....38 C1
Long Cswy *ATH* M46 ....52 B4
  FWTH BL4 ....47 H1
Longcliffe Wk *BOL* BL1 * 20 D5
Longden Dr *BOL* BL1 ....30 A2
Longfellow Av *BOLS/LL* BL3 ....37 H2
Longfield Rd *BOLS/LL* BL3 ....37 H3
Longford Av *BOL* BL1 ....20 A5
Longhirst Cl *BOL* BL1 ....19 H4
Longhurst Rd
  WGNE/HIN WN2 ....42 B4
Long La *BOLE* BL2 ....31 H5
  CHLYE PR6 ....7 G2
  WGNE/HIN WN2 ....42 B4
  WHTN BL5 ....35 E3
Longley Dr *WALK* M28 ....56 D4
Longley St *WALK* M28 ....55 H1
Long Meadow *EDGW/EG* BL7 ..11 G5
Longridge Crs *BOL* BL1 ....19 F5
Longridge Dr *TOT/BURYW* BL8 ..33 H2
Longshaw Av *SWIN* M27 ....57 H2
Longshaw Dr *LHULT* M38 ....47 E4
Longshaw Ford Rd *BOL* BL1 ....19 F2
Longsight *BOLE* BL2 ....21 H2
Longsight La *BOLE* BL2 ....21 H3
Longsight Rd *BOLE* BL2 ....21 H4
Longson St *BOL* BL1 ....31 E1
Long St *SWIN* M27 ....57 H4
Longtown Gdns *BOL* BL1 * 20 C5

Longview Dr *SWIN* M27 ....57 E2
Longwall Av *WALK* M28 ....55 G3
Longworth Av *HOR/BR* BL6 ....15 G4
Longworth Clough
  EDGW/EG BL7 ....10 B2
Longworth La *EDGW/EG* BL7 ....10 B4
Longworth Rd *EDGW/EG* BL7 ..10 A1
  HOR/BR BL6 ....17 E3
Longworth St *BOLE* BL2 ....31 G3
Lonsdale Rd *BOL* BL1 ....29 H2
Lord Av *ATH* M46 * 53 E2
Lord Gv *ATH* M46 ....53 F2
Lords Fold *BOL* BL1 * 19 F5
Lord's Stile La *EDGW/EG* BL7 ..11 F5
Lord St *ATH* M46 ....53 E2
  FWTH BL4 ....40 A5
  HOR/BR BL6 ....16 D3
  TYLD M29 ....53 F5
  WHTN BL5 ....35 G4
Lorne St *BOL* BL1 ....2 E3
  FWTH BL4 ....39 G3
Lorton Cl *WALK* M28 ....54 D5
Lorton Gv *BOLE* BL2 ....32 B2
Lostock Junction La
  HOR/BR BL6 ....28 C4
Lostock La *HOR/BR* BL6 ....27 G4
Lostock Park Dr *HOR/BR* BL6 ..28 A3
Lostock Rd *WHTN* BL5 ....35 E1
Lottery Rw *BOL* BL1 ....3 F4
Loughrigg Cl *TYLD* M29 ....53 H4
Louisa St *BOL* BL1 ....20 B5
  WALK M28 ....47 H4
Louise Gdns *WHTN* BL5 ....43 G2
Louvaine Av *BOL* BL1 ....19 F3
Lovalle St *BOL* BL1 ....30 A1
Lovat Rd *BOLE* BL2 ....32 B3
Lovers' La *ATH* M46 ....51 H1
Lowe Av *ATH* M46 ....51 H1
Lower Bridgeman St *BOLE* BL2 ..3 G6
Lowerbrook Cl *HOR/BR* BL6 ....27 G1
Lowercroft Rd *TOT/BURYW* BL8 ..23 H5
Lower Darcy St *BOLE* BL2 ....31 G5
Lower Drake Fold *WHTN* BL5 ..43 G3
Lower Goodwin Cl *BOLE* BL2 ..22 A4
Lower Hill Dr *CHLYE* PR6 ....7 E3
Lower House Dr *HOR/BR* BL6 ..28 C2
Lower House Wk *EDGW/EG* BL7 ..11 E4
Lower Landedmans *WHTN* BL5 ..43 H1
Lower Leigh Rd *WHTN* BL5 ....43 H3
Lower Makinson Fold
  HOR/BR BL6 * 27 F1
Lower Marlands *EDGW/EG* BL7 ..10 D4
Lower Md *EDGW/EG* BL7 ....10 D3
Lower Meadow *EDGW/EG* BL7 ....4 D3
Lower New Rw *WALK* M28 ....55 E2
Lower Rawson St *FWTH* BL4 ....40 A4
Lower Southfield *WHTN* BL5 ....43 G1
Lower St *FWTH* BL4 ....47 G1
Lower Sutherland St *SWIN* M27 ..57 G1
Lower Tong *EDGW/EG* BL7 ....10 D5
Lowerwood La *BOLE* BL2 ....31 F1
Lowe St *RAD* M26 ....41 H1
Lowick Av *BOLS/LL* BL3 ....39 G2
Lowndes St *BOL* BL1 ....29 H2
Lowry Dr *SWIN* M27 ....57 H2
Lowry Wk *BOL* BL1 ....30 B1
Lowside Av *BOL* BL1 ....28 C4
Lowstern Cl *EDGW/EG* BL7 ....10 D3
Lowther Dr *LEIGH* WN7 ....52 D4
Lowther St *BOLS/LL* BL3 ....39 E3
Loxham St *BOLS/LL* BL3 ....39 H3
Lucas Rd *FWTH* BL4 ....39 E5
Luciol Cl *TYLD* M29 ....54 A2
Lucy St *BOL* BL1 ....29 G1
Ludlow Av *WGNE/HIN* WN2 ....42 C4
Ludlow Dr *LEIGH* WN7 ....52 D4
Lulworth Av *BOLS/LL* BL3 ....38 A3
Lulworth Rd *BOLS/LL* BL3 ....37 G2
Lumber La *WALK* M28 ....56 A3
Lumsden St *BOLS/LL* BL3 ....30 C5
Lum St *BOL* BL1 ....3 G2
Lumwood *BOL* BL1 ....19 H4
Lupin Av *FWTH* BL4 ....39 E4
Luton Gv *ATH* M46 ....44 B5
Luton St *BOLS/LL* BL3 ....39 E1
Lydbrook Cl *BOL* BL1 ....2 C5
Lydford Gdns *BOLE* BL2 ....32 B5
Lydgate Av *BOLE* BL2 ....32 A2
Lydiate Cl *BOLS/LL* BL3 ....38 D3
Lymbridge Dr *HOR/BR* BL6 ....15 H5
Lymefield Dr *WALK* M28 ....55 E4
Lymm Cl *WALK* M28 ....47 E5
Lyndale Av *SWIN* M27 ....57 H5
Lyndene Av *WALK* M28 ....56 C3
Lyndon Cl *TOT/BURYW* BL8 ....23 H1
Lynsted Av *BOLS/LL* BL3 ....39 E2

Lynstock Wy *HOR/BR* BL6 ....27 G4
Lynton Av *SWIN* M27 ....57 H2
Lynton Crs *WALK* M28 ....55 H3
Lynton Rd *BOLS/LL* BL3 ....38 A3
  SWIN M27 ....57 H2
  TYLD M29 ....54 B3
  WGNE/HIN WN2 ....42 B2
Lynwood Av *BOLS/LL* BL3 ....39 F3
Lynwood Gv *ATH* M46 ....44 B5
  BOLE BL2 ....21 H3
Lyon Gv *WALK* M28 ....56 C3
Lyon Rd *FWTH* BL4 ....48 C3
Lyon St *SWIN* M27 ....57 G4
Lytton St *BOL* BL1 ....20 B5

M

Mabel Av *BOLS/LL* BL3 ....39 E2
  WALK M28 ....56 C4
Mabel's Brow *FWTH* BL4 ....48 A1
Mabel St *BOL* BL1 ....30 A2
  WHTN BL5 ....43 H2
Macdonald Av *FWTH* BL4 ....47 E1
Mackenzie Gv *BOL* BL1 ....20 D5
Mackenzie St *BOL* BL1 ....20 D5
Madams Wood Rd
  WALK M28 ....46 D5
Madeley Gdns *BOL* BL1 ....20 C5
Maden St *TYLD* M29 ....53 F5
Madison Gdns *WHTN* BL5 ....36 A3
Madison Pk *WHTN* BL5 ....35 H3
Maesbrook Dr *TYLD* M29 ....53 G3
Mafeking Rd *BOLE* BL2 * 32 A3
Maidstone Cl *LEIGH* WN7 ....51 E1
Makants Cl *ATH* M46 ....45 F2
  TYLD M29 ....54 C3
Makinson Av *HOR/BR* BL6 ....27 G1
Makinson La *HOR/BR* BL6 ....17 H3
Maldon Cl *BOLS/LL* BL3 ....40 C2
Maldon Crs *SWIN* M27 ....57 H5
Maldwyn Av *BOLS/LL* BL3 ....37 H3
Mallard Dr *HOR/BR* BL6 ....16 C4
Mallet Crs *BOL* BL1 ....19 F5
Mallison St *BOL* BL1 ....20 D4
Mallowdale *WALK* M28 ....55 F3
Mallowdale Cl *BOL* BL1 ....28 D4
Maltby Dr *BOLS/LL* BL3 ....38 A3
Malton Av *BOLS/LL* BL3 ....37 G1
Malton Cl *LEIGH* WN7 ....51 E5
Malton Rd *WALK* M28 ....54 C4
Malvern Av *ATH* M46 ....45 F3
  BOL BL1 ....29 G1
  WGNE/HIN WN2 ....42 C4
Malvern Cl *FWTH* BL4 ....38 D4
  HOR/BR BL6 ....17 E2
Malvern Gv *WALK* M28 ....47 H5
Manchester Rd *BOLE* BL2 ....3 G7
  BOLE BL2 ....31 E5
  BOLS/LL BL3 ....39 G2
  FWTH BL4 ....48 D2
  HOR/BR BL6 ....15 H5
  SWIN M27 ....49 H5
  SWIN M27 ....57 F2
  TYLD M29 ....53 H2
  TYLD M29 ....54 A5
  WALK M28 ....56 B1
  WHTN BL5 ....35 H3
Manchester Rd East
  LHULT M38 ....47 E4
Manchester Rd West
  LHULT M38 ....46 C3
Mancroft Av *BOLS/LL* BL3 ....38 B1
Mancroft Ter *BOLS/LL* BL3 * 38 B1
Mandley Cl *BOLS/LL* BL3 ....32 D5
Mandon Cl *RAD* M26 ....33 G5
Manley Av *SWIN* M27 ....49 H4
Manley Cl *LEIGH* WN7 ....51 F5
Manley Crs *WHTN* BL5 ....36 B4
Manley Ter *BOL* BL1 * 20 C3
Manning Rd
  BOLS/LL BL3 ....29 H5
Manor Av *BOLS/LL* BL3 ....41 E3
Manorfield Cl *BOL* BL1 ....29 G1
Manor Gate Rd *BOLE* BL2 ....32 C2
Manor Gv *WGNE/HIN* WN2 ....25 F5
Manorial Dr *LHULT* M38 ....46 C3
Manor Rd *HOR/BR* BL6 ....17 F3
  SWIN M27 ....57 H5
  TYLD M29 ....54 A5
  WGNE/HIN WN2 ....42 B3
Manor St *BOL* BL1 ....3 J3
  FWTH BL4 ....47 G1
  FWTH BL4 ....48 D3
Mansell Wy *HOR/BR* BL6 ....27 F2
Mansfield Gv *BOL* BL1 ....29 H1
Manthorpe Av
  WALK M28 ....56 C4

Maple Av *ATH* M46 ....44 ?
  BOL BL1 * ....29 ?
  HOR/BR BL6 ....27 ?
  WGNE/HIN WN2 ....42 ?
Maple Cl *FWTH* BL4 ....48 ?
Maple Crs *LEIGH* WN7 ....51 ?
Maplefield Dr *WALK* M28 ....55 ?
Maple Gv *WALK* M28 ....55 ?
Maple Rd *FWTH* BL4 ....39 ?
  SWIN M27 ....57 ?
Maple St *BOL* BL1 ....21 ?
  BOLS/LL BL3 ....2 ?
Maplewood Gdns *BOL* BL1 * ....20 ?
Maplewood House *BOL* BL1 ....30 ?
Marcus St *BOL* BL1 ....29 ?
Mardale Av *SWIN* M27 ....57 ?
Mardale Cl *ATH* M46 ....44 ?
  BOLE BL2 ....32 ?
Mardale Dr *BOLE* BL2 ....32 ?
Mardale Rd *SWIN* M27 ....57 ?
Margrove Cha *HOR/BR* BL6 ....28 ?
Maria St *BOL* BL1 ....2 ?
Marion St *BOLS/LL* BL3 ....39 ?
Market Pl *CHLY/EC* PR7 ....15 ?
Market St *ATH* M46 ....44 ?
  BOL BL1 ....2 ?
  BOLS/LL BL3 ....40 ?
  CHLY/EC PR7 ....15 ?
  FWTH BL4 ....39 ?
  RAD M26 ....40 ?
  TOT/BURYW BL8 ....? ?
  TYLD M29 ....53 ?
  WHTN BL5 ....35 ?
Markland Hl *BOL* BL1 ....29 ?
Markland Hill Cl *BOL* BL1 ....29 ?
Markland Hill La *BOL* BL1 ....29 ?
Marklands Rd *HOR/BR* BL6 ....17 ?
Markland St *BOL* BL1 ....? ?
Mark St *WALK* M28 ....54 ?
Marlborough Gdns *FWTH* BL4 ..38 ?
Marlborough Rd *ATH* M46 ....45 ?
Marlborough St *BOL* BL1 ....? ?
Marlbrook Dr *WHTN* BL5 ....43 ?
Marlbrook Ms *WHTN* BL5 * ....43 ?
Marlbrook Wk *BOLS/LL* BL3 ....38 ?
Marld Crs *BOL* BL1 ....19 ?
Marled Hey *EDGW/EG* BL7 ....? ?
Marlow Cl *BOLE* BL2 ....32 ?
Marlow Ct *CHLY/EC* PR7 ....? ?
Marlow Dr *SWIN* M27 ....57 ?
Marlwood Rd *BOL* BL1 ....19 ?
Marnland Gv *BOLS/LL* BL3 ....37 ?
Marnock Cl *WGNE/HIN* WN2 ....50 ?
Marple Av *BOL* BL1 ....21 ?
Mars Av *BOLS/LL* BL3 ....38 ?
Marsden Rd *BOL* BL1 ....? ?
Marsden St *WALK* M28 ....54 ?
  WHTN BL5 ....35 ?
Marsham Rd *WHTN* BL5 ....43 ?
Marshbank *WHTN* BL5 ....35 ?
Marshbrook Cl
  WGNE/HIN WN2 ....42 ?
Marsh Brook Fold *WHTN* BL5 ..42 ?
Marshdale Rd *BOL* BL1 ....29 ?
Marsh Fold La *BOL* BL1 ....30 ?
Marsh Hey Cl *LHULT* M38 ....46 ?
Marsh La *FWTH* BL4 ....40 ?
Marsh Rd *BOLS/LL* BL3 ....40 ?
  LHULT M38 ....? ?
Marsh Rw *WGNE/HIN* WN2 ....16 ?
Marsh St *HOR/BR* BL6 ....16 ?
  WALK M28 ....48 ?
  WHTN BL5 ....35 ?
Mars St *EDGW/EG* BL7 ....? ?
Marston Cl *HOR/BR* BL6 ....27 ?
Martha St *BOLS/LL* BL3 * ....38 ?
Martin Av *BOLS/LL* BL3 ....41 ?
Martindale Gdns *BOL* BL1 ....20 ?
Martin Gv *FWTH* BL4 ....48 ?
Martins Av *CHLY/EC* PR7 ....6 ?
Martinsclough *HOR/BR* BL6 ....28 ?
Martins Ct *WGNE/HIN* WN2 ....42 ?
Martin St *ATH* M46 * ....44 ?
  EDGW/EG BL7 ....? ?
Martlew Dr *ATH* M46 ....45 ?
Marton Av *BOLE* BL2 ....32 ?
Marton Dr *ATH* M46 ....45 ?
Marwood Cl *RAD* M26 ....40 ?
Mary Hulton Ct *WHTN* BL5 ....36 ?
Maryland Av *BOLE* BL2 ....32 ?
Mary St *FWTH* BL4 ....47 ?
  TYLD M29 * ....53 ?
Mary St East *HOR/BR* BL6 ....16 ?
Mary St West *HOR/BR* BL6 ....16 ?
Masbury Cl *BOL* BL1 ....10 ?
Masefield Av *LEIGH* WN7 ....51 ?
  RAD M26 ....41 ?
Masefield Dr *FWTH* BL4 ....39 ?
Masefield Rd *BOLS/LL* BL3 ....40 ?

son Gdns *BOLS/LL* BL3 ....2 C6
son La *ATH* M46 ....53 E1
son St *EDGW/EG* BL7 * 10 C3
OR/BR BL6 ....16 C4
chmoor La HOR/BR BL6 ....17 H3
her Fold Rd WALK M28 ....55 F2
her St ATH M46 ....44 D5
OLS/LL BL3 * 2 D6
WTH BL4 ....40 A5
lock Cl ATH M46 ....52 D1
lock Ct HOR/BR BL6 ....17 G3
thews Av FWTH BL4 ....48 B1
d St BOLE BL2 ....21 G2
anby Gdns LHULT M38 ....47 G5
ydsley St BOL BL1 ....2 E4
twell St BOL BL1 ....20 C3
r Av LEIGH WN7 ....51 F5
rbank St BOLS/LL BL3 ....38 B1
fair HOR/BR BL6 ....17 F4
fair Av RAD M26 ....41 F1
fair Dr ATH M46 ....45 F4
field BOLE BL2 ....21 H2
field Av BOLS/LL BL3 ....39 F2
HLYE PR6 ....7 E5
WTH BL4 ....47 G1
ALK M28 ....47 H5
field St BOLE BL2 ....57 E5
field Houses RAD M26 * 41 G3
field Av ATH M46 ....44 C5
hill Dr WALK M28 ....56 C3
or St BOL BL1 ....2 B5
St BOLE BL2 ....3 H4
DGW/EG BL7 ....5 E3
tree Ct CHLYE PR6 ....6 D4
e St BOLS/LL BL3 ....31 H5
onna St BOL BL1 ....20 A4
voy St BOL BL1 ....20 D5
ean St BOLS/LL BL3 ....39 E1
Meade BOLS/LL BL3 ....38 C3
dland Gv BOL BL1 ....20 D3
dowbank Av ATH M46 ....45 E4
dowbank Rd BOLS/LL BL3 ......37 H3
dowbrook Cl SWIN M27 ....36 C2
dow Cl BOLS/LL BL3 ....40 D3
dowcroft RAD M26 ....33 H5
HTN BL5 ....43 H1
dowfield HOR/BR BL6 ....28 D3
dowfield Dr WALK M28 ....55 F5
dowgate WALK M28 ....56 B3
dow La BOLE BL2 ....32 C3
dow Pit La WGNE/HIN WN2 ...25 F2
dowside Av BOLE BL2 ....31 G2
ALK M28 ....48 A4
dowside La BOLE BL2 ....48 A5
dowside Rd
GNE/HIN WN2 ....42 C4
dows La BOLE BL2 ....22 B4
Meadows RAD M26 ....33 G5
Meadow BOL BL1 ....28 D3
dow Vw CHLYE PR6 ....6 D4
dow Wk FWTH BL4 ....47 H1
dow Wy EDGW/EG BL7 ....4 D3
OR/BR BL6 ....26 A1
OT/BURYW BL8 ....23 G1
LD M29 ....54 A5
dway TYLD M29 ....54 B2
dway Cl HOR/BR BL6 ....17 F4
house St ATH M46 ....44 C5
house La ATH M46 ....44 C5
L BL1 ....2 E3
nley Rd LEIGH WN7 ....53 F4
nley St TYLD M29 ....53 F2
lock Cl FWTH BL4 ....39 F5
way Dr FWTH BL4 ....48 D3
OR/BR BL6 ....17 F4
way Rd WALK M28 ....55 F3
field WHTN BL5 ....43 G2
bourne Ct HOR/BR BL6 ....17 E4
bourne Gv HOR/BR BL6 ....17 E4
bourne Rd BOLS/LL BL3 ....29 H5
bury Dr HOR/BR BL6 ....27 F2
den Crs BOL BL1 * 29 H1
ng Cl CHLYE PR6 * 7 E3
or Dr WALK M28 ....55 G2
or Gv BOL BL1 ....29 H1
ose Av BOL BL1 ....29 G1
IGH WN7 ....51 F2
ose Gdns RAD M26 ....33 G5
ose Rd BOLS/LL BL3 ....40 B2
ose St RAD M26 ....33 G5
ham Pl BOLS/LL BL3 * 38 A1
on Cl TYLD M29 ....53 H3
ALK M28 ....55 G1
on St RAD M26 ....41 H1
ille Rd FWTH BL4 ....48 B2
ille St BOLS/LL BL3 ....39 E1

Memorial Cottages *SWIN* M27 * ...49 H5
Memorial Rd *WALK* M28 ....47 H5
Menai St *BOLS/LL* BL3 * 37 H1
Mendip Cl *BOLE* BL2 ....32 C3
HOR/BR BL6 ....17 E2
Mendip Dr *BOLE* BL2 ....32 C4
Mercer Ct *CHLY/EC* PR7 ....6 D3
Mercia St *BOLS/LL* BL3 ....30 A5
Mere Bank Cl *WALK* M28 ....47 G5
Mereclough Av *WALK* M28 ....56 B2
Meredew Av *SWIN* M27 ....57 G5
Meredith St *BOLS/LL* BL3 ....38 D2
Merefield Cl *WGNE/HIN* WN2 ....42 A4
Merefold *HOR/BR* BL6 ....16 B4
Mere Fold *WALK* M28 ....47 F5
Mere Gdns *BOL* BL1 ....2 C1
Merehall Cl *BOL* BL1 ....2 C1
Merehall Dr *BOL* BL1 ....2 C1
Merehall St *BOL* BL1 ....30 B1
Meremanor *WALK* M28 ....56 B2
Mereside Gv *WALK* M28 ....48 A5
Mere Wk *BOL* BL1 ....2 C1
Meriden Cl *BOL* BL1 ....33 H4
Meriden Gv *HOR/BR* BL6 ....28 D4
Merlewood Dr *SWIN* M27 ....57 E5
TYLD M29 ....53 H3
Merlin Gv *BOL* BL1 ....29 H1
Merrion St *FWTH* BL4 ....39 E5
Mersey Cl *WGNE/HIN* WN2 ....43 E5
Merton Cl *BOLS/LL* BL3 * 30 A5
Merton Gv *TYLD* M29 ....54 A5
Mesne Lea Gv *WALK* M28 * 56 A3
Mesne Lea Rd *WALK* M28 ....56 A3
Metcalfe Ct *LHULT* M38 * 46 D4
Metfield Pl *BOL* BL1 * 30 A2
Methwold St *BOLS/LL* BL3 * 38 A1
The Mews *BOL* BL1 ....29 H2
Mickleton *ATH* M46 ....45 E4
Middlebrook Dr *HOR/BR* BL6 ....28 C4
Middle Turn *EDGW/EG* BL7 ....4 D2
Midford Dr *BOL* BL1 ....10 C5
Midgley St *SWIN* M27 ....57 F5
Midland Cl *LEIGH* WN7 ....51 E5
Milburn Dr *BOLE* BL2 ....32 B2
Mile La *TOT/BURYW* BL8 ....33 H1
Miles St *BOL* BL1 ....20 B5
Milford Rd *BOLE* BL2 ....22 B3
BOLS/LL BL3 ....38 C2
Milk St *TYLD* M29 ....53 G2
Millbank Gdns *BOL* BL1 * 30 A1
Millbeck Gv *BOLS/LL* BL3 * 38 C1
Millbrook Av *ATH* M46 ....45 E3
Mill Brow *WALK* M28 ....56 B5
Mill Court Dr *RAD* M26 ....40 D5
Mill Cft *BOL* BL1 ....2 B1
Milldale Cl *ATH* M46 ....44 C5
HOR/BR BL6 ....28 C3
Miller's La *ATH* M46 ....52 D2
Miller St *BOL* BL1 ....20 C3
RAD M26 ....33 H4
Millfield Dr *WALK* M28 ....55 F5
Millfield Rd *BOLE* BL2 ....32 C3
Millgate *EDGW/EG* BL7 ....10 B2
Mill Hl *BOLE* BL2 * 3 H2
LHULT M38 ....46 C2
Mill Hill Caravan Pk *BOLE* BL2 ....3 H2
Mill Hill St *BOLE* BL2 ....3 H2
Mill La *HOR/BR* BL6 ....17 F3
WGNE/HIN WN2 ....34 B2
WHTN BL5 ....43 G4
Millpond Av *BOLS/LL* BL3 ....39 E2
Millstone Rd *BOL* BL1 ....29 F1
Mill St *ATH* M46 ....53 E2
BOL BL1 ....3 G3
CHLYE PR6 ....7 G3
EDGW/EG BL7 ....10 D4
FWTH BL4 ....39 G5
TOT/BURYW BL8 ....13 H4
WALK M28 ....55 E4
WHTN BL5 ....35 H5
Mill View La *HOR/BR* BL6 ....17 G4
Millwell La *BOL* BL1 ....2 E3
Milner St *RAD* M26 ....41 G2
Milnholme *BOL* BL1 ....19 H4
Milnthorpe Rd *BOLE* BL2 ....32 A2
Milsom Av *BOLS/LL* BL3 ....38 A2
Milton Av *BOLS/LL* BL3 * 37 H2
BOLS/LL BL3 ....40 D1
Milton Crs *FWTH* BL4 ....47 F2
Milton Rd *RAD* M26 ....41 F1
SWIN M27 ....57 F2
Milverton Cl *HOR/BR* BL6 ....28 D5
Milwain Rd *BOL* BL1 * 57 H1
Minehead Av *LEIGH* WN7 ....51 F1
Minerva Rd *FWTH* BL4 ....38 D4
Minnie St *BOLS/LL* BL3 * 37 H1
Minorca St *BOLS/LL* BL3 ....38 C1
Minster Cl *BOLE* BL2 ....21 G5
Minster Gv *TYLD* M29 ....53 H4

Minster Rd *BOLE* BL2 ....21 G5
Minstrel Cl *SWIN* M27 ....57 F4
Miriam St *BOLS/LL* BL3 * 37 H1
Miry La *WHTN* BL5 ....43 G3
Mitre St *BOL* BL1 ....20 C3
Mitton Cl *TOT/BURYW* BL8 ....23 H5
Moatfield Gdns *BOL* BL1 ....2 A1
Mobberley Rd *BOLE* BL2 ....31 H2
Moffat Cl *BOLE* BL2 ....32 B4
Moisant St *BOLS/LL* BL3 ....38 B2
Mold St *BOL* BL1 ....20 C4
Molyneux Rd *WHTN* BL5 ....36 B4
Moncrieffe St *BOLS/LL* BL3 ....3 G5
Monks La *BOLE* BL2 ....21 H5
Montague St *BOLS/LL* BL3 * 37 H2
Monton St *BOLS/LL* BL3 ....38 C2
RAD M26 ....41 H2
Montrose Av *BOLE* BL2 ....31 G1
Montrose Dr *EDGW/EG* BL7 .....11 G5
Montserrat Brow *BOL* BL1 ....18 C4
Montserrat Rd *BOL* BL1 ....19 E5
Monyash Vw *WGNE/HIN* WN2 ...42 B5
Moorby Wk *BOLS/LL* BL3 * 30 C5
Moor Cl *RAD* M26 ....33 G5
Moore's Ct *BOL* BL1 ....30 A2
Moorfield *EDGW/EG* BL7 ....4 D3
WALK M28 ....54 D4
WALK M28 ....56 B3
Moorfield Cha *FWTH* BL4 ....47 H1
Moorfield Cl *SWIN* M27 ....57 E5
Moorfield Gv *BOLE* BL2 ....31 F1
Moorfield Rd *SWIN* M27 ....57 E5
Moor Ga *BOLE* BL2 ....21 H2
Moorgate Cl *BOLE* BL2 ....31 F1
Moorgate Dr *TYLD* M29 ....54 A5
Moorgate Rd *RAD* M26 ....33 G2
Moorhey Rd *LHULT* M38 ....46 D2
Moorland Dr *HOR/BR* BL6 ....17 H4
LHULT M38 ....47 E2
Moorland Gv *BOL* BL1 ....19 G5
Moorlands Vw *BOLS/LL* BL3 ......37 G3
Moor La *BOL* BL1 ....2 D4
LEIGH WN7 ....51 G3
Moor Platt Cl *HOR/BR* BL6 ....17 H4
Moorside *SWIN* M27 ....57 F4
Moorside Av *BOL* BL1 ....19 G5
BOLE BL2 ....33 F1
FWTH BL4 ....47 H1
HOR/BR BL6 ....17 E3
Moorside Rd *SWIN* M27 ....57 F3
TOT/BURYW BL8 ....23 G2
Moorside Vw *TOT/BURYW* BL8 ...23 H1
Moor St *SWIN* M27 ....57 H4
Moor Wy *TOT/BURYW* BL8 ....12 D1
Morar Dr *BOLE* BL2 ....32 C3
Morley Av *SWIN* M27 ....57 F2
Morley Rd *RAD* M26 ....41 F1
Morley St *ATH* M46 ....44 C5
BOLS/LL BL3 ....2 B5
Mornington Rd *ATH* M46 ....44 C5
BOL BL1 ....29 H2
CHLYE PR6 ....7 F1
WGNE/HIN WN2 ....42 B3
Morpeth St *SWIN* M27 ....57 F2
Morris Fold Dr *HOR/BR* BL6 ......28 C4
Morris Gn *BOLS/LL* BL3 ....38 A3
Morris Green La *BOLS/LL* BL3 ...38 A2
Morris Green St *BOLS/LL* BL3 * ..38 A3
Morrison St *BOLS/LL* BL3 ....38 C2
Morris St *BOL* BL1 ....3 G3
TYLD M29 ....53 G2
Mortfield Gdns *BOL* BL1 ....2 A1
Mortfield La *BOL* BL1 ....2 A1
Mortlake Cl *WALK* M28 ....46 D5
Mort La *TYLD* M29 ....54 C1
Mort St *FWTH* BL4 ....39 F5
HOR/BR BL6 ....16 D3
WGNE/HIN WN2 ....42 C3
Morven Gv *BOLE* BL2 ....32 B2
Mosedale Cl *TYLD* M29 ....54 A5
Mosley Common Rd*
WALK M28 ....54 C4
Mosley St *RAD* M26 ....20 B1
Moss Bank Cl *BOL* BL1 ....20 B3
Moss Bank Gv *SWIN* M27 ....57 E1
Moss Bank Pk *BOL* BL1 * 19 F4
Moss Bank Rd *SWIN* M27 ....57 F1
Moss Bank Wy *BOL* BL1 ....29 E1
Mossbrook Dr *LHULT* M38 ....46 D2
Moss Cl *RAD* M26 ....33 F5
Moss Colliery Rd *SWIN* M27 * 49 H5
Mossdale Av *BOL* BL1 ....28 D3
Moss Dr *HOR/BR* BL6 ....17 H4
Mossfield Ct *BOL* BL1 * 2 C1
Mossfield Rd *FWTH* BL4 ....39 F5
FWTH BL4 ....48 B3
SWIN M27 ....57 G1

Moss Fold *TYLD* M29 ....54 A4
Mossland Gv *BOLS/LL* BL3 ....36 D3
Moss La *BOL* BL1 ....19 G4
FWTH BL4 ....48 D3
HOR/BR BL6 ....16 B5
SWIN M27 ....57 F2
WALK M28 ....56 B3
Moss Lea *BOL* BL1 ....20 B3
Moss Meadow *WHTN* BL5 ....35 G3
Moss Shaw Wy *RAD* M26 ....33 G5
Moss St *FWTH* BL4 ....40 A4
Moss View Rd *BOLE* BL2 ....32 A2
Mottershead Av *BOLS/LL* BL3 ...40 C1
Mottram St *HOR/BR* BL6 ....16 D3
Mountain Gv *WALK* M28 ....47 G4
Mountain St *WALK* M28 ....47 G4
Mount Pleasant *BOLS/LL* BL3 * ...31 G5
CHLYE PR6 ....7 F1
Mount Pleasant Rd *FWTH* BL4 ...38 D5
Mount Pleasant St *HOR/BR* BL6 ..27 F1
Mount St Joseph's Rd*
BOLS/LL BL3 ....29 H5
Mount Sion Houses *RAD* M26 * ...41 G3
Mount Sion Rd *RAD* M26 ....41 G3
Mount Skip La *LHULT* M38 ....47 E4
Mount St *BOL* BL1 ....30 C1
HOR/BR BL6 ....27 F1
SWIN M27 ....57 H4
Mowbray St *BOL* BL1 * 29 H1
Moyse Av *TOT/BURYW* BL8 ......23 H2
Muirfield Cl *BOLS/LL* BL3 ....37 F2
Muirfield Dr *TYLD* M29 ....54 A4
Mule St *BOLE* BL2 ....3 H2
Mulgrave Rd *WALK* M28 ....56 C3
Mulgrave St *BOLS/LL* BL3 ....38 A3
SWIN M27 ....57 F2
Mulliner St *BOL* BL1 * 30 D1
Murray St *ATH* M46 ....52 D1
Musgrave Gdns *BOL* BL1 ....30 A2
Musgrave Rd *BOL* BL1 ....30 A2
Mycroft Cl *LEIGH* WN7 ....51 G3
Myrrh St *BOL* BL1 ....20 C4
Myrtle Av *LEIGH* WN7 ....51 G4
Myrtle St *BOL* BL1 ....2 B2
Mytham Rd *BOLS/LL* BL3 ....40 D2
Mytton Rd *BOL* BL1 ....19 H4

Nabbs Fold *TOT/BURYW* BL8 .....13 H1
Nandywell *BOLS/LL* BL3 ....40 D2
Nantwich Wk *BOLS/LL* BL3 * 38 C1
Napier St *SWIN* M27 ....57 F4
Narborough Cl *WGNE/HIN* WN2 ..42 A4
Nasmyth St *HOR/BR* BL6 ....17 E4
Naylor St *ATH* M46 ....44 C5
Near Hey Cl *RAD* M26 ....41 G2
Neasden Gv *BOLS/LL* BL3 * 30 A5
Neath Fold *BOLS/LL* BL3 ....38 B2
Nebo St *BOLS/LL* BL3 ....38 B1
Nebraska St *BOL* BL1 * 30 C1
Nell St *BOL* BL1 ....20 D3
Nel Pan La *LEIGH* WN7 ....51 E3
Nelson Sq *BOL* BL1 ....3 F4
Nelson St *ATH* M46 ....44 B5
BOLS/LL BL3 ....31 E5
BOLS/LL BL3 * 40 D2
FWTH BL4 ....40 A5
HOR/BR BL6 ....17 F4
TYLD M29 ....53 H3
Nene Gv *WGNE/HIN* WN2 ....42 A4
Nesbit St *BOLE* BL2 * 21 F4
Neston Av *BOL* BL1 ....20 D2
Neston Rd *TOT/BURYW* BL8 ......23 H3
Netherfield Rd *BOLS/LL* BL3 .....38 C3
Netherfields *LEIGH* WN7 ....51 F4
Netherwood Wy *WHTN* BL5 ......36 A3
Nevada St *BOL* BL1 * 30 C1
Nevern Cl *BOL* BL1 ....29 F2
Neville Ct *RAD* M26 ....33 F2
Nevis Gv *BOL* BL1 ....20 B2
Nevy Fold Av *HOR/BR* BL6 ....17 H4
Newall Gv *LEIGH* WN7 ....51 H4
Newark Av *RAD* M26 ....33 E5
New Bank St *TYLD* M29 * 53 G3
New Barn St *BOL* BL1 ....29 H1
Newbeck Cl *HOR/BR* BL6 ....27 F1
Newbridge Gdns *BOL* BL1 ....22 A3
New Briggs Fold *EDGW/EG* BL7 ...10 C2
Newbrook Rd *ATH* M46 ....45 F2
New Brunswick St *HOR/BR* BL6 ..16 D4
Newbury Rd *BOLS/LL* BL3 ....40 B2
Newbury Wk *BOL* BL1 * 2 C1
Newby Rd *BOLE* BL2 ....32 A1
New Chapel La *HOR/BR* BL6 ......17 H5
New Church Rd *BOL* BL1 ....19 F5

New City Rd WALK M28....55 E3
New Colliers Rw BOL BL1 *....19 E2
Newcombe Dr LHULT M38....46 D2
New Court Dr EDGW/EG BL7....10 C1
New Drake Gn WHTN BL5....43 G3
Newearth Rd WALK M28....55 F3
New Ellesmere Ap WALK M28....47 G4
New Field Cl RAD M26....41 G2
Newgate Cottages WHTN BL5 *....37 G4
Newgate Dr LHULT M38....46 D2
Newhall Av BOLE BL2....32 D4
New Hall La BOL BL1....29 G2
New Hall Ms BOL BL1....28 D1
New Hall Pl BOL BL1....29 G2
Newhart Gv WALK M28....55 G1
Newhaven Av LEIGH WN7....51 H3
New Heys Wy BOLE BL2....21 H1
New Holder St BOL BL1....2 C4
Newholme Gdns WALK M28....47 G5
Newington Dr BOL BL1 *....30 C1
Newington Wk BOL BL1 *....30 C1
Newland Dr WHTN BL5....45 F1
Newlands Av BOLE BL2....32 B1
  TYLD M29....53 G5
Newlands Dr HOR/BR BL6....26 A3
New La BOLE BL2....31 H1
New Lane Ct BOLE BL2....22 A5
Newlea Cl BOL BL1....20 A5
New Lester Cl TYLD M29....53 H2
New Lester Wy LHULT M38....46 C4
Newmarket Rd BOLS/LL BL3....40 C3
New Meadow HOR/BR BL6....28 C3
Newnham St BOL BL1....20 D4
Newport Rd BOLS/LL BL3....39 E2
Newport St BOL BL1....2 E5
  BOLS/LL BL3....3 F5
  FWTH BL4....47 H1
Newquay Av BOLE BL2....33 F1
New Raven Ct BOLS/LL BL3 *....40 C2
New Riven Ct BOLS/LL BL3....40 C2
New Rd CHLYE PR6....7 H4
  WGNE/HIN WN2....25 E4
Newry St BOL BL1....20 B4
Newsham Cl BOLS/LL BL3....2 A6
New Springs BOL BL1 *....19 H4
Newstead Dr BOLS/LL BL3....37 G3
New St BOLS/LL BL3....21 D5
  TOT/BURYW BL8....23 H1
New Tempest Rd HOR/BR BL6....36 C1
New Tong Fld EDGW/EG BL7....10 C5
Newton St BOL BL1....20 C5
Newton Ter BOL BL1 *....20 C5
Newton Wk BOL BL1....20 C5
Newtown Cl SWIN M27....57 H1
New York BOLS/LL BL3....37 F1
Neyland Cl BOL BL1....29 F3
Nicholas St BOLE BL2....3 H2
Nick Hilton's Brow CHLYE PR6....7 G2
Nick Hilton's La CHLYE PR6....7 H1
Nightingale Rd HOR/BR BL6....15 G4
Nightingale St CHLYE PR6....7 E4
Nile St BOLS/LL BL3....2 E7
Ninehouse La BOLS/LL BL3....38 D1
Nixon Rd BOLS/LL BL3....38 A2
Nixon Rd South BOLS/LL BL3....38 A2
Noble St BOLS/LL BL3....2 C7
Noel St BOL BL1....2 D3
Nook Flds BOLE BL2....22 A5
The Nook WALK M28....56 B3
Norbreck St BOLE BL2....31 G2
Norbury Gv BOL BL1....20 D3
  SWIN M27....57 H2
Norden Ct BOLS/LL BL3....38 C1
Norfolk Cl BOLS/LL BL3....40 D1
  WGNE/HIN WN2....42 C2
Norfolk Dr FWTH BL4....39 H4
Norfolk Rd ATH M46....44 C3
Norfolk St WALK M28....47 H3
Normanby Gv SWIN M27....57 G2
Normanby Rd WALK M28....55 G2
Normanby St BOLS/LL BL3....37 H3
  SWIN M27....57 G2
Normandale Av BOL BL1....29 G1
Normandy Crs RAD M26....41 H4
Norris St BOLS/LL BL3....2 C7
  BOLS/LL BL3....40 C2
  FWTH BL4....47 G1
  TYLD M29 *....53 G3
North Av FWTH BL4....39 E5
  TOT/BURYW BL8....13 H2
North Edge LEIGH WN7....52 B5
Northern Cl BOLS/LL BL3....30 A1
Northfield St BOLS/LL BL3....30 A5
North Gv WALK M28....47 G5
Northland Rd BOL BL1....20 D1
Northlands RAD M26....33 G4
North La TYLD M29....53 G5
Northolt Av LEIGH WN7....51 H3
Northolt Dr BOLS/LL BL3....38 D1

North Rd ATH M46....44 B3
North St ATH M46....45 E5
Northumbria St BOLS/LL BL3....30 A5
North V CHLYE PR6....6 D3
North Wy BOL BL1....21 F3
Northwell St LEIGH WN7....51 G3
Northwold Dr BOL BL1....20 B1
Northwood BOLE BL2....21 H3
Northwood Crs BOLS/LL BL3 *....30 A5
Norton Rd WALK M28....54 C4
Norton St BOL BL1....20 D4
Norway St BOL BL1 *....20 B5
Norwich Cl BOLS/LL BL3....37 E1
Norwood Av TYLD M29....53 G5
Norwood Cl CHLYE PR6....7 E4
  WALK M28....56 A3
Norwood Dr SWIN M27....57 F4
Norwood Gv BOL BL1 *....30 A2
Nottingham Dr BOL BL1....30 C1
Nuffield Cl BOL BL1....29 H1
Nugent Rd BOLS/LL BL3....38 C2
Nunnery Rd BOLS/LL BL3....37 H1
Nuthatch Av WALK M28....55 H3
Nut St BOL BL1....20 B5
Nuttall Av BOLS/LL BL3....41 E2
  HOR/BR BL6....16 C4
Nuttall St ATH M46....45 E5

O

Oak Av BOLS/LL BL3....40 D2
  WGNE/HIN WN2....42 C5
Oakbank Dr BOL BL1....20 B1
Oakbarton HOR/BR BL6....36 C1
Oak Coppice BOL BL1....29 G3
Oakdale BOLE BL2....21 H3
Oakdale Dr TYLD M29....54 A5
Oakdene WALK M28....56 D5
Oakenbottom Rd BOLE BL2....31 H4
Oakenclough Dr BOL BL1....19 F5
Oakes St FWTH BL4....48 B1
Oakfield Av ATH M46....44 C4
Oakfield Cl HOR/BR BL6....17 H5
Oakfield Crs WGNE/HIN WN2....25 C5
Oakfield Dr LHULT M38....46 C5
Oakfield Gv FWTH BL4....47 G2
Oakford Wk BOLS/LL BL3....38 A1
Oak Gates EDGW/EG BL7....10 C5
Oakhill Cl BOLE BL2....32 C3
Oakhurst Gv WHTN BL5....43 E1
Oakland Gv BOL BL1 *....19 G5
Oaklands BOL BL1....29 F3
Oaklands Rd SWIN M27....57 F5
Oakleigh Av BOLS/LL BL3....39 E3
Oakley Pk BOL BL1....29 F3
The Oaklings WGNE/HIN WN2....42 C5
Oaks Av BOLE BL2....21 G3
Oaks La BOLE BL2....21 F2
Oak St ATH M46....52 A2
  TYLD M29....53 G2
Oak Tree Ct ATH M46....52 A2
Oakwood Av SWIN M27....49 G4
  WALK M28....56 B1
Oakwood Dr BOL BL1....29 F2
  WALK M28....56 B1
Oakworth Dr BOL BL1....20 B2
Oban Gv BOL BL1....20 C2
Oban St BOL BL1 *....20 B4
Oban Wy WGNE/HIN WN2 *....25 H5
Octagon Ct BOL BL1 *....2 E4
Offerton St HOR/BR BL6....16 C4
Ogden St SWIN M27....57 H4
Okehampton Cl RAD M26....33 G5
Olaf St BOLE BL2....31 F1
Old Barn Pl EDGW/EG BL7....11 E4
Old Chapel La CHLYE PR6 *....7 E5
Old Clough La WALK M28....56 B3
Old Colliers Rw BOL BL1....19 E2
Old Doctors St TOT/BURYW BL8....13 H5
Old Eagley Ms BOL BL1....20 D1
Oldfield Cl WHTN BL5....35 H5
Old Fold Rd WGNE/HIN WN2....25 H5
  WHTN BL5....42 D1
Old Gn BOLE BL2....22 A1
Old Greenwood La HOR/BR BL6....27 F1
Old Hall Clough HOR/BR BL6....28 C3
Old Hall La HOR/BR BL6....28 C1
  WALK M28....56 A4
Old Hall Mill La ATH M46....52 A3
Old Hall St FWTH BL4....48 A1
Old Hall St North BOL BL1 *....2 E4
Oldhams La BOL BL1....20 B2
Old Kiln La BOL BL1....18 D5
Old La HOR/BR BL6....17 H5
  LHULT M38....46 D3
  WHTN BL5....35 F5

Old Lord's Crs HOR/BR BL6....16 D2
Old Manor Pk ATH M46....52 A1
Old Nans La BOLE BL2....22 B5
Old Nursery Fold BOLE BL2....22 A3
Old Oak Cl BOLE BL2....32 D5
Old Oake Cl WALK M28 *....56 A1
Old Quarry La EDGW/EG BL7....10 D3
Old Rake HOR/BR BL6....17 F1
Old Rd BOL BL1....20 C4
Old School La CHLY/EC PR7....14 C2
Oldstead Gv BOLS/LL BL3....37 F1
Old Swan Cl EDGW/EG BL7 *....10 C5
Old Towns Cl TOT/BURYW BL8....13 H5
Old Vicarage WHTN BL5....43 G3
Old Vicarage Gdns WALK M28....47 H5
Old Vicarage Rd HOR/BR BL6....17 H4
Old Wells Cl LHULT M38....47 E2
Old Will's La HOR/BR BL6....16 D1
Olga St BOL BL1....20 B5
Oliver St ATH M46....44 D5
Olive St BOLS/LL BL3....38 B1
Ollerbrook Ct BOL BL1....20 D5
Ollerton St BOL BL1....20 D1
  CHLYE PR6....7 E4
Openshaw Pl FWTH BL4....39 F5
Orchard Av BOL BL1....20 D4
  WALK M28....55 F4
Orchard Cl LEIGH WN7....51 H4
Orchard Gdns BOLE BL2....22 B4
Orchard La LEIGH WN7....51 H4
The Orchard WHTN BL5....35 G4
Orchid Av FWTH BL4....39 F4
Ordsall Av LHULT M38....47 E4
Organ St WGNE/HIN WN2....42 D5
Oriel St BOLS/LL BL3....30 A5
Oriole Cl WALK M28....55 F4
Oriole Dr WALK M28....55 F3
Orlando St BOLE BL2....3 G7
Ormond St BOLS/LL BL3....31 H5
Ormrod St BOLE BL2....21 G2
  BOLS/LL BL3....2 D5
  FWTH BL4....39 G5
Ormside Cl WGNE/HIN WN2....42 D5
Ormskirk Cl TOT/BURYW BL8....33 H2
Ormston Av HOR/BR BL6....16 D2
Ormston Gv WGNE/HIN WN2....51 H4
Ornatus St BOL BL1 *....20 D2
Orwell Rd BOL BL1....19 H5
Osborne Ct ATH M46....44 C5
Osborne Gv BOL BL1....30 A1
  LEIGH WN7....52 D5
Osbourne Cl FWTH BL4....39 H4
Oscar St BOL BL1 *....20 A5
Oscott Av LHULT M38....47 E3
Osmund Av BOLE BL2....31 H3
Osprey Av WHTN BL5....43 E2
Oswald St BOLS/LL BL3....38 A1
Oswestry Cl TOT/BURYW BL8....13 C4
Otterbury Cl TOT/BURYW BL8....23 H5
Oulton St BOL BL1....21 E2
Outwood Av SWIN M27....49 F4
Outwood Gv BOL BL1....20 C2
Overdale Dr BOL BL1....29 G3
Overdene Cl HOR/BR BL6....28 B4
Overgreen BOLE BL2....22 A4
Overshores Rd EDGW/EG BL7....4 A2
Owenington Gv LHULT M38....47 E3
Owlwood Cl LHULT M38....46 C5
Owlwood Dr LHULT M38....46 C5
Owsten Ct HOR/BR BL6....16 B4
Oxford Cl FWTH BL4....38 D5
Oxford Gv BOL BL1....2 A1
Oxford Rd ATH M46....44 B3
  BOLS/LL BL3....40 B2
  HOR/BR BL6....27 H2
Oxford St BOL BL1....2 E4
  CHLY/EC PR7....14 D1
  LEIGH WN7....51 H4
  WGNE/HIN WN2....42 B1
Ox Ga BOLE BL2....21 H2
Ox Hey Cl HOR/BR BL6....27 G2
Ox Hey La HOR/BR BL6....27 H5
Oxlea Gv WHTN BL5....43 G1

P

Packer St BOL BL1....20 A5
Padbury Wy BOLE BL2....22 A5
Paddison St SWIN M27....57 G4
Paddock Cl ATH M46....45 E3
The Paddock WALK M28....56 A4
Paderborn Ct BOL BL1....2 C5
Pailton Cl HOR/BR BL6....28 D4
Paisley Pk FWTH BL4....39 H4
Paiton St BOL BL1....30 A3
Palace St BOL BL1....2 E2
Palatine St BOL BL1....2 E3

Paley St BOL BL1....3
Palin St WGNE/HIN WN2....42
Pall Ml HOR/BR BL6 *....8
Palmer Gv LEIGH WN7....51
Pansy Rd FWTH BL4....39
Panton St HOR/BR BL6....27
Paper Mill Rd EDGW/EG BL7....10
Paramel Av BOLS/LL BL3....32
Paris St BOLS/LL BL3....37
Park Av BOL BL1 *....20
Park Bank ATH M46....45
Park Cottages BOL BL1 *....20
Parkdale Rd BOLE BL2....31
Parkdene Cl BOLE BL2....21
Park Edge WHTN BL5....36
Parkfield Av FWTH BL4....47
  TYLD M29....52
Parkfield Cl LEIGH WN7....52
  TYLD M29....53
Parkfield Dr TYLD M29....53
Parkfield Rd BOLS/LL BL3....38
Parkgate TOT/BURYW BL8....23
Parkgate Dr BOL BL1....20
Park Gv RAD M26....41
  WALK M28....55
Parkham Cl WHTN BL5....43
Park Hill St BOL BL1....2
Parkinson St BOLS/LL BL3....30
Parklands Dr WGNE/HIN WN2....25
The Parklands RAD M26....41
Park La HOR/BR BL6....17
  WGNE/HIN WN2....50
Park Meadow WHTN BL5....36
Park Rd BOL BL1....20
  BOLS/LL BL3....40
  CHLY/EC PR7....14
  RAMS BL0....13
  WALK M28....55
  WGNE/HIN WN2....42
  WHTN BL5....35
  WHTN BL5....36
Park Rw BOL BL1....20
Parkside Av WGNE/HIN WN2....42
Parkside Av WALK M28....55
Parkside St BOLE BL2 *....31
Parks Nook FWTH BL4....47
Parkstone Cl TOT/BURYW BL8....23
Park St ATH M46....45
  BOL BL1....2
  FWTH BL4....48
  TYLD M29....53
Park Vw FWTH BL4....48
Park View Rd BOLS/LL BL3 *....38
Parkway LHULT M38....46
  WHTN BL5....43
Parkway Gv LHULT M38....46
Parkwood Dr WHTN BL5....45
Parnham Cl RAD M26....32
Parr Cl FWTH BL4....39
Parrfield Rd WALK M28....55
Parr Fold Av WALK M28....55
Parrot St BOLS/LL BL3....30
Parr St TYLD M29....53
Parsonage Dr WALK M28....55
Parsonage Rd RAD M26 *....49
  WALK M28....55
Parsonage Wy LEIGH WN7....51
Partington Ct FWTH BL4....39
Partington La SWIN M27....57
Partington St BOLS/LL BL3....38
  BOL BL1....35
Part St WHTN BL5....35
Paton Av BOLS/LL BL3....39
Patricia Dr WALK M28....56
Patterdale Rd BOLE BL2....22
Patterson St BOLS/LL BL3....35
  WHTN BL5....42
Paulette St BOL BL1....20
Paulhan St BOLS/LL BL3....38
Pauline St WGNE/HIN WN2....42
Pavilion Gdns WHTN BL5....35
Pavilion Wk RAD M26....33
Peabody St BOLS/LL BL3....38
Peace St ATH M46....45
  BOLS/LL BL3....30
  TYLD M29....53
Peacock Fold LEIGH WN7....51
Peak Av ATH M46....44
Peak St BOL BL1....20
Pear Tree Ct WGNE/HIN WN2....25
Pear Tree Dr FWTH BL4....47
Pear Tree Gv TYLD M29....54
Peatfield Av SWIN M27....57
Pedder St BOL BL1....20
Peel Cl ATH M46....45
Peel Dr LHULT M38....46
Peel Gv WALK M28....56

l Hall Av TYLD M29....................53 H2
l La LHULT M38...........................46 D4
l Park Crs LHULT M38..............46 D4
l St CHLYE PR6..............................7 F5
WTH BL4......................................40 A5
VHTN BL5.....................................35 G4
lwood Av LHULT M38................47 E4
lwood Gv ATH M46.....................53 E1
amoid St BOL BL2.....................31 F1
ham St BOLS/LL BL3..................38 A2
on Av SWIN M27..........................57 F1
berton St BOL BL1 *.................20 C3
HULT M38....................................47 F4
broke Cl HOR/BR BL6.............16 C3
broke Dr
CNE/HIN WN2............................43 E5
broke St BOL BL1.......................2 B2
arth Rd BOLS/LL BL3.................37 H1
deen Cl RAD M26........................53 G4
dennis Av HOR/BR BL6..............28 D5
dennis Cl RAD M26.....................33 E5
dennis Crs WGNE/HIN WN2.....42 C5
dle Av BOL BL1.............................20 C1
dlebury Fold BOLS/LL BL3......36 D3
dlebury La WGN WN1................24 A4
dlebury St BOL BL1....................20 D4
dle Cl BOL BL1...............................20 B4
dle Dr HOR/BR BL6.....................17 E2
garth Rd HOR/BR BL6...............17 E3
gwern Av BOLS/LL BL3..............29 H5
keth Av TYLD M29.......................53 H5
nine Cl HOR/BR BL6...................17 E2
nine Gv LEIGH WN7....................51 E3
nine Rd HOR/BR BL6..................17 E2
nington Cl LHULT M38..............46 C4
CNE/HIN WN2............................34 A4
nington Green La
CNE/HIN WN2............................34 A3
nington La
CNE/HIN WN2............................24 C1
nington Rd BOLS/LL BL3..........38 D2
nington St
OT/BURYW BL8........................23 G3
ALK M28..56 A1
n St BOLE BL4..............................39 G5
OR/BR BL6...................................17 E4
rhyn Gv ATH M46.......................44 C3
rice Cl RAD M26...........................33 F5
rice Fold WALK M28....................55 F4
rith Av BOL BL1............................29 G1
ALK M28..56 B1
sford Ct BOLE BL2......................22 A1
swick Rd WGNE/HIN WN2.......43 F5
tland Ter BOLE BL2....................30 C1
ydarren Vw BOLS/LL BL3........39 G3
cy St BOL BL1 *............................20 D5
WTH BL4 *.....................................48 A1
endale Ri BOL BL1......................20 C3
ch St BOLS/LL BL3.......................38 A1
WIN M27..57 F4
erborough Dr BOL BL1...............50 D1
erborough Wk BOL BL1............30 C1
erhead Cl BOL BL1......................30 B1
er Martin St HOR/BR BL6.........16 D3
ersfield Wk BOL BL1..................30 C1
er St TYLD M29............................53 F2
HTN BL5..42 C1
el Cl TYLD M29.............................53 G3
eril St BOLS/LL BL3....................37 H2
rist Gn WHTN BL5......................43 G2
Pewfist Spinney
HTN BL5..43 F1
Pewfist WHTN BL5......................43 G1
asant Cl WALK M28....................55 F5
thean St BOLE BL2......................3 H3
WTH BL4..39 G4
ps Av FWTH BL4...........................47 H1
p St BOLS/LL BL3.........................30 B5
ips St LEIGH WN7........................51 G3
ps St WALK M28...........................47 G4
ebe St BOLS/LL BL3 *................38 A1
enix St BOL BL1............................3 G1
WTH BL4..47 H1
Av ATH M46..................................52 A1
Rd BOLS/LL BL3.........................38 B1
ngton Rd FWTH BL4...................48 B2
AD M26..33 H5
ngton St BOLS/LL BL3................2 D7
ng Fld EDGW/EG BL7.................10 C3
ing St BOLS/LL BL3.....................39 E1
lott Rd BOL BL1.............................21 F4
Gv FWTH BL4..............................39 F5
WIN M27..57 F4
ALK M28..56 A3
HTN BL5..43 G1

Pine Meadow RAD M26 ....49 E2
Pine St BOL BL1..............................20 D5
TYLD M29.....................................53 G2
Pinewood Cl BOL BL1..................20 C5
Pinfold Cl WHTN BL5...................43 F2
Pinfold Rd WALK M28.................55 G2
Pinnacle Dr EDGW/EG BL7........10 B2
Pioneer Cl HOR/BR BL6..............17 E3
Pioneer Rd HOR/BR BL6..............17 E3
Pitcombe Cl BOL BL1...................10 B5
Pitfield La BOLE BL2....................22 B4
Pitfield St BOLE BL2......................3 J4
Pitt St RAD M26.............................41 G2
Pixmore Av BOL BL1.....................21 F3
Plantation Av WALK M28.............47 G4
Plantation Rd EDGW/EG BL7......5 F7
Platt Fold Rd LEIGH WN7...........52 A5
Platt Hill Av BOLS/LL BL3..........37 G1
Platt La WHTN BL5........................44 B2
Platt St LEIGH WN7......................51 H5
Playfair St BOL BL1.......................20 D1
Pleasant Gdns BOL BL1................2 C1
Pleasant St TOT/BURYW BL8.....23 H3
Pleasington Dr
TOT/BURYW BL8........................23 G5
Plevna St BOLE BL2........................3 H3
Plodder La FWTH BL4..................38 B5
WHTN BL5.....................................37 G5
Ploughfields WHTN BL5.............35 G2
Plowden Av BOLS/LL BL3............38 A2
Plymouth Dr FWTH BL4..............38 D5
Plymouth Gv RAD M26.................33 F5
Pocket Nook Rd
HOR/BR BL6................................36 B2
Polegate Dr LEIGH WN7.............51 F1
Pole St BOLE BL2............................31 F1
Pondwater Cl WALK M28............46 D5
Poolfield Cl RAD M26...................41 G2
Pool St BOL BL1................................2 D3
Pool Ter BOL BL1...........................19 G5
Poplar Av BOL BL1........................20 D3
BOLE BL2.....................................21 G1
HOR/BR BL6.................................27 G1
Poplar Gv WGNE/HIN WN2........50 D1
WHTN BL5.....................................35 G5
Poplar Rd SWIN M27....................57 H4
WALK M28....................................56 A1
The Poplars CHLY/EC PR7...........14 D1
Poplar St TYLD M29......................53 G2
Porchester Dr RAD M26..............33 E5
Porterfield Dr TYLD M29............53 G3
Portfield Cl BOL BL1.....................29 F2
Porthleven Crs TYLD M29...........54 A3
Portland Pl HOR/BR BL6.............17 E4
Portland Rd WALK M28...............47 G3
Portland St BOLS/LL BL3............20 C5
Portugal St BOLE BL2.....................3 J4
Pott St SWIN M27..........................57 H1
Poulton Av BOLE BL2...................32 A3
Powys St ATH M46.........................53 E2
Praeton Cl ATH M46......................52 A2
Preesall Cl TOT/BURYW BL8.......33 H2
Prenton Wy TOT/BURYW BL8....23 H2
Presall St BOLE BL2 *....................31 G2
Prescot Av ATH M46......................45 E4
TYLD M29.....................................54 A2
Prescott St BOLS/LL BL3 *..........38 A1
LEIGH WN7..................................51 H5
WALK M28....................................47 F5
Prestbury Rd BOL BL1..................21 E2
Presto Gdns BOLS/LL BL3 *........37 H1
Prestolee Rd BOLS/LL BL3..........40 C4
RAD M26..41 E4
Preston St BOLS/LL BL3..............39 F1
Presto St BOLS/LL BL3.................37 H1
FWTH BL4......................................40 A4
Prestwich St ATH M46..................44 B4
Prestwood Cl BOLS/LL BL3.........30 A1
Prestwood Dr BOL BL1.................30 B1
Prestwood Rd FWTH BL4.............39 E4
Pretoria Rd BOLE BL2...................32 A3
Price St FWTH BL4.........................39 H4
Priestley Rd WALK M28................57 E3
Priestners Wy LEIGH WN7..........51 G5
Primrose Av FWTH BL4................39 E4
WALK M28....................................55 F1
Primrose Bank
TOT/BURYW BL8........................13 G5
WALK M28....................................55 F1
Primrose Cl BOLE BL2..................22 C3
Primrose St BOL BL1....................20 D3
FWTH BL4......................................48 A1
Primrose St North TYLD M29....53 G2
Primula Cl BOL BL1.......................20 D3
Prince's Av BOLS/LL BL3.............40 D1
TYLD M29.....................................53 G5
Princess Av ATH M46...................44 C3
FWTH BL4......................................48 B3
Princess Gv FWTH BL4.................39 H5

Princess Rd CHLYE PR6.................7 F4
HOR/BR BL6................................28 B3
Princess St BOL BL1........................3 G4
RAD M26..41 G2
Prince St BOL BL1............................2 D1
Princethorpe Cl HOR/BR BL6.....28 D4
Printers La EDGW/EG BL7...........21 G1
Printshop La ATH M46..................53 E2
Priory La LEIGH WN7...................51 F2
Priory Pl BOLE BL2.......................21 G5
Priory Rd SWIN M27....................57 G3
Progress St BOL BL1.....................30 D1
Prospect Av FWTH BL4................47 H1
Prospect Dr TOT/BURYW BL8....13 H5
Prospect Hl BOLE BL2..................22 B3
Prospect Pl FWTH BL4.................47 G1
Prospect St BOL BL1.....................30 D1
TYLD M29.....................................53 F2
Prosser Av ATH M46.....................52 A1
Providence St BOLS/LL BL3..........3 F7
Pryce St BOL BL1.............................2 D1
Punch La BOLS/LL BL3.................36 D3
Punch St BOLS/LL BL3...................2 B6
The Pungle WHTN BL5.................43 F3
Purbeck Dr HOR/BR BL6.............27 H2
Purbeck Wy TYLD M29.................53 G4
Purcell Cl BOL BL1.........................30 B1
Purple St BOL BL1............................3 F3

Q

Quakerfields WHTN BL5.............43 F1
Quakers Fld TOT/BURYW BL8.....13 H4
Quarlton Dr TOT/BURYW BL8....12 D1
Quarry Pond Rd WALK M28........46 D5
Quarry Rd FWTH BL4...................48 C1
Quebec Pl BOLS/LL BL3...............30 A5
Quebec St BOLS/LL BL3...............30 B5
Queen Ann Dr WALK M28............55 F4
Queen's Av ATH M46....................55 E5
EDGW/EG BL7..............................11 E5
Queensbrook BOL BL1...................2 C3
Queensbury Cl BOL BL1...............20 B2
Queens Cl WALK M28...................54 B4
Queensgate BOL BL1....................29 H2
Queens Pk BOL BL1 *.....................2 A4
Queens Rd BOLS/LL BL3..............37 H1
Queen St BOL BL1............................2 D4
FWTH BL4......................................39 H5
HOR/BR BL6.................................16 C4
LHULT M38....................................47 F5
WHTN BL5.....................................35 G5
Queensway FWTH BL4..................48 B2
WALK M28.....................................55 F3

R

Radbourne Gv BOLS/LL BL3........37 F1
Radcliffe Gv LEIGH WN7.............51 H4
Radcliffe Moor Rd BOLE BL2......32 D5
RAD M26..33 J4
Radcliffe Rd BOLE BL2...................3 J4
BOLS/LL BL3................................32 A5
BOLS/LL BL3................................40 C1
Radelan Gv RAD M26....................41 F1
Radley Cl BOL BL1.........................29 G1
Radnor Cl WGNE/HIN WN2.........42 C5
Radstock Cl BOL BL1....................10 C5
Radway TYLD M29........................54 A2
Raglan St BOL BL1........................20 B2
Raikes La BOLS/LL BL3................31 H5
Raikes Rd BOLS/LL BL3...............31 H5
Raikes Wy BOLS/LL BL3..............31 H5
Railway Rd CHLY/EC PR7..............7 E5
Railway St ATH M46......................44 B4
FWTH BL4......................................40 A4
WGNE/HIN WN2.........................42 A1
Raimond St BOL BL1....................20 A4
Rainbow Dr ATH M46...................44 C1
Rainford St BOLE BL2...................21 G1
Rainham Dr BOL BL1....................30 C1
Rainshaw St BOL BL1....................20 D3
Rake La SWIN M27........................49 H5
Ralph St BOL BL1...........................20 B5
Ramsay Av FWTH BL4..................47 F1
Ramsay St BOL BL1.......................20 C3
Ramsbottom Rd HOR/BR BL6.....16 D4
TOT/BURYW BL8........................12 C2
Ramsden Fold SWIN M27............57 H1
Ramsden St BOLS/LL BL3............31 H5
Ramsey Cl ATH M46......................44 D3
Ram St LHULT M38.......................46 D4
Ramwell Gdns BOLS/LL BL3........2 A7
Ramwells Brow EDGW/EG BL7...10 D4
Ramwells Ct EDGW/EG BL7 *.....11 F4

Ramwells Ms EDGW/EG BL7 *...11 F4
Randal St BOLS/LL BL3................38 A1
Randolph Rd FWTH BL4...............48 B1
Randolph St BOLS/LL BL3.............2 A5
Rands Clough Dr WALK M28.......55 F5
Range St BOLS/LL BL3.................38 B1
Ranicar Steet WGNE/HIN WN2...43 E5
Rankine Ter BOLS/LL BL3 *...........2 B7
Rannoch Rd BOLE BL2.................32 B3
Ranworth Cl BOL BL1...................21 E1
Raphael St BOL BL1......................20 B5
Rasbottom St BOLS/LL BL3............2 B6
Ratcliffe Rd WGNE/HIN WN2......25 G4
Ratcliffe St LEIGH WN7...............51 H5
TYLD M29.....................................53 H2
Rathybank Cl BOL BL1.................19 H5
BOL BL1...30 A1
Raveden Cl BOL BL1.....................20 A4
Ravenfield Gv BOL BL1 *...............2 B1
Ravenhurst Dr BOL BL1..............28 D4
Raven Rd BOLS/LL BL3................37 G1
Ravenscraig Rd LHULT M38........47 F2
Ravensdale Rd BOL BL1...............28 D4
Ravens Holme BOL BL1................29 E3
Ravens Wd BOL BL1......................29 E3
Ravenswood Dr BOL BL1.............29 E3
WGNE/HIN WN2.........................42 A2
Rawcliffe Av BOLE BL2.................32 B3
Rawlinson La CHLY/EC PR7...........6 D3
Rawlinson St HOR/BR BL6..........16 D3
Rawlyn Rd BOL BL1......................29 F1
Rawson Av FWTH BL4..................40 A4
Rawson Rd BOL BL1......................30 A1
Rawson St FWTH BL4...................39 H4
Rawsthorne St BOL BL1...............20 C5
TYLD M29.....................................54 B3
Rayden Crs WHTN BL5.................43 G2
Raymond St SWIN M27................57 H2
The Reach WALK M28...................56 A1
Recreation St BOLE BL2...............22 A2
BOLS/LL BL3................................38 C1
Rectory Gdns WHTN BL5.............43 G4
Red Bank Rd RAD M26.................33 H5
Redbrook Cl FWTH BL4 *.............40 A4
Redcar Rd BOL BL1.......................19 H3
BOLS/LL BL3................................40 C2
Redcot BOL BL1 *...........................29 H3
Reddish Cl BOLE BL2...................22 A2
Redgate Wy FWTH BL4................38 D4
Redhill Gv BOL BL1......................30 C1
Redisher Cl RAMS BL0.................13 H1
Redisher Cft RAMS BL0...............13 H1
Redisher La TOT/BURYW BL8.....13 G1
Red La BOLE BL2...........................31 H1
Redpol Av LEIGH WN7.................52 B5
Redpoll Cl WALK M28...................55 F4
Red Rock La RAD M26..................49 F2
WGN WN1......................................24 B2
Redshank Cl LEIGH WN7.............52 A5
Redshaw Av BOLE BL2..................21 G1
Redstart Gv WALK M28................55 H3
Redstock Cl WHTN BL5................36 A4
Red St ATH M46............................45 E5
Redthorpe Cl BOLE BL2...............31 F1
Redwater Cl WALK M28................55 E5
Red Waters LEIGH WN7...............52 A5
Redwing Rd TOT/BURYW BL8.....13 H2
Redwood WHTN BL5....................43 F2
Reeceton Gdns BOL BL1...............29 G3
Reedham Cl BOL BL1....................30 A2
Reedley Dr WALK M28..................55 G3
Reedmace Cl WALK M28..............56 A2
Reedymoor WHTN BL5................43 G4
Reeves St LEIGH WN7..................51 H5
Regaby Gv WGNE/HIN WN2........42 C3
Regan St BOL BL1..........................20 B4
Regent Av LHULT M38..................47 G4
Regent Dr HOR/BR BL6................28 B3
LEIGH WN7..................................52 D4
Regent Rd HOR/BR BL6...............28 B4
Regents Hl HOR/BR BL6..............28 C4
Regent St ATH M46.......................53 E1
Regent Wk FWTH BL4 *...............39 H5
Regina Crs LEIGH WN7................53 E5
Reginald St BOLS/LL BL3 *..........37 G3
SWIN M27......................................57 F2
Renfrew Dr BOLS/LL BL3.............37 F2
Renfrew Rd WGNE/HIN WN2......25 H5
Renton Rd BOLS/LL BL3...............37 H2
Reservoir St WGNE/HIN WN2.....34 B2
Reynolds Cl WHTN BL5................45 F2
Reynolds Dr WHTN BL5...............45 F1
Rhine Cl TOT/BURYW BL8...........13 H5
Rhode St TOT/BURYW BL8..........23 H1
Rhosleigh Av BOL BL1..................20 C3
Ribble Av BOLE BL2......................32 A3
Ribble Dr FWTH BL4.....................48 D3
WALK M28....................................54 D5

Ribblesdale Rd *BOLS/LL* BL3 ......38 B1
Ribbleton Cl *TOT/BURYW* BL8 ......33 H1
Ribchester Gv *BOLE* BL2 ....32 A1
Richard Gwyn Cl *WHTN* BL5 ......43 F3
Richard St *RAD* M26 ....41 H2
Richelieu St *BOLS/LL* BL3 ....39 E1
Richmond Cl *TOT/BURYW* BL8 ......23 H1
Richmond Dr *LEIGH* WN7 ....53 E4
WALK M28 ....55 E3
Richmond Gdns *BOLS/LL* BL3.......39 F2
Richmond Gv *FWTH* BL4 * 51 H3
LEIGH WN7 ....52 D5
Richmond Rd *WALK* M28 ....54 C4
WGNE/HIN WN2 ....42 C5
Richmond St *HOR/BR* BL6 ....15 G5
Ridgemont Cl *HOR/BR* BL6 ....17 H4
Ridgeway *BOL* BL1 * 2 E3
Ridgway Gates *BOL* BL1 * 2 E3
Ridgmont Dr *HOR/BR* BL6 ....17 H4
WALK M28 ....54 D5
Ridgway *HOR/BR* BL6 ....15 G5
Riding Cl *TYLD* M29 ....54 B4
Riding Ga *BOL* BL2 ....22 A1
Riding Gate Ms *BOLE* BL2 ....22 A1
Riding St *CHLYE* PR6 ....7 E5
Ridyard St *LHULT* M38 ....47 C4
Riefield *BOL* BL1 ....19 H4
Rigby Av *BOL* BL2 * 15 G5
Rigby Ct *BOLS/LL* BL3 ....38 D1
Rigby Gv *LHULT* M38 ....46 C4
Rigby La *BOLE* BL2 ....21 H2
Rigbys Houses *CHLY/EC* PR7 * 14 C1
Rigby St *BOLS/LL* BL3 ....38 D1
WGNE/HIN WN2 ....42 A2
Riley Ct *BOL* BL1 ....30 D1
Riley La *WGNE/HIN* WN2 ....25 F3
Riley St *ATH* M46 ....52 A2
Ringley Gv *BOL* BL1 ....20 C2
Ringley Mdw *RAD* M26 ....49 E1
Ringley Old Brow *RAD* M26..........49 E1
Ringley Rd *RAD* M26...................40 D5
RAD M26 ....49 E1
Ringley Rd West *RAD* M26...........41 G5
Ringlow Av *SWIN* M27 ....57 E4
Ringlow Park Rd *SWIN* M27 ....57 E5
Ringway Av *LEIGH* WN7 ....51 H3
Ripley Dr *WN7* WN7 ....51 H5
Ripley St *BOLE* BL2 ....29 F1
Ripon Av *BOL* BL1 ....29 F1
Ripon Cl *BOLS/LL* BL3 ....40 B2
Ripon St *BOL* BL1 ....29 F1
Rishton Av *BOLS/LL* BL3 ....38 D3
Rishton La *BOLS/LL* BL3 ....38 D2
Riverbanks *BOLS/LL* BL3 ....31 G5
The Riverbank *RAD* M26 ....40 D5
Riverside *BOL* BL1 ....20 D5
Riverside Dr *RAD* M26 ....40 D5
Riversleigh Cl *BOL* BL1 ....19 F4
Riversmeade *EDGW/EG* BL7 ....11 G5
LEIGH WN7 ....52 A5
River St *BOLE* BL2 ....3 G4
Riverview Wk *BOL* BL1 * 30 A4
Rivington Av *CHLYE* PR6 ....7 E5
Rivington Dr *WGNE/HIN* WN2 ......50 B2
Rivington La *CHLYE* PR6 ....15 H1
HOR/BR BL6 ....8 B3
Rivington St *ATH* M46 ....46 D1
HOR/BR BL6 ....15 H5
Rix St *BOL* BL1 ....20 C5
Rixton Dr *TYLD* M29 ....53 H3
Roading Brook Rd *BOLE* BL2 ....22 D4
Robertshaw St *LEIGH* WN7 ....51 G4
Robert St *ATH* M46 * 53 E2
BOLE BL2 * 22 A2
Robinson St *HOR/BR* BL6 ....16 D4
WALK M28 ....55 G2
Rochester Av *BOLE* BL2 ....32 A1
WALK M28 ....55 G2
Rock Av *BOL* BL1 ....20 A5
Rock Fold *EDGW/EG* BL7 * 10 D3
Rockhaven Av *HOR/BR* BL6 ....17 E3
Rock St *HOR/BR* BL6 ....16 D4
Rock Ter *EDGW/EG* BL7 ....10 D5
Rodgers Cl *WHTN* BL5 ....43 G2
Rodgers Wy *WHTN* BL5 ....43 G2
Rodmell Cl *EDGW/EG* BL7 ....10 D5
Rodney St *ATH* M46 * 52 C1
Roebuck St *WGNE/HIN* WN2 ....43 E5
Roe Gn *WALK* M28 ....56 C3
Roe Green Av *WALK* M28 ....56 C3
Rogerstead *BOLS/LL* BL3 * 30 A4
Roland Rd *BOLS/LL* BL3...............30 A5
Roman St *RAD* M26 ....41 G2
Romer St *BOLE* BL2....................31 G3
Romford Av *LEIGH* WN7.............51 H1
Romford Pl *WGNE/HIN* WN2 ....42 A3
Romiley Crs *BOLE* BL2 ....31 H2
Romiley Dr *BOLE* BL2 ....31 H2
Romney Cha *BOL* BL1 ....20 C3
Romney Rd *BOL* BL1 ....19 E5

Romsley Dr *BOLS/LL* BL3.............38 A2
Roocroft Ct *BOL* BL1 ....30 B1
Roocroft Sq *HOR/BR* BL6 ....15 G5
Roosevelt Rd *FWTH* BL4 ....48 B1
Rosamond St *BOLS/LL* BL3 ....38 A1
Roscoe Ct *WHTN* BL5 ....43 H1
Roscoe Lowe Brow
CHLYE PR6 ....7 H5
Roscow Av *BOLE* BL2..................32 A2
Roscow Rd *FWTH* BL4 ....48 C2
Rose Acre *WALK* M28 ....55 F4
Rosebank *HOR/BR* BL6 ....28 C3
Rosebank Cl *BOLE* BL2 ....33 E1
Roseberry St *BOLS/LL* BL3 ....38 A1
Rosebery St *WHTN* BL5 ....35 H5
Rosebury Gv *LEIGH* WN7 ....52 B5
Rosedale Av *ATH* M46.................44 C5
BOL BL1 ....20 C2
Rose Gv *FWTH* BL4 ....48 B1
Rose Hl *BOLE* BL2 ....3 H7
Rose Hill Cl *EDGW/EG* BL7 ....11 E5
Rosehill Rd *SWIN* M27 ....57 H1
Rose Lea *BOLE* BL2 ....22 A3
Rosemary La *WHTN* BL5 ....45 H2
Roseneath Gv *BOLS/LL* BL3 ....38 B2
Roseneath Rd *BOLS/LL* BL3 ....38 B2
Rose St *BOLE* BL2 ....3 G7
Rosewood *WHTN* BL5 ....43 E2
Rossall Cl *BOLE* BL2 ....31 G3
Rossall Rd *BOLE* BL2 ....31 G2
Rossall St *BOLE* BL2 ....31 G3
Ross Dr *SWIN* M27 ....49 G4
Rossini St *BOL* BL1 ....20 B4
Rostherne Gdns *BOLS/LL* BL3 ......37 H1
Rothay Cl *BOLE* BL2 ....32 B1
Rothbury Cl *TOT/BURYW* BL8......37 H1
Rothbury Ct *BOLS/LL* BL3 ....37 H2
Rotherhead Cl *HOR/BR* BL6 ....16 B5
Rothesay Rd *BOLS/LL* BL3 * 37 H2
Rothwell Crs *LHULT* M38.............46 C2
Rothwell La *LHULT* M38 ....46 C3
Rothwell Rd *CHLYE* PR6 ....7 F5
Rothwell St *BOLS/LL* BL3 ....2 C7
WALK M28 ....48 B5
Roughlee Av *SWIN* M27 ....57 F4
Round Hill Wy *BOL* BL1 * 3 F1
Roundthorn La *WHTN* BL5 ....43 G1
Rowan Av *HOR/BR* BL6 ....27 G1
The Rowans *BOL* BL1 ....29 E3
CHLYE PR6 ....7 E4
Rowena St *BOLS/LL* BL3..............39 G3
Rowe St *TYLD* M29 * 53 H3
Rowland Av *ATH* M46 ....52 D1
Rowsley Av *BOL* BL1 ....29 G1
Rowton St *BOLE* BL2 ....21 F4
Roxalina St *BOLS/LL* BL3 ....38 C1
Roxby Cl *WALK* M28 ....47 F5
Royal Court Dr *BOL* BL1 * 2 E1
Royal Dr *LEIGH* WN7 ....52 D5
Royds St *TOT/BURYW* BL8 ....13 H5
Royland Av *BOLS/LL* BL3 ....39 E2
Royle St *WALK* M28 ....55 H1
Roynton Rd *HOR/BR* BL6.............16 D1
Royston Av *BOLE* BL2...................3 K1
Royston Cl *TOT/BURYW* BL8 ....13 H3
Roy St *BOLS/LL* BL3 ....37 H5
Ruabon Crs *WGNE/HIN* WN2 ....42 B4
Ruby St *BOL* BL1 ....20 D4
Rudford Gdns *BOLS/LL* BL3 ....38 D1
Rudolph St *BOLS/LL* BL3..............38 D2
Rufford Cl *BOLS/LL* BL3...............38 B3
Rufford Gv *BOL* BL1 ....38 B3
Ruins La *BOLE* BL2 ....22 A3
Rumworth Rd *HOR/BR* BL6..........28 C4
Rumworth St *BOLS/LL* BL3 ....38 B3
Runnymede Ct *BOLS/LL* BL3 * 2 A7
Rupert St *BOLS/LL* BL3...............38 D2
Rush Acre Cl *RAD* M26 ....41 G2
Rushey Fld *EDGW/EG* BL7............10 D4
Rushey Fold La *BOL* BL1..............20 B5
Rusheylea Cl *BOL* BL1 ....20 B5
Rushford Gv *BOL* BL1 ....20 D3
Rushlake Dr *BOL* BL1 ....30 C1
Rushton Av *LEIGH* WN7 ....51 F3
Rushton Rd *BOL* BL1 ....29 H1
Rushton St *WALK* M28 ....55 H1
Ruskin Av *FWTH* BL4 ....48 B1
Ruskin Rd *BOLS/LL* BL3...............40 D1
Rusland Dr *BOLE* BL2 ....30 A2
Russell Cl *BOL* BL1 ....30 A5
Russell Ct *FWTH* BL4 * 40 A5
LHULT M38 ....47 C5
Russell St *ATH* M46 ....44 C5
FWTH BL4.............................47 H1
LHULT M38 ....47 C5
WGNE/HIN WN2 ....51 E1
Rutherford Dr *WHTN* BL5 ....45 F1
Rutherglen Dr *BOLS/LL* BL3 ....29 F4
Ruth St *BOLE* BL2 ....2 C2

Rutland Av *ATH* M46 ....45 F3
SWIN M27 ....57 H1
Rutland Cl *BOLS/LL* BL3 ....40 D1
Rutland Gv *BOL* BL1 ....30 A1
FWTH BL4 * 47 G1
Rutland Rd *TYLD* M29 ....53 F1
WALK M28 ....55 H2
WGNE/HIN WN2 ....42 B2
Rutland St *BOLS/LL* BL3 ....38 B1
SWIN M27 ....57 G2
Rydal Av *WGNE/HIN* WN2 ....42 A3
Rydal Cl *HOR/BR* BL6 ....15 G4
TYLD M29 ....53 G4
Rydal Ct *BOL* BL1 * 29 F1
Rydal Crs *SWIN* M27 ....57 H5
WALK M28 ....56 A2
Rydal Gv *FWTH* BL4 ....46 D1
Rydal Rd *BOL* BL1 ....29 G2
BOLS/LL BL3 ....40 C2
Ryder St *BOL* BL1 ....20 A5
Ryde St *BOLS/LL* BL3 * 37 G1
Rydley St *BOLE* BL2 ....3 J5
Ryeburn Dr *BOLE* BL2 ....21 F2
Ryecroft Av *TOT/BURYW* BL8.......23 H1
Ryecroft Rd *WHTN* BL5 ....35 F2
Ryefield St *BOL* BL1 ....31 E1
Rye Hl *WHTN* BL5 * 35 H5
Ryelands *WHTN* BL5 ....35 H5
Ryelands Ct *WHTN* BL5 * 35 H5
Ryley Av *BOLS/LL* BL3 ....29 H5
Ryley St *BOLS/LL* BL3 * 2 A6

S

Sabden Rd *BOL* BL1 * 19 E5
Sackville St *BOLE* BL2 * 31 G3
Saddleback Cl *WALK* M28............55 F5
Saddle St *BOLE* BL2 ....21 F5
Sadler St *BOLS/LL* BL3 ....39 E1
St Andrews Ct *BOL* BL1 * 2 E4
St Andrews Rd *HOR/BR* BL6.........28 A3
RAD M26 ....33 H4
St Andrew's Vw *RAD* M26 ....33 H4
St Anne's Av *ATH* M46................53 E2
St Annes Meadow
TOT/BURYW BL8......................13 H5
St Annes Rd *HOR/BR* BL6 ....17 H5
St Anns St *SWIN* M27 ....57 G3
St Ann St *BOL* BL1 ....30 C1
St Aubin's Rd *BOLE* BL2 ....3 J6
St Augustine St *BOL* BL1 ....20 B5
St Austell Av *TYLD* M29 ....54 A3
St Austell Dr *TOT/BURYW* BL8......13 H2
St Bartholomew St
BOLS/LL BL3 ....39 E1
St Bede's Av *BOLS/LL* BL3 ....37 H3
St Bees Rd *BOLE* BL2 ....21 C5
St Brides Cl *HOR/BR* BL6 ....16 C3
St Catherines Dr *FWTH* BL4..........38 D5
St Clair Rd *TOT/BURYW* BL8 * 13 H1
St Clare Ter *HOR/BR* BL6 * 27 E1
St David's Crs *WGNE/HIN* WN2.....25 F5
St Dominics Ms *BOLS/LL* BL3........38 A2
St Edmund St *BOL* BL1 ....2 D3
St Elizabeth's Rd
WGNE/HIN WN2 ....25 F5
St Ethelbert's Av *BOLS/LL* BL3 ......29 H5
St George's Av *WHTN* BL5 ....43 G4
St George's Ct *BOL* BL1 * 2 E2
TYLD M29 ....53 F3
St George's Crs *WALK* M28 ....55 H1
St George's Pl *ATH* M46 * 44 B4
St George's Rd *BOL* BL1...............2 E2
St Georges Sq *BOL* BL1 * 3 F2
St George's St *BOL* BL1 * 3 F2
TYLD M29 ....53 F3
St Germain St *FWTH* BL4 ....39 G5
St Gregorys Cl *FWTH* BL4............47 G1
St Helena Rd *BOL* BL1 ....2 C2
St Helens Rd *BOLS/LL* BL3 ....38 A1
WHTN BL5 ....37 G4
St Heliers St *BOLS/LL* BL3 ....38 B1
St James Av *BOLE* BL2 ....32 A2
St James Crs *WGNE/HIN* WN2 ......50 B3
St James St *FWTH* BL4................47 F1
WHTN BL5 ....43 H3
St John's Av *WHTN* BL5 ....35 F2
St Johns Ct *HOR/BR* BL6 ....36 B1
WHTN BL5 ....35 G2
St John's Rd *HOR/BR* BL6 ....36 B2
WALK M28 ....54 D4
WGNE/HIN WN2 ....25 F5
St John's St *FWTH* BL4 ....40 A5
St John St *ATH* M46 ....44 D5
HOR/BR BL6 ....16 D4
WALK M28 ....47 G4
St Johns Wd *HOR/BR* BL6 ....36 B1

St Joseph St *BOL* BL1 20
St Katherines Dr *HOR/BR* BL6.......15
St Kilda Av *FWTH* BL4 48
St Leonard's Av *HOR/BR* BL6........27
St Margaret's Cl *BOL* BL1 * 29
St Margaret's Rd *BOL* BL1 29
St Mark's Crs *WALK* M28 55
St Mark's St *BOLS/LL* BL3 30
St Mark's Vw *BOLS/LL* BL3 * 30
St Marks Wk *BOLS/LL* BL3 38
St Mary's Av *BOLS/LL* BL3 29
St Mary's Cl *ATH* M46 53
WGNE/HIN WN2 * 25
St Mary's Rd *WALK* M28 47
WGNE/HIN WN2 25
St Matthews Gra *BOL* BL1 * 30
St Matthews Wk *BOL* BL1 * 30
St Mawes Ct *RAD* M26 * 49
St Michael's Av *ATH* M46 52
BOLS/LL BL3
St Michaels Cl *TOT/BURYW* BL8 ...33
St Osmund's Dr *BOLE* BL2 32
St Osmund's Gv *BOLE* BL2 32
St Paul's Cl *CHLYE* PR6 7
St Pauls Ct *WALK* M28 55
St Pauls Rd *WALK* M28 * 56
St Peter's Av *BOL* BL1 19
St Peters Rd *SWIN* M27 57
St Peter's Ter *FWTH* BL4 47
St Peter's Wy *BOL* BL1 * 3
BOLE BL2 3
BOLS/LL BL3 39
St Philip's Av *BOLS/LL* BL3 38
St Richards Cl *ATH* M46 44
St Stephen's Cl *BOLE* BL2 31
St Thomas St *BOL* BL1 * 2
St Williams Av *BOLS/LL* BL3 38
Salcombe Av *BOLE* BL2 33
Salcombe Gv *BOLE* BL2 33
Sale La *TYLD* M29 54
WALK M28 54
Salford Rd *WHTN* BL5 37
Salisbury Av *WGNE/HIN* WN2.......42
Salisbury Rd *HOR/BR* BL6 27
RAD M26 33
SWIN M27 57
Salisbury St *BOLS/LL* BL3 38
Salisbury Ter *BOLS/LL* BL3 41
Salisbury Wy *TYLD* M29 53
Salop St *BOLE* BL2 3
Saltergate *BOLS/LL* BL3 35
Salters Ct *ATH* M46 44
Salterton Dr *BOLS/LL* BL3 37
Saltram Cl *RAD* M26...................33
Saltwood Gv *BOL* BL1 30
Samuel St *ATH* M46 53
Sandalwood *WHTN* BL5 43
Sand Banks *BOL* BL1 20
Sanderling Cl *WHTN* BL5 43
Sanderson Cl *WALK* M28 56
Sandfield Dr *HOR/BR* BL6 28
Sandford Cl *BOLE* BL2 22
Sandgate Av *RAD* M26 48
Sandgate Cl *LEIGH* WN7 51
Sandham St *BOLS/LL* BL3 38
Sandham Wk *BOLS/LL* BL3 * 38
Sandhill Cl *BOLS/LL* BL3 38
Sand Hole Rd *FWTH* BL4 48
Sandhurst Cl *BOLE* BL2 32
Sandhurst Dr *BOLE* BL2 32
Sandileigh Dr *BOL* BL1 21
Sandiway Cl *WHTN* BL5 35
Sandon St *BOLS/LL* BL3 38
Sandown Crs *BOLS/LL* BL3 40
Sandown Rd *BOLE* BL2................22
Sandpiper Cl *FWTH* BL4 48
Sandray Cl *BOLS/LL* BL3 29
Sandridge Cl *FWTH* BL4 40
Sandringham Cl *CHLY/EC* PR7 14
Sandringham Dr *LEIGH* WN7........53
Sandringham Rd *HOR/BR* BL6.......17
WALK M28 55
WGNE/HIN WN2 55
Sandwich St *WALK* M28 55
Sandwick Crs *BOLS/LL* BL3 30
Sandwood Av *BOLS/LL* BL3 38
Sandyacre Cl *WHTN* BL5 35
Sandybrook Cl *TOT/BURYW* BL8...38
Sandygate Cl *SWIN* M27 57
Sandy Gv *SWIN* M27 57
Sandyhills *BOLS/LL* BL3 38
Sandy La *CHLY/EC* PR7 14
WGNE/HIN WN2 42
Sandy Pk *WGNE/HIN* WN2...........42
Sandy Wy *WGNE/HIN* WN2..........42
Sapling Rd *BOLS/LL* BL3 30
Sarah St *WGNE/HIN* WN2 50
Saunders Ms *CHLY/EC* PR7 14
Saunton Av *BOLE* BL2 32

ck Av *BOLE* BL2 .... 32 A3
lle Rd *RAD* M26 .... 33 H3
lle St *BOLE* BL2 .... 3 G4
ours Ter *BOLS/LL* BL3 * 30 A5
st *BOL* BL1 .... 20 C5
y Av *EDGW/EG* BL7 .... 10 D4
on St *RAD* M26 .... 41 H2
at Rw *HOR/BR* BL6 * 18 C4
dale Av *BOL* BL1 .... 29 G1
gill Rd *BOLS/LL* BL3 .... 37 G1
thwood Cl *BOLE* BL2 .... 22 A2
vfell Av *BOLE* BL2 .... 21 F5
ofield La *ATH* M46 .... 43 H5
oles Bank *HOR/BR* BL6 ...... 16 C3
sley St *BOLE* BL2 .... 31 E5
ol Brow *WALK* M28 .... 56 B5
ol Hl *BOL* BL1 .... 2 D1
ol La *EDGW/EG* BL7 .... 4 D1
GNE/HIN* WN2 .... 24 C2
ol St *ATH* M46 .... 52 B1
DLS/LL* BL3 .... 40 D2
DGW/EG* BL7 .... 10 D5
OR/BR* BL6 .... 17 E4
IGH* WN7 .... 51 G3
AD* M29 .... 41 H2
LD* M29 .... 53 F3
LD* M29 .... 53 F5
HTN* BL5 .... 35 G5
ell St *TOT/BURYW* BL8 ...... 23 H2
ton Av *BOLE* BL2 .... 32 B3
ton St *BOL* BL1 * 30 A2
La *WGNE/HIN* WN2 .... 25 H4
t Av *WGNE/HIN* WN2 .... 42 A2
st *RAD* M26 .... 49 F1
th St *BOL* BL1 .... 35 G3
vcroft St *BOLE* BL2 .... 31 F1
orth Av *ATH* M46 .... 44 C4
orth Rd *BOL* BL1 .... 20 C2
hwaite Cl *TYLD* M29 .... 53 G4
hwaite Rd *FWTH* BL4 .... 46 D1
on Rd *BOL* BL1 .... 20 A5
nd Av *ATH* M46 .... 44 D4
OL* BL1 .... 29 H3
DLS/LL* BL3 .... 40 B1
nd St *BOL* BL1 .... 19 F3
ion St *BOL* BL1 .... 2 E5
ion Cl *ATH* M46 .... 44 C5
ion Gdns *RAD* M26 .... 40 C5
ion La *RAD* M26 .... 40 C5
ion St *BOLS/LL* BL3 * 40 D2
LULT* M38 .... 46 D3
HTN* BL5 .... 35 G5
efield Dr *BOL* BL1 .... 19 H4
efield Rd *RAD* M26 .... 41 H5
emoor V *BOLE* BL2 .... 22 B5
dey Dr *WHTN* BL5 .... 43 G3
wick Cl *ATH* M46 .... 45 E5
HTN* BL5 .... 43 H2
ley Av *LHULT* M38 .... 47 F4
t St *BOL* BL1 .... 30 A3
on Av *ATH* M46 .... 44 C3
on Dr *SWIN* M27 .... 57 F5
ALK* M28 .... 56 C5
on La *HOR/BR* BL6 .... 27 G1
on Rd *BOL* BL1 .... 19 H5
WIN* M27 .... 57 H2
ourne Cl *WHTN* BL5 .... 36 A4
ourne St *LEIGH* WN7 .... 51 H4
rk Rd *BOL* BL1 .... 20 B2
yn St *BOLE* BL2 .... 3 H5
CH* WN7 .... 51 H5
nicar La *WGN* WN1 .... 24 A5
e Cl *TOT/BURYW* BL8 .... 23 H5
e St *BOLS/LL* BL3 .... 38 C2
DLS/LL* BL3 .... 41 E3
n Oaks *LEIGH* WN7 .... 52 A5
noaks Dr *BOLS/LL* BL3 ...... 38 C2
rn Wy *WGNE/HIN* WN2 ...... 43 E5
rn Wy *FWTH* BL4 .... 48 D3
ell Wy *LHULT* M38 .... 46 D5
nour Cl *BOL* BL1 .... 21 G1
nour Gv *FWTH* BL4 * 39 E4
nour Rd *BOL* BL1 .... 20 D4
nour St *BOLE* BL2 .... 21 G1
kleton Gv *BOL* BL1 .... 19 F5
le La *CHLY/EC* PR6 .... 6 B3
well Gv *LEIGH* WN7 .... 51 H3
ly La *EDGW/EG* BL7 .... 21 F1
tesbury Av *HOR/BR* BL6 ...... 27 H2
tesbury Rd *SWIN* M27 ...... 57 H4
erley La *ATH* M46 .... 45 F4
erley Rd *TYLD* M29 .... 53 F2
espeare Av *RAD* M26 ...... 41 G1
espeare Rd *SWIN* M27 ...... 57 F3
bourne Rd *WALK* M28 ...... 47 G5
ebrook Cl *ATH* M46 .... 52 A1
emere Ct *ATH* M46 .... 52 A1

Shalewood Ct *ATH* M46 ...... 52 A1
Shalfleet Cl *BOLE* BL2 ...... 22 A2
Shanklin Wk *BOLS/LL* BL3 ...... 31 G5
Shap Dr *WALK* M28 .... 56 B1
Sharman St *BOLS/LL* BL3 ...... 31 F5
Sharnford Cl *BOLE* BL2 ...... 3 J6
Sharples Av *BOL* BL1 .... 20 C1
Sharples Dr *TOT/BURYW* BL8 ...... 23 H3
Sharples Gn *EDGW/EG* BL7 ...... 4 D3
Sharples Hall Dr *BOL* BL1 ...... 20 D1
Sharples Hall Fold *BOL* BL1 ...... 20 D1
Sharples Hall Ms *BOL* BL1 ...... 20 D1
Sharples Pk *BOL* BL1 .... 20 D3
Sharp St *WALK* M28 .... 48 A5
Shaving La *WALK* M28 .... 55 H2
Shawbrook Av *WALK* M28 ...... 55 F3
Shawbury Cl *HOR/BR* BL6 ...... 25 H1
Shawes Dr *CHLYE* PR6 ...... 7 G5
Shaw Rd *HOR/BR* BL6 .... 16 D2
Shaw St *BOLS/LL* BL3 .... 2 C7
FWTH BL4 * 39 G3
Shearwater Av *TYLD* M29 ...... 53 G3
Shearwater Dr *WALK* M28 ...... 47 G5
WHTN BL5 .... 43 F2
The Sheddings *BOLS/LL* BL3 ...... 39 E1
Sheep Gate Dr *TOT/BURYW* BL8 ...... 23 G2
Sheep House La *HOR/BR* BL6 ...... 8 B2
Sheephouse La *HOR/BR* BL6 ...... 8 C2
Shelbourne Av *BOL* BL1 ...... 19 H5
Shelley Rd *LHULT* M38 * 47 E3
WHTN M27 .... 57 F3
Shelley St *LEIGH* WN7 .... 51 E4
Shelley Wk *BOL* BL1 .... 30 B1
Shepherd Cross St *BOL* BL1 ...... 30 A1
Shepherds Cl *HOR/BR* BL6 ...... 15 C4
TOT/BURYW BL8 .... 13 H3
Shepherd's Dr *HOR/BR* BL6 ...... 18 A4
Shepherd St *TOT/BURYW* BL8 ...... 13 H4
Shepley Av *BOLS/LL* BL3 ...... 30 A5
Shepton Cl *BOL* BL1 .... 10 B5
Sherborne Av *WGNE/HIN* WN2 ...... 42 C3
Sherbourne Cl *RAD* M26 ...... 33 F5
Sherbourne Rd *BOLE* BL2 ...... 29 G1
Sheriffs Dr *TYLD* M29 .... 54 B2
Sheriff St *BOLE* BL2 .... 31 F1
Sheringham Dr *SWIN* M27 ...... 57 H5
Sheringham Pl *BOLS/LL* BL3 ...... 30 B5
Sherwood Av *RAD* M26 ...... 33 H2
TYLD M29 .... 53 C5
Sherwood Cl *TOT/BURYW* BL8 ...... 13 H5
Sherwood St *BOL* BL1 .... 20 D4
Shield Dr *WALK* M28 .... 57 E3
Shiel St *WALK* M28 .... 47 H5
Shiffnall St *BOLE* BL2 .... 3 G5
Shillingford Rd *FWTH* BL4 ...... 39 G5
Shillingstone Cl *BOLE* BL2 ...... 22 C4
Shillingten Cl *WALK* M28 ...... 46 D5
Shilton Gdns *BOLS/LL* BL3 ...... 2 C7
Shipgate *BOL* BL1 .... 3 F3
Shipham Cl *LEIGH* WN7 ...... 51 F4
Shipton St *BOL* BL1 .... 29 H1
Shireburn Av *BOLE* BL2 ...... 31 G2
Shires Cl *WGNE/HIN* WN2 ...... 42 A4
Shorefield Mt *EDGW/EG* BL7 ...... 10 C4
Shoreswood *BOL* BL1 .... 20 B2
Shorland St *SWIN* M27 .... 57 E4
Shorrocks St *TOT/BURYW* BL8 ...... 23 H4
Shortland Pl *WGNE/HIN* WN2 ...... 50 C5
Shrewsbury Rd *BOLS/LL* BL3 ...... 29 H2
Shrewsbury Wy *WGNE/HIN* WN2 ...... 42 B2
Shudehill Rd *WALK* M28 ...... 55 E2
Shurdington Rd *ATH* M46 ...... 45 F3
Shurmer St *BOLS/LL* BL3 ...... 38 A1
Shuttle Hillock Rd
WGNE/HIN WN2 .... 50 B4
Shuttle St *TYLD* M29 .... 53 F2
WGNE/HIN WN2 .... 50 B4
Sidford Cl *BOLS/LL* BL3 .... 31 H5
Sidney St *BOLS/LL* BL3 .... 3 F7
Siemens St *HOR/BR* BL6 ...... 17 E5
Silchester Wy *BOLE* BL2 ...... 32 A1
Silkhey Gv *WALK* M28 .... 55 H2
Silk St *WHTN* BL5 * 35 G4
Silverdale Rd *BOL* BL1 .... 30 A3
FWTH BL4 .... 39 E4
WHTN WN2 .... 42 B3
Silverton Gv *BOL* BL1 .... 20 D3
Silverwell La *BOL* BL1 .... 3 F4
Silverwell St *BOL* BL1 .... 3 F4
HOR/BR BL6 .... 16 D3
Silverwell Yd *BOL* BL1 * 3 F4
Silvester St *HOR/BR* BL6 * 15 H5
Simonbury Cl *TOT/BURYW* BL8 ...... 23 H5
Simpson Gv *WALK* M28 ...... 55 E5
Simpson Rd *WALK* M28 ...... 55 F5
Sindsley Gv *BOLS/LL* BL3 ...... 38 C2
Sindsley Rd *SWIN* M27 ...... 57 F1
Singleton Av *BOLE* BL2 ...... 32 B3
HOR/BR BL6 .... 17 E2

Singleton Gv *WHTN* BL5 ...... 36 B5
Singleton St *RAD* M26 .... 41 F1
Sion St *RAD* M26 .... 41 H1
Sixpools Gv *WALK* M28 ...... 55 G3
Sixth Av *BOL* BL1 .... 29 H3
BOLS/LL BL3 .... 40 B1
Skagen Ct *BOL* BL1 .... 30 C1
Skelton St *BOLE* BL2 .... 32 B2
Skelwith Av *BOLS/LL* BL3 ...... 38 D3
Skipton Av *WGNE/HIN* WN2 ...... 42 C4
Skipton Cl *TOT/BURYW* BL8 ...... 23 H4
Skipton St *BOLE* BL2 .... 31 G3
Skipton Wk *BOLE* BL2 ...... 31 G3
Slackey Brow *FWTH* BL4 ...... 49 E3
Slackey Fold *WGNE/HIN* WN2 ...... 50 D2
Slack Fold La *FWTH* BL4 ...... 38 B4
Slack La *BOLE* BL2 .... 12 A5
WHTN BL5 .... 35 H3
Slack's La *CHLYE* PR6 .... 7 G2
Slade St *BOLS/LL* BL3 .... 40 C2
Slaidburn Av *BOLE* BL2 .... 32 B4
Slaidburn Dr *TOT/BURYW* BL8 ...... 23 G4
Slater Av *HOR/BR* BL6 ...... 16 D5
Slaterfield *BOLS/LL* BL3 ...... 30 C5
Slater La *BOL* BL1 .... 3 H1
BOL BL1 .... 31 E1
Slater's Nook *WHTN* BL5 ...... 35 G4
Slater St *BOL* BL1 .... 2 D1
FWTH BL4 .... 39 G2
Sledmere Cl *BOL* BL1 ...... 20 D5
Slimbridge Cl *BOLE* BL2 ...... 32 C1
Sloane St *BOLS/LL* BL3 ...... 37 H2
Smallbridge Cl *WALK* M28 ...... 55 G3
Smallbrook La *LEIGH* WN7 ...... 43 G5
Smeaton St *HOR/BR* BL6 * 17 E2
Smedley Av *BOLS/LL* BL3 ...... 39 E2
Smethurst La *BOLS/LL* BL3 ...... 37 H3
Smithills Croft Rd *BOL* BL1 ...... 19 H4
Smithills Dean Rd *BOL* BL1 ...... 19 G2
Smithills Dr *BOL* BL1 .... 19 F5
Smith La *EDGW/EG* BL7 ...... 10 D4
Smith's La *WGNE/HIN* WN2 ...... 50 C3
Smith's Rd *BOLS/LL* BL3 ...... 3 K5
Smith St *ATH* M46 * 44 C5
WALK M28 .... 47 H5
WGNE/HIN WN2 .... 25 G5
Smithwood Av *WGNE/HIN* WN2 ...... 42 B2
Smithy Cft *EDGW/EG* BL7 ...... 10 D4
Smithy Hl *BOLS/LL* BL3 ...... 37 G1
Smyrna St *RAD* M26 .... 41 H1
Snape St *RAD* M26 .... 33 H5
Snipe St *BOLS/LL* BL3 .... 30 D5
Snowden St *BOL* BL1 .... 2 C2
Snowdon Dr *HOR/BR* BL6 ...... 17 E2
Snow Hill Rd *BOLS/LL* BL3 ...... 31 H5
Snydale Cl *WHTN* BL5 .... 36 A3
Snydale Wy *BOLS/LL* BL3 ...... 36 B3
Sofa St *BOL* BL1 .... 29 H1
Soham Cl *WGNE/HIN* WN2 ...... 42 A4
Soho St *BOL* BL1 .... 2 E5
Solent Dr *BOLS/LL* BL3 .... 38 B2
Solway Cl *BOLS/LL* BL3 ...... 38 B2
SWIN M27 .... 49 G4
Somerdale Av *BOL* BL1 ...... 29 F2
Somersby Dr *EDGW/EG* BL7 ...... 10 D4
Somersby Wk *BOLS/LL* BL3 * 30 D5
Somerset Av *TYLD* M29 ...... 45 F5
Somerset Rd *ATH* M46 .... 44 C4
BOL BL1 .... 29 H2
Somerton Rd *BOLE* BL2 ...... 32 B4
Somerville Av *BOL* BL1 ...... 20 A4
Somerville Sq *BOL* BL1 ...... 20 A4
Somerville St *BOL* BL1 ...... 20 A4
Sonning Dr *BOLS/LL* BL3 ...... 37 G3
South Av *FWTH* BL4 .... 49 E3
Southbrook Gv *BOLS/LL* BL3 ...... 38 D2
Southcourt *LEIGH* WN7 ...... 51 E5
Southdown Dr *WALK* M28 ...... 54 D5
South Dr *BOLE* BL2 .... 32 C3
Southend St *BOLS/LL* BL3 ...... 38 A2
Southern St *WALK* M28 ...... 47 H5
Southfield Dr *WHTN* BL5 ...... 43 H1
Southfield St *BOLS/LL* BL3 ...... 39 F1
Southgate *BOLE* BL2 .... 22 A3
South Gv *WALK* M28 .... 55 E5
Southgrove Av *BOL* BL1 ...... 20 C1
Southleigh Dr *BOLE* BL2 ...... 32 A4
Southmoor Wk *BOLS/LL* BL3 * 30 C5
Southover *WHTN* BL5 .... 48 A2
South Royd St *TOT/BURYW* BL8 ...... 13 H5
South St *ATH* M46 .... 52 E2
BOLS/LL BL3 .... 38 C2
South Vw *ATH* M46 .... 44 C5
South View St *BOLE* BL2 ...... 31 G3
Southwell Cl *BOL* BL1 .... 2 C1
Southwood Cl *BOLS/LL* BL3 ...... 38 D3
Sovereign Fold Rd *LEIGH* WN7 ...... 51 G3
Sowerby Cl *TOT/BURYW* BL8 ...... 23 H5

Spa Crs *LHULT* M38 .... 47 E2
Spa Gv *LHULT* M38 .... 47 E2
Spa La *LHULT* M38 .... 47 E2
Spa Rd *ATH* M46 .... 44 C3
BOL BL1 .... 2 B5
Sparta Av *WALK* M28 .... 55 G1
Spencer Av *BOLS/LL* BL3 ...... 41 E2
Spenser Av *RAD* M26 .... 41 C1
Spindle Cft *FWTH* BL4 ...... 47 H1
Spindlepoint Dr *WALK* M28 ...... 55 G3
Spindle Wk *WHTN* BL5 ...... 35 H3
Spingfield St *BOLS/LL* BL3 ...... 39 E1
Spiningdale *LHULT* M38 ...... 46 B2
Spinners Ms *BOL* BL1 .... 2 D1
Spinney Nook *BOLE* BL2 ...... 21 H5
The Spinney *EDGW/EG* BL7 ...... 11 G2
WALK M28 * 57 E5
Spinningfields *BOL* BL1 * 2 A1
Spinning Meadow *BOL* BL1 ...... 2 B1
Spinning Mdw *BOL* BL1 ...... 2 B1
Sportside Av *WALK* M28 ...... 47 H5
Sportside Cl *WALK* M28 ...... 47 H5
Sportside Gv *WALK* M28 ...... 47 H4
Springburn Cl *HOR/BR* BL6 ...... 27 F1
WALK M28 .... 55 G5
Spring Cl *TOT/BURYW* BL8 ...... 23 G1
Spring Clough Av *WALK* M28 ...... 56 B1
Spring Clough Dr *WALK* M28 ...... 56 B1
Springfield Rd *BOLE* BL2 ...... 49 E2
Springfield Gdns *FWTH* BL4 ...... 48 C2
Springfield Rd *ATH* M46 ...... 45 F2
BOL BL1 .... 10 C5
CHLYE PR6 .... 7 E4
FWTH BL4 .... 39 E4
FWTH BL4 .... 48 B2
HOR/BR BL6 .... 27 F2
Spring Gdns *BOLE* BL2 ...... 22 B3
HOR/BR BL6 .... 16 D3
Springlawn *BOL* BL1 .... 29 F2
Springlawns *BOL* BL1 * 29 F2
Springside Av *WALK* M28 ...... 48 A5
Springside Cl *WALK* M28 ...... 48 A5
Springside Gv *WALK* M28 ...... 48 A5
Spring St *BOLS/LL* BL3 ...... 30 D5
FWTH BL4 .... 39 H4
TOT/BURYW BL8 .... 13 G5
TOT/BURYW BL8 .... 23 H3
Spring Vale Dr *TOT/BURYW* BL8 ...... 23 G1
Spring Vale St *TOT/BURYW* BL8 ...... 23 H1
Springwater Cl *BOLE* BL2 ...... 22 A4
Squires La *TYLD* M29 .... 53 E3
Squirrel La *HOR/BR* BL6 ...... 16 C3
Stafford Rd *SWIN* M27 .... 57 H3
WALK M28 .... 55 H1
Stainforth Cl *TOT/BURYW* BL8 ...... 23 H4
Stainton Cl *RAD* M26 .... 41 H1
Stainton Rd *RAD* M26 ...... 33 G5
Stamford St *ATH* M46 ...... 45 E4
Stanbourne Dr *BOL* BL1 ...... 20 D3
Stancliffe Gv *WGNE/HIN* WN2 ...... 55 G4
Standfield Dr *WALK* M28 ...... 55 E4
Standish St *TYLD* M29 .... 53 G3
Stanford Cl *RAD* M26 * 49 E1
Stanhope St *LEIGH* WN7 ...... 51 F5
Stanier Pl *HOR/BR* BL6 ...... 17 E5
Stanley Cl *WHTN* BL5 .... 44 A1
Stanley Dr *LEIGH* WN7 ...... 51 F3
Stanley Gv *HOR/BR* BL6 ...... 27 F1
Stanley La *WGNE/HIN* WN2 ...... 25 G3
Stanley Ms *BOLE* BL2 .... 31 H3
Stanley Park Wk *BOLE* BL2 ...... 31 G2
Stanley Rd *BOL* BL1 .... 29 H1
FWTH BL4 .... 38 C5
RAD M26 .... 33 G4
WALK M28 .... 55 H1
WGNE/HIN WN2 .... 25 G4
Stanley St *ATH* M46 .... 52 C1
Stanley St South *BOLS/LL* BL3 ...... 2 C5
Stanmere Ct *TOT/BURYW* BL8 ...... 12 D1
Stanmoor Dr *WGNE/HIN* WN2 ...... 25 C5
Stanmore Dr *BOLS/LL* BL3 ...... 30 A5
Stanrose Cl *EDGW/EG* BL7 ...... 10 C3
Stansfield Cl *BOLE* BL2 * 31 G3
Stansfield Rd *BOLE* BL2 ...... 3 J2
Stanway Av *BOLS/LL* BL3 * 2 B6
Stanway Cl *BOLS/LL* BL3 * 2 B6
Stanwell Rd *SWIN* M27 ...... 57 G4
Stanworth Av *BOLE* BL2 ...... 32 A3
Stapleford Cl *WHTN* BL5 ...... 45 G2
Staplehurst Cl *LEIGH* WN7 ...... 51 E1
Stapleton Av *BOL* BL1 .... 29 E2
Starbeck Cl *TOT/BURYW* BL8 ...... 23 H5
Starcliffe St *BOLS/LL* BL3 ...... 39 H3
Starkie Rd *BOLE* BL2 .... 3 K3
BOLE BL2 .... 31 F1
Starkie St *WALK* M28 .... 56 C3
Star La *HOR/BR* BL6 .... 16 B4
Starling Dr *FWTH* BL4 ...... 46 D1
Starling Rd *RAD* M26 ...... 33 G2

Starmount Cl *BOLE* BL2.................32 C4
Station Rd *CHLY/EC* PR7..............14 D1
   EDGW/EG BL7.........................4 C5
   FWTH BL4..................................48 B1
   HOR/BR BL6..............................26 A1
   SWIN M27...................................57 H2
   TOT/BURYW BL8.....................13 H3
Station St *BOLS/LL* BL3....................3 F6
Staton Av *BOLE* BL2.........................31 G2
Staveley Av *BOL* BL1.......................20 C1
Steele Gdns *BOLE* BL2....................31 H5
Stephenson St *HOR/BR* BL6.........16 D5
Stephens St *BOLE* BL2....................32 A2
Sterndale Rd *WALK* M28.................54 D5
Sterratt St *BOL* BL1............................2 A4
Stetchworth Dr *WALK* M28.............55 F4
Stevenson Rd *SWIN* M27................57 G3
Stevenson St *WALK* M28.................47 F5
Stewart Av *FWTH* BL4.....................47 F1
Stewart St *BOL* BL1.........................30 C1
Steynton Cl *BOL* BL1.......................29 F2
Stirling Rd *BOL* BL1.........................20 A5
   WGNE/HIN WN2......................42 B4
Stitch-Mi-Lane *BOLE* BL2..............22 B5
Stockdale Gv *BOLE* BL2.................32 B1
Stockley Av *BOLE* BL2....................22 A5
Stocks Cottages *HOR/BR* BL6 * 17 F3
Stocksfield Dr *LHULT* M38..............46 D3
Stocks Park Dr *HOR/BR* BL6.........17 F4
Stockton Rd *FWTH* BL4...................39 G3
Stockton St *SWIN* M27....................57 G4
Stoneacre *HOR/BR* BL6...................27 H2
Stoneacre Ct *SWIN* M27.................57 H4
Stoneacre Dr *CHLYE* PR6..................7 E3
Stonebridge Cl *HOR/BR* BL6.........28 C4
Stonechat Cl *WALK* M28..................55 F3
Stoneclough Ri *RAD* M26................40 D5
Stoneclough Rd *FWTH* BL4............48 B1
Stonedelph Cl *BOLE* BL2................33 F1
Stonefield *TYLD* M29........................54 A2
Stonegate Fold *CHLYE* PR6.............7 F3
Stonehaven *BOLS/LL* BL3...............37 F2
Stone Hill Rd *FWTH* BL4.................47 H2
Stonehouse *EDGW/EG* BL7...........11 F5
Stone Lea Wy *ATH* M46...................52 A1
Stoneleigh Dr *RAD* M26..................48 D1
Stonemead *BOLS/LL* BL3...............38 D3
Stonesteads Dr *EDGW/EG* BL7....11 E4
Stonesteads Wy *EDGW/EG* BL7....11 E4
Stone St *BOLE* BL2...........................31 F1
Stoney Bank *RAD* M26.....................49 E4
Stoneycroft Av *HOR/BR* BL6.........17 F3
Stoneycroft Cl *HOR/BR* BL6...........17 F3
Stoney La *CHLY/EC* PR7.................14 C3
Stoneyside Av *WALK* M28...............48 A4
Stoneyside Gv *WALK* M28..............48 A5
Stonor Rd *CHLY/EC* PR7...................6 D5
Stonyhurst Av *BOL* BL1..................20 C2
Stopes Rd *BOLS/LL* BL3..................40 D2
Store St *HOR/BR* BL6.......................17 E3
Stott La *BOLE* BL2............................31 F1
Stott Rd *SWIN* M27...........................57 F5
Stourbridge Av *LHULT* M38............47 E2
Stour Rd *TYLD* M29...........................53 H3
Stowell Ct *BOL* BL1..........................30 C1
Stowell St *BOL* BL1...........................30 C1
The Straits *TYLD* M29.......................54 A5
The Strand *HOR/BR* BL6.................17 F4
Strangford St *RAD* M26...................41 F1
Stranton Dr *WALK* M28....................57 E3
Stratford Av *BOL* BL1......................29 H1
Stratford Cl *FWTH* BL4....................38 D4
Strathmore Rd *BOLE* BL2...............32 A1
Stratton Rd *SWIN* M27....................57 H2
Strawberry Hill Rd *BOLE* BL2..........3 J7
The Stray *BOL* BL1............................21 F3
Street Elmfield St *BOL* BL1............20 D5
Streetgate *LHULT* M38.....................47 E3
Street Kirklees *TOT/BURYW* BL8...13 H5
Street La *RAD* M26...........................33 G2
Stretton Rd *BOLS/LL* BL3...............37 H1
Stuart Av *WGNE/HIN* WN2.............42 A5
Studley Ct *TYLD* M29.......................53 E3
Sudbury Dr *HOR/BR* BL6................28 C5
Sudren St *TOT/BURYW* BL8...........23 H4
Suffolk Cl *BOLS/LL* BL3...................32 D5
Sulby St *RAD* M26............................40 D5
Summerfield Dr *TYLD* M29.............53 H5
Summerfield Rd *BOLS/LL* BL3.......39 F1
   WALK M28.................................56 C4
Summer St *HOR/BR* BL6.................16 D5
Sumner Av *BOLE* BL2......................33 F4
Sumner St *ATH* M46........................44 C5
   WGNE/HIN WN2......................25 H5
Sunadale Cl *BOL* BL1.......................29 H5
Sundridge Cl *BOLS/LL* BL3............37 G2
Sunleigh Rd *WGNE/HIN* WN2........42 A2
Sunlight Rd *BOL* BL1........................30 A3
Sunningdale Av *RAD* M26...............33 F5

Sunningdale Gv *LEIGH* WN7..........52 D4
Sunningdale Wk *BOLS/LL* BL3 * 30 A5
Sunning Hill St *BOLS/LL* BL3..........38 B1
Sunny Bank *RAD* M26.....................40 C5
Sunnybank Rd *BOL* BL1..................20 A5
   TYLD M29...................................53 H5
Sunny Bower St
   TOT/BURYW BL8....................23 G1
Sunny Garth *WHTN* BL5..................35 G5
Sunnymead Av *BOL* BL1.................20 D3
Sunnyside Rd *BOL* BL1...................20 A5
Surrey Cl *BOLS/LL* BL3...................40 D1
Sussex Cl *WGNE/HIN* WN2.............42 C3
Sutcliffe St *BOL* BL1........................20 C1
Sutherland Gv *FWTH* BL4...............39 G5
Sutherland Rd *BOL* BL1..................20 C2
Sutherland St *FWTH* BL4................39 G5
   SWIN M27...................................57 G2
Sutton La *CHLYE* PR6........................7 F4
Sutton Rd *BOLS/LL* BL3...................37 F1
Swan La *WGNE/HIN* WN2...............41 G5
Swan Rd *TOT/BURYW* BL8.............13 H2
Sweetlove's Gv *BOL* BL1................20 C2
Sweetlove's La *BOL* BL1.................20 C2
Swinside Rd *BOLE* BL2....................32 B2
Swinton St *BOLE* BL2.......................32 A3
Swithemby St *HOR/BR* BL6...........16 C5
Sycamore Av *RAD* M26....................41 H5
   TYLD M29...................................54 B2
   WGNE/HIN WN2......................42 B5
Sycamore Rd *ATH* M46....................45 E5
   TOT/BURYW BL8....................23 H2
The Sycamores *RAD* M26...............48 D2
Sycamore Wk *HOR/BR* BL6............17 C5
Syderstone Cl *WGNE/HIN* WN2....42 A4
Sydney St *SWIN* M27........................57 F3

T

Tabley Rd *BOLS/LL* BL3...................37 H1
Tackler Cl *SWIN* M27........................57 H4
Tadmor Cl *LHULT* M38......................46 D4
Taibenny Cl *BOL* BL1.......................29 F2
Talbot Av *BOLS/LL* BL3....................40 C1
Talbot Ct *BOL* BL1.............................20 D3
Tamar Cl *FWTH* BL4.........................48 D3
Tamarin Cl *SWIN* M27.......................57 E2
Tamer Gv *LEIGH* WN7.......................51 E1
Tanfield Dr *RAD* M26........................48 D1
Tanhouse Av *TYLD* M29...................54 B4
Tanworth Wk *BOL* BL1.....................20 C5
Tarbet Dr *BOLE* BL2.........................32 B4
Tarleton Av *ATH* M46.......................44 B3
Tarleton Cl *TOT/BURYW* BL8.........33 H1
Tarleton Pl *BOLS/LL* BL3.................37 G2
Tarnbrook Dr *WGNE/HIN* WN2......25 F5
Tarn Gv *WALK* M28...........................56 B2
Tarvin Wk *BOL* BL1............................20 C5
Tattersall Av *BOL* BL1......................19 E5
Taunton Av *LEIGH* WN7..................49 F5
Taunton Cl *BOL* BL1 * 30 A1
Taunton Dr *FWTH* BL4.....................38 D4
Tavistock Rd *BOL* BL1........................2 A5
   WGNE/HIN WN2......................42 C4
Tavistock St *ATH* M46......................44 B5
Taylor Gv *WGNE/HIN* WN2.............43 E5
Taylor Rd *WGNE/HIN* WN2.............43 E5
Taylor's La *BOLE* BL2........................32 D3
Taylor St *BOLS/LL* BL3 * 3 F5
   HOR/BR BL6............................16 D4
   LEIGH WN7................................51 F3
Tayton Cl *TYLD* M29.........................54 A2
Taywood Rd *BOLS/LL* BL3..............36 D3
Teak Dr *FWTH* BL4............................49 F4
Teal St *BOLS/LL* BL3........................38 D1
Tebworth Dr *WGNE/HIN* WN2........42 A4
Telford Crs *LEIGH* WN7...................51 F3
Telford St *ATH* M46..........................52 A1
   HOR/BR BL6.............................17 E5
Tellers Cl *ATH* M46...........................44 D5
Temperance St *BOLS/LL* BL3...........2 C7
Tempest Cha *HOR/BR* BL6.............36 B1
Tempest Ct *HOR/BR* BL6 * 36 C1
Tempest Rd *HOR/BR* BL6................36 C2
Tempest St *BOLS/LL* BL3................37 H1
Templecombe Dr *BOL* BL1.............20 B1
Temple Dr *BOL* BL1..........................20 A4
Temple Rd *BOL* BL1.........................20 A4
Templeton Cl *WHTN* BL5.................35 G5
Tenby Av *BOL* BL1.............................29 G1
Tenby St *BOL* BL1..............................20 B5
Tennyson Av *LEIGH* WN7................51 E3
   RAD M26...................................41 G1
Tennyson Rd *FWTH* BL4..................47 F2
   SWIN M27...................................57 F3
Tennyson St *BOL* BL1......................30 C1
Tensing Av *ATH* M46........................44 C3

Ternhill Cl *FWTH* BL4.......................39 G5
Tetbury Dr *BOLE* BL2.......................32 B2
Thaxted Pl *BOL* BL1.........................30 A2
Thelwall Av *BOLE* BL2......................31 H2
Thetford Cl *WGNE/HIN* WN2..........42 A4
Thicketford Brow *BOLE* BL2...........31 H1
Thicketford Cl *BOLE* BL2................21 G5
Thicketford Rd *BOLE* BL2...............31 G1
Third Av *BOL* BL1..............................29 H3
   BOLS/LL BL3............................40 B1
Third St *BOL* BL1...............................19 F3
Thirlmere Av *HOR/BR* BL6..............17 E5
   TYLD M29...................................53 C4
Thirlmere Cl *CHLYE* PR6...................7 F4
Thirlmere Dr *LHULT* M38................47 E3
Thirlmere Gv *FWTH* BL4..................38 C5
Thirlmere Rd *HOR/BR* BL6.............15 C4
   WGNE/HIN WN2......................42 A3
   WHTN BL5.................................45 F1
Thirlspot Cl *BOL* BL1.......................20 C1
Thirsk Rd *BOLS/LL* BL3....................40 C3
Thistleton Rd *BOLS/LL* BL3.............37 F2
Thomas Dr *BOLS/LL* BL3.................30 B5
Thomas Holden St *BOL* BL1.............2 C2
Thomas More Cl *FWTH* BL4............48 B2
Thomasson Cl *BOL* BL1...................30 C1
Thomas St *ATH* M46.........................46 C3
   BOLS/LL BL3............................30 B5
   FWTH BL4..................................40 A5
   WGNE/HIN WN2......................42 D5
   WHTN BL5 * 35 G2
Thompson Av *BOLE* BL2.................33 F1
Thompson Rd *BOL* BL1...................29 H1
Thompson St *BOLS/LL* BL3............30 D5
   HOR/BR BL6............................16 C4
Thoresby Cl *RAD* M26......................33 E5
Thornbank *BOLS/LL* BL3.................30 A4
Thornbeck Dr *BOL* BL1...................29 F1
Thornbeck Rd *BOL* BL1...................29 F1
Thorncliffe Rd *BOL* BL1..................20 D2
Thorne St *FWTH* BL4.......................39 G4
Thorneyholme Cl *HOR/BR* BL6....28 C4
Thornfield Crs *LHULT* M38.............46 D3
Thornfield Dr *SWIN* M27.................57 G4
Thornfield Gv *LHULT* M38..............46 D3
Thornfield Rd *TOT/BURYW* BL8....13 F5
Thornham Dr *BOL* BL1....................20 D1
Thornhill Dr *WALK* M28...................56 A3
Thorn Lea *ATH* M46.........................53 E1
   BOLE BL2..................................21 H3
Thornlea Av *SWIN* M27...................57 F5
Thorn Lea Cl *BOL* BL1.....................20 A5
Thornley Av *BOL* BL1.......................20 A5
Thornley Ms *BOL* BL1 * 20 A5
Thornmere Cl *SWIN* M27................57 E1
Thorn Rd *SWIN* M27.........................57 G5
Thorns Av *BOL* BL1...........................20 B4
Thorns Cl *BOL* BL1............................20 B4
Thorns Rd *BOL* BL1...........................20 B4
Thorn St *BOL* BL1..............................20 D5
Thornton Av *BOL* BL1......................29 F1
Thornton Cl *BOLS/LL* BL3..............41 E3
   FWTH BL4..................................47 F1
   WALK M28.................................54 C4
Thornton Rd *WALK* M28..................54 C4
Thornton St *BOLE* BL2......................3 H3
Thornway *WALK* M28.......................55 H4
Thorn Well *WHTN* BL5.....................43 G1
Thornydyke Av *BOL* BL1.................20 D2
Thorpe Av *SWIN* M27.......................57 G2
Thorpe St *BOL* BL1...........................20 B5
   WALK M28.................................47 H4
Thorsby Cl *EDGW/EG* BL7..............10 D4
Threadfold Wy *EDGW/EG* BL7......10 D5
Threlkeld Rd *BOL* BL1.....................10 B5
Thurlestone Av *BOLE* BL2...............33 F1
Thurlstone Av *BOL* BL1...................10 B5
Thurlwood Cft *WHTN* BL5..............35 G4
Thursby Rd *BOLS/LL* BL3................38 A2
Thursford Gv *HOR/BR* BL6.............25 H1
Thurstane St *BOL* BL1.....................20 A5
Thurston Cl *BOLS/LL* BL3.................3 F7
Thynne St *BOLS/LL* BL3....................3 F7
   FWTH BL4..................................39 G4
Tig Fold Rd *FWTH* BL4....................38 C5
Tildsley St *BOLS/LL* BL3.................38 C1
Tilside Gv *HOR/BR* BL6...................28 B4
Timberbottom *BOLE* BL2.................21 G3
Timsbury Cl *BOLE* BL2.....................32 B5
Tindle St *WALK* M28.........................48 B5
Tinkersfield *LEIGH* WN7.................51 F4
Tinsley Gv *BOLE* BL2.........................3 K1
Tin St *BOLS/LL* BL3............................2 D7
Tintagel Ct *RAD* M26........................33 E5
Tintagel Rd *WGNE/HIN* WN2..........42 C4
Tintern Av *BOLE* BL2........................21 F5
   TYLD M29...................................54 A4
Tipton Cl *RAD* M26..........................33 F5
Tithe Barn Crs *BOL* BL1..................21 F3
Tithe Barn St *WHTN* BL5................35 G4
Tiverton Av *LEIGH* WN7..................51 F1

Tiverton Cl *RAD* M26........................3
   TYLD M29...................................5
Tiverton Wk *BOL* BL1 * 3
Toddington La *WGNE/HIN* WN2....2
Toll St *RAD* M26................................4
Tomlinson St *HOR/BR* BL6.............1
Tomlin Sq *BOLE* BL2........................3
Tommy La *BOLE* BL2........................3
Tonge Bridge Wy *BOLE* BL2...........3
Tonge Fold Rd *BOLE* BL2................3
Tonge Moor Rd *BOLE* BL2..............3
Tonge Old Rd *BOLE* BL2.................3
Tonge Park Av *BOLE* BL2................3
Tongfields *EDGW/EG* BL7...............1
Tong Head Av *BOL* BL1....................2
Tong Rd *BOLS/LL* BL3......................3
Tong St *FWTH* BL4............................3
Top o th Brow *BOLE* BL2 * 3
Top o' th' La *BOLS/LL* BL3 * 3
Toppings Gn *EDGW/EG* BL7............1
Topping St *BOL* BL1..........................3
Topp St *FWTH* BL4............................4
Topp Wy *BOL* BL1.............................3
Tor Av *TOT/BURYW* BL8.................1
Tor Heg Ms *TOT/BURYW* BL8........1
Torkington Av *SWIN* M27................5
Toronto St *BOLE* BL2........................3
Torra Barn Cl *EDGW/EG* BL7..........1
Torridon Rd *BOLE* BL2.....................3
Torrington Av *BOL* BL1....................2
Torrisdale Cl *BOLS/LL* BL3.............3
Torside Wy *SWIN* M27.....................3
Torver Dr *BOLE* BL2..........................3
Tottington Rd *BOLE* BL2..................3
   EDGW/EG BL7.........................1
Tower Buildings *HOR/BR* BL6 * 1
Tower Ct *EDGW/EG* BL7..................1
   TOT/BURYW BL8....................1
Tower Gv *LEIGH* WN7......................5
Towers Av *BOLS/LL* BL3...................3
Tower St *EDGW/EG* BL7...................1
Towncroft La *BOL* BL1.......................2
Townsend Rd *SWIN* M27.................5
Townsfield Rd *WHTN* BL5...............3
Toxhead Cl *HOR/BR* BL6.................2
Trafford Dr *LHULT* M38...................3
Trafford Gv *FWTH* BL4.....................3
Trafford St *FWTH* BL4......................3
Trawden Av *BOL* BL1........................2
Tredgold St *HOR/BR* BL6................1
Treen Rd *TYLD* M29..........................5
Tree Tops *EDGW/EG* BL7.................1
Tregaron Gv *WGNE/HIN* WN2........2
Trencherbone Rd *RAD* M26.............4
Trent Dr *WALK* M28..........................5
   WGNE/HIN WN2......................2
Trentham Av *FWTH* BL4...................3
Trentham Cl *FWTH* BL4....................3
Trentham St *FWTH* BL4....................3
   SWIN M27 * 5
Trent Wy *FWTH* BL4.........................4
Treswell Cl *WGNE/HIN* WN2...........5
Trevarrick Ct *HOR/BR* BL6..............1
Trevore Dr *WGN* WN1......................2
Trevor Rd *SWIN* M27........................5
Trillo Av *BOLE* BL2............................3
Trinity Crs *WALK* M28......................5
Trinity St *BOLS/LL* BL3.....................3
Troon Cl *BOLS/LL* BL3......................3
Troutbeck Cl *TOT/BURYW* BL8......1
Troutbeck Dr *TYLD* M29...................5
Truro Rd *TYLD* M29...........................5
Tucker's Hill Brow *HOR/BR* BL6....2
Tudor Av *BOL* BL1.............................2
   FWTH BL4..................................4
Tudor St *BOLS/LL* BL3 * 3
Tulip Av *FWTH* BL4...........................4
   FWTH BL4..................................4
Turf St *RAD* M26................................4
Turks Rd *RAD* M26............................4
Turk St *BOL* BL1.................................3
Turnberry *BOLS/LL* BL3....................3
Turnberry Cl *TYLD* M29....................5
Turncroft Wy *WALK* M28.................5
Turner Av *WGNE/HIN* WN2.............4
Turner Bridge Rd *BOLE* BL2...........3
Turnerford Cl *EDGW/EG* BL7..........1
Turner St *BOL* BL1.............................3
   WHTN BL5.................................3
Turnstone Cl *LEIGH* WN7................5
Turnstone Rd *BOLE* BL2...................3
Turton Ct *BOL* BL1............................4
Turton Hts *BOLE* BL2........................3
Turton Rd *BOLE* BL2.........................3
   TOT/BURYW BL8....................4
Turton St *BOL* BL1.............................3
Twisse Rd *BOLE* BL2.........................3
Two Brooks La *TOT/BURYW* BL8...1
Tybyrne Cl *WALK* M28......................3

esley Old Rd ATH M46 ....52 D1
esley Pas TYLD M29 ....53 F2
esley Rd ATH M46 ....52 D1
e Ct WALK M28 ....47 G5
esbank WALK M28 ....55 G1
esbank Cottages
ALK M28 * 47 G5

U

nda St BOLS/LL BL3 ....38 A3
swater Cl BOLS/LL BL3 ....40 B2
swater St BOL BL1 ....20 D5
water Rd TYLD M29 ....53 G4
erton Rd WHTN BL5 ....45 F1
on Buildings BOLE BL2 ....3 F5
n Ct BOLE BL2 * 21 E5
n Rd BOLE BL2 ....21 E5
n St EDGW/EG BL7 ....10 B2
VIN M27 ....57 G3
YLD M29 ....53 F2
worth Av TYLD M29 ....53 H3
worth St LEIGH WN7 ....51 G4
AD M26 ....41 H1
nd Dr LHULT M38 ....46 D2
er George St TYLD M29 ....53 G3
er Lees Dr WHTN BL5 ....36 A4
er Rd EDGW/EG BL7 ....10 D3
n La TYLD M29 ....54 A3
n Rd ATH M46 ....45 E4
n Wy TOT/BURYW BL8 ....23 H2
ey St BOL BL1 ....20 B5

V

ene Cl FWTH BL4 ....47 H1
ene Dr FWTH BL4 ....47 H1
ALK M28 ....55 H3
on HOR/BR BL6 ....16 C4
AD M26 ....49 E1
e Coppice HOR/BR BL6 ....16 C4
St BOLE BL2 ....32 C3
DGW/EG BL7 ....4 D5
etts La BOL BL1 ....30 A1
ey MI EDGW/EG BL7 * 10 D4
y Av BOLE BL2 ....21 F4
comme St BOL BL1 ....20 C3
ey Rd BOLS/LL BL3 ....37 G1
e House Cl HOR/BR BL6 ....15 H5
dale Av SWIN M27 ....57 F5
ce St BOLS/LL BL3 ....38 A1
nor Av BOL BL1 ....20 D4
ena Av FWTH BL4 ....39 E4
ure Av BOL BL1 ....29 E2
mont St BOL BL1 ....2 A1
e Av SWIN M27 ....57 G3
ham Wk BOLS/LL BL3 ....38 C1
on Rd TOT/BURYW BL8 ....13 H3
on St BOL BL1 ....2 C2
on Wk BOL BL1 ....40 A5
on Wk BOL BL1 ....2 D1
rage Cl CHLYE PR6 ....7 E4
rage Rd HOR/BR BL6 ....15 H5
VIN M27 ....57 G3
ALK M28 ....47 G4
rage Rd West HOR/BR BL6 ....15 G5
rage St BOLS/LL BL3 ....2 B7
rs Hall Gdns WALK M28 ....54 D5
er Cl SWIN M27 ....57 H1
erman St BOL BL1 ....20 B5
ers Rw FWTH BL4 ....39 F4
ers St BOLS/LL BL3 ....2 B7
ria Av WGNE/HIN WN2 ....50 A2
ria Cl WALK M28 * 55 E5
GNE/HIN WN2 ....25 F4
ria Ct FWTH BL4 ....39 G3
ria Gv BOL BL1 ....30 A1
ria La SWIN M27 ....57 F3
ria Rd BOL BL1 ....28 D3
VTH BL4 ....48 C2
OR/BR BL6 ....17 E4
ria Sq BOL BL1 ....2 E4
ria St BOLE BL2 ....33 E1
VTH BL4 ....39 F4
OR/BR BL6 ....15 H5
IGH WN7 ....51 G5
OT/BURYW BL8 ....13 G5
ALK M28 ....55 E1
HTN BL5 ....35 H5
ria Ter WGNE/HIN WN2 ....50 B3
ria Wy LEIGH WN7 ....51 G4
ory Rd BOLS/LL BL3 ....40 C1

Victory St BOL BL1 * 30 A2
View St BOLS/LL BL3 ....38 B1
Vigo Av BOLS/LL BL3 ....37 H2
Viking St BOLS/LL BL3 ....39 E1
Vincent St BOL BL1 ....2 A1
BOL BL1 ....30 A4
Violet Av FWTH BL4 ....39 E4
Virginia St BOLS/LL BL3 ....37 H1

W

Waddington Cl
TOT/BURYW BL8 ....23 G5
Waddington Rd BOL BL1 ....20 D5
Wade Bank WHTN BL5 ....35 H5
Wadebridge Dr
TOT/BURYW BL8 ....23 H5
Wade St BOLS/LL BL3 ....38 D2
Wadsley St BOL BL1 ....2 C1
Waggoners Ct SWIN M27 ....57 H4
Waggon Rd BOLE BL2 ....31 H2
Wagner St BOL BL1 ....20 B4
Wagtail Cl WALK M28 ....55 H3
Wainscot Cl TYLD M29 ....53 H4
Wakefield Dr SWIN M27 ....49 F4
Wakefield Ms EDGW/EG BL7 ....10 D5
Waldeck St BOL BL1 ....30 A2
Waldon Cl BOLS/LL BL3 ....38 A1
WGNE/HIN WN2 ....42 B4
Walkden Dr WALK M28 ....47 F5
Walkden Market Pl
WALK M28 * 47 H5
Walkden Rd WALK M28 ....55 H2
Walkdens Av ATH M46 ....52 A1
Walker Av BOLS/LL BL3 ....38 D2
Walker Cl FWTH BL4 ....48 C2
Walker Fold Rd BOL BL1 ....18 D3
Walkers Ct FWTH BL4 ....39 H5
Walker St BOL BL1 ....2 B5
WHTN BL5 ....35 G5
The Walk ATH M46 ....44 D5
The Walkway BOLS/LL BL3 ....29 F5
Wallbrook Crs LHULT M38 ....47 E2
The Walled Gdn SWIN M27 ....57 F5
Walley St BOL BL1 ....20 C4
Walls St WGNE/HIN WN2 ....51 E1
Wallsuches HOR/BR BL6 ....17 H5
Wallwork Rd TYLD M29 ....54 B5
Walmer Rd WGNE/HIN WN2 ....42 C3
Walmley Gv BOLS/LL BL3 ....38 A2
Walnut Cl SWIN M27 ....49 F4
Walnut Gv LEIGH WN7 ....51 H3
Walnut St BOL BL1 ....20 D4
Walshaw Brook Cl
TOT/BURYW BL8 ....23 H3
Walshaw Dr SWIN M27 ....57 H4
Walshaw La
TOT/BURYW BL8 ....23 H3
Walshaw Rd
TOT/BURYW BL8 ....23 H3
Walsh St HOR/BR BL6 ....16 D3
Walter St RAD M26 ....33 H4
WALK M28 ....55 H1
Walton Ct BOLS/LL BL3 ....38 D1
Walton Pl FWTH BL4 ....48 A1
Walton St ATH M46 * 45 E4
CHLY/EC PR7 ....15 E1
Wanborough Cl
LEIGH WN7 ....51 H4
Wapping St BOL BL1 ....20 B5
Warbeck Cl WGNE/HIN WN2 ....42 A5
Warbreck Cl BOLE BL2 ....32 B3
Warburton Pl ATH M46 ....44 D5
Warburton St BOL BL1 ....20 D5
Wardend Cl LHULT M38 * 47 E2
Wardens Bank WHTN BL5 ....43 G3
Wardle Cl RAD M26 ....33 G5
Wardle St BOLE BL2 ....3 K7
Wardley Av WALK M28 ....55 F1
Wardley Hall La WALK M28 ....56 C3
Wardley Hall Rd WALK M28 ....56 D2
Wardley Rd TYLD M29 ....54 B3
Wardley Sq TYLD M29 ....54 B3
Wardley St SWIN M27 ....57 H3
Wardour St BOLS/LL BL3 ....37 H1
Wardour St ATH M46 ....52 D1
Wareing St TYLD M29 ....53 F3
Wareing Wy BOLS/LL BL3 ....2 C5
The Warke WALK M28 ....56 B5
Warlow Dr LEIGH WN7 ....51 F2
Warren Cl ATH M46 ....45 E4
Warren Dr SWIN M27 ....57 F5
Warren Rd WALK M28 ....48 A5
Warton Cl TOT/BURYW BL8 ....33 H1
Warwick Av SWIN M27 ....57 F1
Warwick Dr WGNE/HIN WN2 ....42 B2
Warwick Gdns BOLS/LL BL3 ....37 H3

Warwick Rd ATH M46 ....44 C3
RAD M26 ....33 H4
TYLD M29 ....53 G1
WALK M28 ....55 G2
WGNE/HIN WN2 * 25 G5
Warwick St BOL BL1 ....20 C3
CHLY/EC PR7 ....14 D1
SWIN M27 ....57 H2
Wasdale Av BOLE BL2 ....32 B1
Washacre WHTN BL5 ....43 H1
Washacre Cl WHTN BL5 ....43 H1
Washbrook Av WALK M28 ....55 F2
Washburn Cl WHTN BL5 ....43 H1
Washington St BOLS/LL BL3 ....30 A4
Washwood Cl LHULT M38 * 47 F2
Watergate Dr WHTN BL5 ....46 A1
Watergate La WHTN BL5 ....46 A1
Waterhouse Knock
HOR/BR BL6 ....15 E2
Water La FWTH BL4 ....48 A2
RAD M26 ....41 H2
Water Lane St RAD M26 ....41 H1
Waterloo St BOL BL1 ....30 D1
Watermans Cl HOR/BR BL6 ....17 E3
Watermillock Gdns BOL BL1 ....20 D4
Water's Edge FWTH BL4 ....39 E3
WALK M28 ....56 B1
Waterslea Dr BOL BL1 ....29 F3
Watersmead Cl BOL BL1 ....20 D5
Watersmead St BOL BL1 ....20 D5
Waters Meeting Rd BOL BL1 ....20 D4
Water's Nook Rd WHTN BL5 ....36 A5
Water St ATH M46 ....44 D5
BOL BL1 ....3 F3
CHLY/EC PR7 ....15 E1
EDGW/EG BL7 ....10 B2
Watling St TOT/BURYW BL8 ....12 B2
TOT/BURYW BL8 ....33 H2
Watson Rd FWTH BL4 ....38 D5
Watson St SWIN M27 ....57 H1
Watton Cl SWIN M27 * 57 H1
Watts St HOR/BR BL6 ....16 D5
Waverley Av FWTH BL4 ....48 B2
Waverley Gv LEIGH WN7 * 52 D5
Waverley Rd BOL BL1 ....20 C4
WALK M28 ....55 F2
Wavertree Av ATH M46 ....44 B4
Wayfarer Dr TYLD M29 ....53 G3
Wayfarers Wy SWIN M27 ....57 G4
Wayfaring WHTN BL5 ....35 H3
Wayoh Cft EDGW/EG BL7 ....4 A3
Wayside Gv WALK M28 ....48 A4
Wealdstone Gv BOLE BL2 * 21 F5
Wearish La WHTN BL5 ....43 H5
Weaste Av LHULT M38 ....47 G2
Weaver Av WALK M28 ....55 E1
Weavers Ct BOLS/LL BL3 ....2 D7
Weavers Gn FWTH BL4 ....47 H1
Webb St HOR/BR BL6 ....17 F3
Weber Dr BOLS/LL BL3 ....30 B5
Webster St BOLS/LL BL3 ....2 A7
Weeton Av BOLE BL2 ....32 B3
Welbeck Rd BOL BL1 ....29 G2
WALK M28 ....56 D5
Weldon Av BOLS/LL BL3 ....37 G3
The Welland WHTN BL5 ....35 G5
Wellbank Cl BOLS/LL BL3 ....40 D2
Wellbank St TOT/BURYW BL8 ....23 F1
Wellfield Rd BOLS/LL BL3 ....30 A5
WGNE/HIN WN2 ....42 C4
Welling St BOLE BL2 ....31 F1
Wellington Dr TYLD M29 ....54 C3
Wellington Ms EDGW/EG BL7 ....4 D5
Wellington Rd ATH M46 ....45 E4
EDGW/EG BL7 ....4 D5
SWIN M27 ....57 G3
Wellington St BOLS/LL BL3 ....2 B5
FWTH BL4 ....39 H5
WHTN BL5 ....35 G5
Wellington Wk BOLS/LL BL3 ....2 C5
Well Rd LEIGH WN7 ....51 F2
Wells Cl TYLD M29 ....53 H4
Wellstock La LHULT M38 ....46 D2
Well St BOL BL1 ....2 D3
BOLE BL2 ....33 E1
TYLD M29 ....53 F3
Wemsley Gv BOLE BL2 ....31 F1
Wendover Dr BOLS/LL BL3 ....29 E5
Wenlock Cl HOR/BR BL6 ....17 E1
Wenlock St SWIN M27 ....57 F3
Wentbridge Rd BOL BL1 ....2 B2
Wentworth Av FWTH BL4 ....47 G1
Wentworth Cl RAD M26 ....41 F1
Wentworth Rd SWIN M27 ....57 F5
Wesley Cl WHTN BL5 ....35 G5
Wesley Ct WALK M28 * 47 H4
Wesley Dr WALK M28 ....56 B3
Wesley Ms BOLE BL2 * 3 J4

The Wesleys FWTH BL4 ....38 D5
Wesley St ATH M46 * 45 E5
BOLS/LL BL3 * 30 C5
EDGW/EG BL7 ....11 E4
FWTH BL4 ....48 A1
SWIN M27 ....57 H3
TOT/BURYW BL8 ....13 G5
WHTN BL5 ....35 C3
West Av FWTH BL4 ....39 F5
WALK M28 ....47 G5
Westbank Rd HOR/BR BL6 ....28 D4
West Bank St ATH M46 ....53 E2
Westbourne Av BOLS/LL BL3 ....39 E2
LEIGH WN7 ....51 H4
SWIN M27 ....49 F3
Westbrook Cl BOLE BL2 ....3 G6
Westbrook Ct BOLE BL2 * 3 G6
Westbrook Rd SWIN M27 ....57 G4
Westbrook St BOLE BL2 ....3 H6
Westbury Cl WHTN BL5 ....36 A4
Westby Gv BOLE BL2 ....3 K2
Westcliffe Rd BOL BL1 ....20 D1
West Cl ATH M46 ....53 E2
Westcott Cl BOLE BL2 ....22 A2
Westcourt Rd BOLS/LL BL3 ....38 B2
Westend St FWTH BL4 ....39 F5
Westerdale Cl TYLD M29 ....53 H3
Westerdale Dr BOLS/LL BL3 ....29 G5
Westerton Ct BOLS/LL BL3 ....2 A7
Westfield Rd BOLS/LL BL3 ....37 H3
Westgate Av BOL BL1 ....30 A3
RAMS BL0 ....13 H2
Westgate Dr SWIN M27 ....57 H5
TYLD M29 ....54 A5
West Gv WHTN BL5 ....43 G2
Westgrove Av BOL BL1 * 20 C1
Westhoughton Rd CHLY/EC PR7 ....6 D3
Westlake Gv WGNE/HIN WN2 ....42 D4
Westland Av BOL BL1 ....29 G1
FWTH BL4 ....47 G2
Westleigh La LEIGH WN7 ....51 F1
Westmarsh Cl BOL BL1 * 30 C1
West Meade BOLS/LL BL3 ....38 C3
SWIN M27 ....57 G5
Westmeade Rd WALK M28 ....47 G3
Westminster Av FWTH BL4 ....39 G5
RAD M26 ....41 F1
Westminster Dr LEIGH WN7 ....53 E5
Westminster Rd BOL BL1 ....20 C2
WALK M28 ....55 H1
Westminster St FWTH BL4 ....39 G5
SWIN M27 ....57 F2
Westmorland Rd TYLD M29 ....53 G1
Weston Av SWIN M27 ....49 H4
Weston St ATH M46 ....45 E4
BOLS/LL BL3 ....38 D1
Westover St SWIN M27 ....57 G2
Westrees LEIGH WN7 ....52 A4
West St BOL BL1 ....30 A3
FWTH BL4 ....40 A4
WGNE/HIN WN2 ....42 D5
West Vw HOR/BR BL6 ....17 G2
West Wk EDGW/EG BL7 ....10 B2
West Wy BOL BL1 ....21 F4
LHULT M38 ....47 E3
Westwell Gv LEIGH WN7 ....51 G3
Westwell St LEIGH WN7 ....51 G3
Westwood Av WALK M28 ....55 E1
Westwood Cl FWTH BL4 ....39 H5
Westwood Rd BOL BL1 ....30 A2
Westworth Cl BOL BL1 ....2 B1
Wetheral Cl WGNE/HIN WN2 ....43 E5
Wetheral Dr BOLS/LL BL3 ....38 C2
Weybourne Gv BOLE BL2 ....21 F3
Weycroft Cl BOLE BL2 ....32 C4
Weymouth Dr WGNE/HIN WN2 ....42 C4
Weymouth St BOL BL1 ....20 C5
Weythorne Dr BOL BL1 ....20 D3
Whalley Av BOL BL1 ....19 F4
Whalley Dr TOT/BURYW BL8 ....23 H5
Whalley Gv LEIGH WN7 ....51 F2
Wharfedale WHTN BL5 ....35 H3
Wharton Hall Cl TYLD M29 ....53 H2
Wharton La LHULT M38 ....46 C3
Wheatfield St BOLE BL2 ....3 K7
Wheatley Rd SWIN M27 ....57 F1
Wheeldale Cl BOL BL1 ....20 C5
Whimbrel Rd TYLD M29 ....54 A4
Whins Av FWTH BL4 ....38 C5
Whins Crest HOR/BR BL6 ....28 C3
Whinslee Dr HOR/BR BL6 ....28 C3
Whiston Dr BOLE BL2 ....31 G4
Whitbeam Gv WGNE/HIN WN2 ....50 A1
Whitburn Cl BOLS/LL BL3 ....37 E1
Whitby Cl TOT/BURYW BL8 ....23 H5
Whitchurch Gdns BOL BL1 ....20 C5
Whiteacres SWIN M27 ....57 E4
Whitebeam Wk WHTN BL5 ....35 H3
White Birk Cl TOT/BURYW BL8 ....13 H2

Y

Z

Index - featured places

...rton Industrial Centre
H M46 ....44 D4
...rton Public Baths
H M46 ....44 C5
...dale Health Centre
OL BL1 ....30 A1
...Lane Industrial Estate
H M46 ....44 C4
...mont Hospital
OR/BR BL6 ....28 B2
...mont Primary School
OLS/LL BL3 ....29 E5
...ch House Infant
...epartment
OL BL1 ....29 H3
...Fold Medical Centre
H M46 ....52 B1
...Hive Industrial Estate
OR/BR BL6 ....27 G3
...ershaw CE Primary
...hool
GNE/HIN WN2 ....50 B3
...nshaw Hall School
GW/EG BL7 ....21 F1
...op Bridgeman CE Primary
...hool
OLS/LL BL3 ....38 C1
...krod Church School
OR/BR BL6 ....15 G5
...krod Primary School
OR/BR BL6 ....26 A2
...kshaw Primary School
LE BL2 ....32 C4
...n Business Centre
LE BL2 ....3 G5
...n CC
LE BL2 ....39 E3
...n Community College
LE BL2 ....3 G6
...n Gates Retail Park
L BL1 ....3 F1
...n Golf Club
OR/BR BL6 ....28 A2
...n Institute
LS/LL BL3 ....2 C6
...n Little Theatre
L BL1 ....2 C4
...n Muslim Girls School
OLS/LL BL3 ....38 B1
...n Old Links Golf Club
L BL1 ....18 D4
...n Open Golf Club
LE BL2 ....21 H4
...n Parish CE Primary
...hool
LE BL2 ....3 J3
...n Road Industrial
...ate
HTN BL5 ....35 H4
...n Rugby Union FC
L BL1 ....2 A1
...n Running Track
OR/BR BL6 ....27 E3
...n School Boys Division
L BL1 ....30 A3
...n School Girls Division
L BL1 ....29 H3
...n Sixth Form College
...rth Campus
L BL1 ....19 H3
...n Sports Arena
LE BL2 ....27 E3
...n Wanderers FC
OR/BR BL6
...eebok Stadium)
OR/BR BL6 ....27 F3
...hstown Methodist
...mary School
LK M28 ....54 D5
...dary Industrial Estate
LE BL2 ....32 C3
...ness Primary School
LS/LL BL3 ....40 B2
...kley Municipal Golf Club
ULT M38 ....46 C2
...ey Fold Trading Estate
LE BL2 ....33 E4
...shaw CC
LE BL2 ....21 G2
...dwood Primary School
LS/LL BL3 ....38 A1
...htmet FC
LE BL2 ....32 B3
...htmet Golf Club
LE BL2 ....32 C1
...htmet Industrial Estate
LE BL2 ....32 B3
...ewater Primary
...hool
ULT M38 ....47 G4

Bridgewater School
WALK M28 ....56 C5
Britannia Business Park
BOLE BL2 ....21 F5
Broadoak Primary School
SWIN M27 ....57 E5
Brookfield High School
WGNE/HIN WN2 ....42 A4
Brownlow Business Centre
BOL BL1 ....30 B1
Brownlow Fold Community
Learning Centre
BOL BL1 ....30 B1
Brownlow Fold Primary School
BOL BL1 ....30 B1
Burnden Industrial Estate
BOLS/LL BL3 ....39 F1
Bury Industrial Estate
BOLE BL2 ....32 B2
Cambrian Business Park
BOLS/LL BL3 ....30 B5
Cams Lane Primary School
RAD M26 ....41 H2
Cannon Street Health Centre
BOLS/LL BL3 ....2 B7
Canon Slade School
BOLE BL2 ....21 F3
Carlton Industrial Centre
....3 G5
Castle Hill Primary School
BOLE BL2 ....21 F5
Castle Hill St Philips CE Primary
School
WGNE/HIN WN2 ....42 B2
Central Industrial Estate
BOLS/LL BL3 ....30 D5
Century Mill Industrial Estate
FWTH BL4 ....39 F5
Chanters Industrial Estate
ATH M46 ....53 F1
Cherry Tree Primary School
FWTH BL4 ....38 C5
Chorley Golf Club
CHLYE PR6 ....7 E1
Chorley New Road Primary
School
HOR/BR BL6 ....17 E5
Chowbent Primary School
ATH M46 ....45 E5
Christchurch Ainsworth CE
Primary School
BOLE BL2 ....33 E1
Christchurch CE Primary School
TOT/BURYW BL8 ....23 H3
Christs Church CE Primary
School
BOLE BL2 ....22 B5
Christ the King RC Primary
School
WALK M28 ....56 A1
Church Road Primary School
BOL BL1 ....19 G5
Cineworld
BOL BL1 ....21 E4
Clarendon CP School
BOLS/LL BL3 ....30 C5
Claypool Primary School
HOR/BR BL6 ....27 G1
Cleggs Lane Industrial Site
LHULT M38 ....47 F2
Clevelands Preparatory School
BOL BL1 ....29 G3
Clifton Country Park
SWIN M27 ....49 G3
Clifton Primary School
SWIN M27 ....49 H5
Cobden Mill Industrial Estate
FWTH BL4 ....39 F4
Collier Brook Industrial Estate
ATH M46 ....44 C5
Comtech Business Park
WHTN BL5 ....35 G2
Constellation Trading Estate
RAD M26 ....33 H4
Crompton Fold Primary School
BOLE BL2 ....32 A3
Crompton Place Shopping
Centre
BOL BL1 ....2 E4
David Lloyd Fitness Centre
BOL BL1 ....2 B3
Deakins Business Park
EDGW/EG BL7 ....10 B2
Deane Golf Club
BOLS/LL BL3 ....29 G5
Deane Leisure Centre
BOLS/LL BL3 ....37 F1
The Deans CP School
SWIN M27 ....57 G3

Deans Road Industrial Estate
SWIN M27 ....57 F3
Derby Shopping Centre
BOLS/LL BL3 ....2 A7
De Vere Whites Hotel
HOR/BR BL6 ....27 F3
Devonshire Road Primary
School
BOL BL1 ....29 C2
Dodd Lane Industrial Estate
WHTN BL5 ....34 D1
Doffcocker Lodge Nature
Reserve
BOL BL1 ....29 E1
Douglas Valley Business Park
WGN WN1 ....24 A5
Dukesgate Primary School
LHULT M38 ....47 E3
Dunscar Golf Club
EDGW/EG BL7 ....10 B4
Dunscar Industrial Estate
EDGW/EG BL7 ....10 C5
Duxbury Jubilee Park Golf Club
CHLY/EC PR7 ....6 B1
Eagley Infant School
EDGW/EG BL7 ....11 E4
Eagley Junior School
EDGW/EG BL7 ....11 F4
Edge Fold Industrial Estate
FWTH BL4 ....38 A4
Edgworth CC
EDGW/EG BL7 ....5 E3
Egerton CC
EDGW/EG BL7 ....10 B1
Egerton & Dunscar Health
Centre
EDGW/EG BL7 ....10 D4
Egerton House Hotel
EDGW/EG BL7 ....10 C2
Egerton Primary School
EDGW/EG BL7 ....10 B1
Ellenbrook Primary School
WALK M28 ....55 F4
Ellesmere Bowling & Tennis Club
WALK M28 ....55 H3
Ellesmere Golf Club
WALK M28 ....56 B2
Ellesmere Retail Park
WALK M28 ....47 G5
Ellesmere Shopping Centre
LHULT M38 ....47 G5
Europa Trading Estate
RAD M26 ....48 D1
Express Trading Estate
FWTH BL4 ....47 H2
Fall Birch Hospital Lodge
HOR/BR BL6 ....28 A1
Farnworth Cemetery
FWTH BL4 ....40 A4
Farnworth Leisure Centre
FWTH BL4 ....39 H5
Farnworth Little Theatre
FWTH BL4 ....39 H5
Farnworth Park Industrial
Estate
FWTH BL4 ....39 H4
Farnworth Social Circle CC
FWTH BL4 ....47 G1
Firsdale Industrial Estate
LEIGH WN7 ....51 E5
Firwood Industrial Estate
BOLE BL2 ....21 G5
Firwood Special School
BOLE BL2 ....21 G5
Fishbrook Industrial Estate
FWTH BL4 ....48 B1
Fowler Industrial Estate
HOR/BR BL6 ....17 E5
Fred Longworth High School
TYLD M29 ....53 E2
Garrett Hall Primary School
TYLD M29 ....54 B4
Gaskell Primary School
BOL BL1 ....2 B1
The Gates Primary School
WHTN BL5 ....35 H3
The Gates Shopping Centre
BOL BL1 ....2 E3
George Tomlinson School
FWTH BL4 ....48 A2
Gilnow Mill Industrial Estate
BOL BL1 ....30 A4
Gilnow Primary School
BOL BL1 ....30 A4
Grasmere Street Health Centre
LEIGH WN7 ....51 G5
Great Lever & Farnworth Golf
Club
FWTH BL4 ....38 B4

Greenbank Industrial Estate
WGNE/HIN WN2 ....42 C5
Green Fold Special School
FWTH BL4 ....38 D5
Green Hall Primary School
ATH M46 ....45 F4
Greenhill Primary School
TOT/BURYW BL8 ....33 H1
Greenmount CC
TOT/BURYW BL8 ....13 H3
Greenmount Primary School
TOT/BURYW BL8 ....13 G2
Grimeford Industrial Estate
CHLYE PR6 ....15 H1
Haigh Hall Country Park
WGNE/HIN WN2 ....24 D4
Haigh Hall Golf Complex
WGNE/HIN WN2 ....24 D4
Hall i' th' Wood Museum
BOL BL1 ....21 E3
Halliwell Industrial Estate
BOL BL1 ....20 B4
Harcourt Industrial Centre
WALK M28 ....47 H3
Hardy Mill Primary School
BOLE BL2 ....22 B3
Harper Green School
FWTH BL4 ....39 F4
Harrop Fold School
WALK M28 ....47 F5
Hart Common Golf Club
WHTN BL5 ....42 D1
Harwood Golf Club (Bolton)
BOLE BL2 ....22 C3
Harwood Health Centre
BOLE BL2 ....21 H2
Harwood Meadows Primary
School
BOLE BL2 ....22 B4
Haslam Park Primary School
BOLS/LL BL3 ....29 H5
Hayward School
BOLS/LL BL3 ....38 A3
Hayward Sports Centre
BOLS/LL BL3 ....38 A3
Heathfield Primary School
BOLS/LL BL3 ....37 G3
Heaton CC
BOL BL1 ....19 G5
Heaton Cemetery
BOL BL1 ....29 H4
Heaton Medical Centre
BOL BL1 ....29 F1
Hesketh Fletcher CE High School
ATH M46 ....52 C1
Higher Folds Primary School
LEIGH WN7 ....52 D4
Highfield Primary School
FWTH BL4 ....39 E5
High Lawn Primary School
BOL BL1 ....20 C1
Highlea Secondary School
WALK M28 ....54 D3
Hilton Lane Primary School
WALK M28 ....47 E5
Hindley All Saints CE Primary
School
WGNE/HIN WN2 ....42 A3
Hindley Green Primary School
WGNE/HIN WN2 ....50 D1
Hindley High School - Arts
College
WGNE/HIN WN2 ....42 B3
Hindley Leisure Centre
WGNE/HIN WN2 ....42 B3
Hindsford CE Primary School
ATH M46 ....53 E2
Holiday Inn
BOL BL1 ....2 E2
Holly Bank Industrial Estate
RAD M26 ....41 H2
Holly Mount RC Primary
School
TOT/BURYW BL8 ....13 F3
Hollywood Bowl
HOR/BR BL6 ....27 F2
Holy Family RC School
WALK M28 ....54 C4
Holy Infant RC Primary School
BOL BL1 ....20 C3
Horwich Business Park
HOR/BR BL6 ....16 D5
Horwich Golf Club
HOR/BR BL6 ....17 F5
Horwich Leisure Centre
HOR/BR BL6 ....17 E4
Horwich Parish CE Primary
School
HOR/BR BL6 ....17 E3

Howe Bridge Crematorium
 ATH M46 ....51 H2
Howe Bridge Sports Centre
 ATH M46 ....52 B2
Hulton Hospital
 BOLS/LL BL3 ....37 G2
Inscape House Special School
 WALK M28 ....56 A2
James Brindley Primary School
 WALK M28 ....55 G2
Johnson Fold Community
 Primary School
 BOL BL1 ....19 F4
Jumbles Country Park
 BOLE BL2 ....11 H3
Kearsley West Primary School
 FWTH BL4 ....48 A1
Kenyon Business Park
 BOLS/LL BL3 ....2 D7
Kershaw Business Centre
 BOLS/LL BL3 ....2 B7
Kilhey Court Hotel
 WGN WN1 ....14 A5
Kingshill School
 TYLD M29 ....53 F3
Ladybridge High School
 BOLS/LL BL3 ....37 F1
Ladybridge Primary School
 BOLS/LL BL3 ....29 F5
Ladywood School
 BOLS/LL BL3 ....40 D1
Last Drop Village Hotel
 EDGW/EG BL7 ....11 E3
Leigh Centurions RLFC
 LEIGH WN7 ....51 G5
Leigh FC
 LEIGH WN7 ....51 G5
Leigh Infirmary
 LEIGH WN7 ....52 A4
Lever Edge Primary School
 BOLS/LL BL3 ....38 B3
Leverhulme Park Athletics
 Stadium
 BOLS/LL BL3 ....31 H4
Lever Park School
 HOR/BR BL6 ....17 E4
Linnyshaw Industrial Estate
 FWTH BL4 ....48 A2
Little Hulton Skills Centre
 WALK M28 ....47 E4
Little Lever School Specialist
 Language College
 BOLS/LL BL3 ....40 A2
Little Theatre
 TYLD M29 ....53 F3
Liverpool Castle
 HOR/BR BL6 ....16 B1
Lords College
 BOLE BL2 ....3 G6
Lord Street Primary School
 HOR/BR BL6 ....16 D3
Lostock Industrial Estate
 HOR/BR BL6 ....27 G3
Lostock Primary School
 HOR/BR BL6 ....28 C4
Lowercroft Primary School
 TOT/BURYW BL8 ....23 G5
Lyon Road Industrial Estate
 FWTH BL4 ....48 A3
Mandelay Health Centre
 BOL BL1 ....20 C1
Manor Golf Club
 FWTH BL4 ....48 D4
Market Place Shopping Centre
 BOL BL1 ....2 E3
Markland Hill Primary School
 BOL BL1 ....29 F2
Marriott Worsley Park Hotel &
 Country Club
 WALK M28 ....56 A4
Masefield Primary School
 BOLS/LL BL3 ....40 D1
Meadowbank Primary School
 ATH M46 ....44 C4
Mental Health Centre
 BOLE BL2 ....32 B1
Mesne Lea Primary School
 WALK M28 ....56 A2
Methodist Cemetery
 BOLE BL2 ....22 A3
Middlebrook Retail & Leisure
 Park
 HOR/BR BL6 ....27 F2
Mill Street Industrial Estate
 BOL BL1 ....3 G3
Moorgate Primary School
 BOLE BL2 ....3 K1
Moorside High School
 SWIN M27 ....57 F4

Moorside Leisure Centre
 SWIN M27 ....57 F4
Moorside Primary School
 SWIN M27 ....57 F4
Mornington High School
 WGNE/HIN WN2 ....42 B3
Morris Green Business Park
 BOLS/LL BL3 ....38 A1
Moses Gate Country Park
 FWTH BL4 ....40 A3
Mossfield CP School
 SWIN M27 ....57 H2
Mount St Joseph Business &
 Enterprise College
 BOLS/LL BL3 ....38 D3
Mytham Primary School
 BOLS/LL BL3 ....40 D2
Newlands Medical Centre
 BOL BL1 ....29 G3
Newton Westpark Primary
 School
 LEIGH WN7 ....51 E3
Nortex Business Centre
 BOL BL1 ....30 A2
North Walkden Primary School
 WALK M28 ....47 G3
Oakhill Trading Estate
 WALK M28 ....47 F3
The Oaks Primary School
 BOL BL1 ....20 D1
Octagon Theatre
 BOL BL1 ....2 E4
Our Lady of Lourdes RC Primary
 School
 FWTH BL4 ....39 E5
Our Lady RC Primary School
 WGNE/HIN WN2 ....25 G5
Our Lady & The Lancashire
 Martyrs RC Primary School
 WALK M28 ....47 E5
Overdale Crematorium
 BOL BL1 ....29 G4
Oxford Grove Primary School
 BOL BL1 ....30 A1
Paragon Business Park
 HOR/BR BL6 ....27 G2
Parklee Primary School
 ATH M46 ....52 C1
Parochial CE Primary School
 WHTN BL5 ....35 G5
Parsonage Retail Park
 LEIGH WN7 ....51 G5
Pearlbrook Industrial Estate
 HOR/BR BL6 ....16 D4
Peel Hall CP School
 LHULT M38 ....46 D5
Pikes Lane Primary School
 BOLS/LL BL3 ....2 A6
Pike View Medical Centre
 HOR/BR BL6 ....16 D3
Pilot Industrial Estate
 BOLS/LL BL3 ....39 F1
Plodder Lane Primary School
 FWTH BL4 ....39 F4
Premier Travel Inn
 HOR/BR BL6 ....27 H2
 SWIN M27 ....57 G5
Prestolee Primary School
 RAD M26 ....40 D5
Prestwich Industrial Estate
 ATH M46 ....44 B4
The Quadrangle Business
 Centre
 WGNE/HIN WN2 ....42 D4
Queensbridge Primary School
 FWTH BL4 ....39 G5
Radcliffe Borough AFC
 RAD M26 ....41 G1
Radcliffe CC
 RAD M26 ....41 G1
Radcliffe Hall CE Primary
 School
 RAD M26 ....41 G1
Radcliffe Riverside School
 RAD M26 ....41 H2
Raikes Lane Industrial Estate
 BOLS/LL BL3 ....39 F1
Ramada Hotel
 HOR/BR BL6 ....26 C3
Ravenside Retail Park
 BOLE BL2 ....3 F6
Red Lane Community School
 BOLE BL2 ....32 B1
Reebok Museum
 HOR/BR BL6 ....27 F2
Regent Park Golf Course
 HOR/BR BL6 ....28 B3
Ridgmont Cemetery
 HOR/BR BL6 ....17 F4

Rivington & Blackrod High
 School
 HOR/BR BL6 ....16 D1
Rivington Country Park
 HOR/BR BL6 ....8 C4
Rivington Park Independent
 School
 HOR/BR BL6 ....8 B3
Rivington Primary School
 HOR/BR BL6 ....8 B3
Roscow Fold Primary School
 BOLE BL2 ....32 A2
Royal Bolton Hospital
 FWTH BL4 ....38 D3
Rumworth School
 BOLS/LL BL3 ....29 F5
Sacred Heart Catholic Primary
 School
 WGNE/HIN WN2 ....42 D5
Sacred Heart RC Primary School
 ATH M46 ....53 E2
 WHTN BL5 ....35 H4
St Ambrose Barlow RC High
 School & Salford College
 SWIN M27 ....57 H4
St Andrews CE Primary School
 RAD M26 ....33 G4
 WHTN BL5 ....37 G5
St Andrews Methodist Primary
 School
 WALK M28 ....47 F5
St Bede CE Primary School
 BOLS/LL BL3 ....38 A3
St Bernard RC Primary School
 BOLS/LL BL3 ....29 E5
St Brendan RC Primary School
 BOLE BL2 ....22 A3
St Catherines CE Primary School
 HOR/BR BL6 ....16 D4
St Charles RC Primary School
 SWIN M27 ....57 F3
St Columbas RC Primary School
 BOLE BL2 ....21 G3
St Davids CE Primary School
 WGNE/HIN WN2 ....25 F3
St Edmunds RC Primary School
 LHULT M38 ....47 F4
St Ethelbert RC Primary School
 BOLS/LL BL3 ....29 H5
St Gabriels RC Primary School
 LEIGH WN7 ....53 E4
St Georges Central CE Primary
 School
 TYLD M29 ....53 G2
St Georges CE Primary School
 ATH M46 ....44 B4
 WHTN BL5 ....43 F1
St Georges RC High School
 WALK M28 ....55 G1
St Gregory RC Primary School
 FWTH BL4 ....40 A5
St James CE Primary School
 FWTH BL4 ....47 F1
St James CE Secondary School
 FWTH BL4 ....39 E5
St James (Daisy Hill) CE Primary
 School
 WHTN BL5 ....43 H3
St John CE Primary School
 FWTH BL4 ....40 A5
St Johns CE Infant School
 LEIGH WN7 ....51 H5
St Johns CE Primary School
 WGNE/HIN WN2 ....42 D5
St Johns Mosley Common CE
 Primary School
 WALK M28 ....54 D3
St John the Evangelist RC
 Primary School
 EDGW/EG BL7 ....10 D5
St Josephs Catholic Primary
 School
 CHLYE PR6 ....7 F5
St Josephs RC Primary
 School
 BOL BL1 ....20 A5
 LHULT M38 ....47 E3
St Josephs RC School
 HOR/BR BL6 ....27 G1
St Marks CE Primary School
 WALK M28 ....56 B5
St Mary CE Primary School
 BOLS/LL BL3 ....37 F1
St Mary RC Primary School
 HOR/BR BL6 ....17 F5
St Mary's Catholic Cemetery
 WALK M28 ....56 D3
St Marys CE Primary School
 TOT/BURYW BL8 ....12 D2

St Marys RC Primary School
 SWIN M27 5
St Matthew CE Primary School
 BOL BL1 3
 BOLS/LL BL3 4
St Maxentius CE Primary School
 BOLE BL2 2
St Michael CE Primary School
 BOLS/LL BL3 3
St Michaels CE Primary Howe
 Bridge School
 ATH M46 5
St Osmunds & St Andrews
 Primary School
 BOLE BL2 3
St Paul CE Primary School
 BOL BL1 1
St Paul's Cemetery
 BOL BL1 1
St Pauls CE Primary School
 CHLYE PR6 ....
 WALK M28 5
St Pauls Peel CE Primary School
 LHULT M38 4
St Peter CE Primary School
 FWTH BL4 4
St Peter & St Paul RC Primary
 School
 BOLS/LL BL3 5
St Peters CE Primary School
 SWIN M27 5
St Peters Smithills Dean CE
 Primary School
 BOL BL1 1
St Philips CE Primary School
 ATH M46 4
St Saviour Primary School
 Ringley
 RAD M26 4
St Stephen & All Martyrs CE
 Primary School
 BOLE BL2 3
St Stephens CE Primary School
 FWTH BL4 4
 TYLD M29 4
St Teresa RC Primary School
 BOLS/LL BL3 3
St Thomas CE Primary School
 BOL BL1 1
 WHTN BL5 5
St Thomas of Canterbury RC
 Primary School
 BOL BL1 2
St William RC Primary School
 BOLS/LL BL3 3
Salford College
 SWIN M27 5
 WALK M28 5
Scot Lane End CE Primary
 School
 HOR/BR BL6 6
Scot Lane Industrial Estate
 HOR/BR BL6 6
Seven Brooks Medical Centre
 ATH M46 4
Shakerley CE Primary School
 TYLD M29 5
Sharples Primary School
 BOL BL1 1
Shepherd Cross Industrial
 Estate
 BOL BL1 2
Smithills Hall Museum
 BOL BL1 1
Smithills School
 BOL BL1 1
Southside Industrial Park
 ATH M46 4
Spa Road Industrial Estate
 BOL BL1 3
Spindle Point Primary School
 FWTH BL4 4
SS Simon & Jude CE Primary
 School
 BOLS/LL BL3 3
Stirling Industrial Estate
 HOR/BR BL6 1
Stone Hill Industrial Estate
 FWTH BL4 4
Sunning Hill Primary School
 BOLS/LL BL3 3
Sunset Business Centre
 FWTH BL4 4
Swinton Cemetery
 SWIN M27 5
The Swinton County High School
 SWIN M27 5
Swinton Leisure Centre
 SWIN M27 5

Special School
/HIN WN2 ....**42** B3
sson Memorial Special
ol
BL1 ....**29** H3
eigh Salesian College
L BL1 ....**20** B3
e Bridge Industrial Estate
OLE BL2 ....**3** J2
e CC
OLE BL2 ....**21** G4
e Fold Health Centre
OLE BL2 ....**31** G3
e Moor Health Centre
OLE BL2 ....**31** G1
e Moor Primary School
OLE BL2 ....**31** F1
o' th' Brow Primary School
OLE BL2 ....**22** A5
ngton Health Centre
T/BURYW BL8 ....**13** G5
ngton High School
T/BURYW BL8 ....**23** H1
ngton Primary School
T/BURYW BL8 ....**23** H2
ngate Business Centre
ULT M38 ....**46** C3
Hall & Albert Halls
L BL1 ....**2** E4
elodge
R/BR BL6 ....**16** A3
sure House School of
ke Up
R/BR BL6 ....**17** E3
y Retail Park
LE BL2 ....**3** H6
n & Edgworth CE/
thodist Primary School
GW/EG BL7 ....**5** E4

Turton Golf Club
EDGW/EG BL7 ....**11** E2
Turton High School
EDGW/EG BL7 ....**11** F5
Turton Leisure Centre
EDGW/EG BL7 ....**11** E2
Turton Tower
EDGW/EG BL7 ....**11** G1
Twelve Apostles RC Primary
School
LEIGH WN7 ....**51** F3
Two Porches School
ATH M46 ....**44** D5
Two Porches Special School
ATH M46 ....**44** C4
Tyldesley Cemetery
TYLD M29 ....**54** B3
Tyldesley Primary School
TYLD M29 ....**53** H4
Tyldesley Swimming Pool
ATH M46 ....**53** E2
University of Bolton
BOLS/LL BL3 ....**2** C6
University of Bolton Chadwick
Campus
BOLE BL2 ....**3** J5
The Valley Community
School
BOL BL1 ....**20** D5
The Valley Leisure Centre
BOL BL1 ....**21** E4
Victoria Industrial Estate
LEIGH WN7 ....**51** G5
Victory Trading Estate
BOLS/LL BL3 ....**31** E5
Vue Cinema
HOR/BR BL6 ....**27** F2
Wadsworth Industrial Park
BOLS/LL BL3 ....**38** C1

Walkden High School
WALK M28 ....**56** A1
Walmsley CE Primary
School
EDGW/EG BL7 ....**10** C3
Walshaw Sports Club
TOT/BURYW BL8 ....**23** H2
Wardley CE Primary School
SWIN M27 ....**57** G1
Wardley Industrial Estate
WALK M28 ....**57** E2
Washacre Primary School
WHTN BL5 ....**43** H1
Waterloo Industrial Park
....**3** G1
The Water Place
BOL BL1 ....**2** E5
Waterside Industrial Park
BOLS/LL BL3 ....**39** G2
Wesley Methodist Primary
School
RAD M26 ....**33** G5
West End Trading Estate
SWIN M27 ....**57** H2
Westhoughton CC
WHTN BL5 ....**35** G5
Westhoughton Clinic
WHTN BL5 ....**35** G5
Westhoughton Golf Club
WHTN BL5 ....**35** F4
Westhoughton High School &
Specialist Technology College
WHTN BL5 ....**35** H4
Westhoughton Industrial
Estate
WHTN BL5 ....**35** G3
Westhoughton Primary
School
WHTN BL5 ....**35** H4

Westleigh Methodist Primary
School
LEIGH WN7 ....**51** F2
Westleigh St Pauls CE Primary
School
LEIGH WN7 ....**51** G3
Wharton Primary School
LHULT M38 ....**46** C2
Wigan Golf Club
WGN WN1 ....**14** B5
Wigan RUFC
WGN WN1 ....**24** B5
Wingates Industrial Estate
WHTN BL5 ....**35** F2
Withins High School
BOLE BL2 ....**22** A5
Wolfenden Primary School
BOL BL1 ....**20** C5
Woodlands Hospital
WALK M28 ....**46** D4
Worsley Business Park
TYLD M29 ....**54** D3
Worsley Road Industrial Estate
FWTH BL4 ....**47** G2
Worsley Trading Estate
LHULT M38 ....**46** C3
Worthington Lakes Business
Park
WGN WN1 ....**24** A2

Acknowledgements

ls address data provided by Education Direct

station information supplied by Johnsons

n centre information provided by:

n Centre Association   Britains best garden centres

le Garden Centres

atement on the front cover of this atlas is sourced, selected and quoted
reader comment and feedback form received in 2004

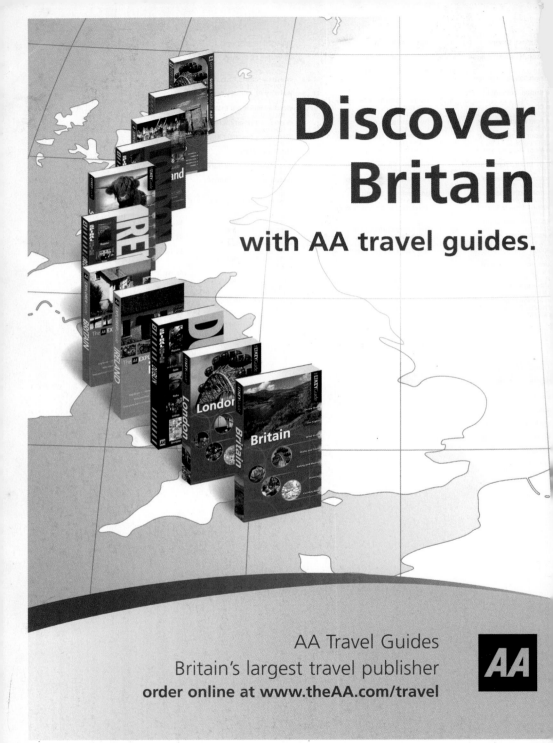

Discover
Britain

with AA travel guides.

AA Travel Guides
Britain's largest travel publisher
order online at www.theAA.com/travel

AA